NORTH DEVON

HISTORY

Peter Christie

EDWARD GASKELL
PUBLISHING

NORTH DEVON
HISTORY

British Library Cataloguing in Publication
A catalogue record for this book is available from
the British Library

ISBN 1- 898546 - 08 - 8

Typeset and printed by
THE LAZARUS PRESS
Cranford House
6 Grenville Street
Bideford
DEVON
EX39 2EA

INTRODUCTION

These articles stem from a chance remark in 1980. I had been talking to the then editor of the *Bideford Gazette* Phil Day when he casually suggested I write an article on Bideford's history as he was always looking for pieces to use in weeks when news was scarce. I went away and came up with the story of a local shipwreck from 1750 which was duly printed in February 1981. Pleased with the reception this received I wrote another which saw print three months later. The interval between this one and the next fell to three weeks and from then on I began turning out articles virtually every week. In September 1984 I was asked to do the same for the *North Devon Journal* and when the *Gazette* split into two editions (Bideford/Barnstaple) in November 1984 I found myself sometimes writing three articles a week to meet the demand. The *Gazette* dropped its dual editions within a few months and stopped printing my contributions altogether in August 1987 as did the *Journal* in October 1992. Over the eleven years a total of 496 articles were published and since the series finished many people have often asked when I would be republishing them. Being involved with other writing projects I didn't have any time to spare until this year when I finally sorted out a batch of those I think deserved a more permanent posterity in book form. A few have been updated and I have attempted to supply references for those who would like to follow up the original material. My thanks are due to Felicity James who has retyped all of them, Edward Gaskell for undertaking the paperwork associated with publishing a book and the staffs of the North Devon Athenaeum and North Devon Record Office for helping in so many ways. I enjoyed researching and writing the articles enormously – I hope you will enjoy reading them.

Peter Christie

CONTENTS

PEOPLE

1. WHITE WITCHES AND WIZARDS TO CURE ALL ILLS

It is well known that the last witches hung in England (in 1682) came from Bideford. After this date it seems that society came to its senses and abandoned the old superstitious beliefs in evil powers. I say 'seems' because every now and again there was a resurgence in belief in various parts of the country. One such event occurred in Combe Martin in October 1827.

A report is found in the *Journal* of that date which begins by attacking the ignorant villagers. Indeed it noted that in few parishes "are they more abundant than in the parish of Combmartin". A belief in witchcraft still reigned there "with all its fears and all its charms and sickness of a cow, or the death of a sheep, is by many considered the malicious doing of some dealer in familiar spirits".

This attack was sparked off by a local girl called Ann Mary Norman who, "is at this time severely afflicted with hysteria". Her illness took the form of violent spasms where, "her body is strangely distorted, and assumes various attitudes, which the human frame in a healthy state is incapable of."

Her family and fellow villagers had concluded that she had been "overlooked" (i.e. given the evil eye) and because she was bewitched, "Medical application is of no avail – consequently it is not resorted to, but the patient is left to combat the violence of the disorder and no assistance afforded to suffering nature".

Doctors may not have been called in but a local "conjuror" or white witch was summoned (we would call him a wizard today). He prescribed "a charm to counteract the malign influence of hurtful spite". The wizard's name is not given but he was said to live in Barnstaple and to be an ex-agricultural labourer who had "abandoned the sickle and the plough for the sublimer pursuits of studying the evolutions of the planets, dispensable charms to expel the foul fiend, and weighing plums and sugar." Not only did he make a charm for the girl but he also told the girl's relations that 25 people in Combe Martin used witchcraft!

The denouement of the case wasn't long in coming though we have to turn to the pages of the local parish register to find it.

There on December 13th 1827 the vicar noted the burial of one Ann Mary Norman aged 19. Clearly the talisman hadn't worked. Whether black magic was involved or not we can never know, but it is worth noting the burial thirteen days later of 3 year old James Norman, followed seven months later by 8 year old John Norman – which suggests a family succumbing to disease rather than spells.

I am unsure if Combe Martin still has this reputation of containing both simpletons and witches – one hopes not, though it could provide a wonderful theme for a local tourist attraction!

North Devon Journal 15.6.1989

2. FOLK-BELIEFS EXPOSED

The eighteenth century was a period of great intellectual advancement that swept away many of the old folk-beliefs of our ancestors. One belief, witchcraft, was very tenacious and indeed still exists today. In September 1836 a case came before the court in Barnstaple that highlights just how entrenched were such ideas. Under the headline "A White Witch" the *Journal* published an account of the case.

James Wheeler "a small farmer" of Instow, was charged by Maria Incledon of Marwood, "a simple looking joskin" with defrauding her. Maria's father had been robbed of some clothing and other articles and "having heard that the defendant was a conjuror" with the power to locate stolen property she decided to hire him.

She, with "a kindred softpate" Jane Wybron went to Instow to "procure the aid of the 'larned man' touching her father's loss." Wheeler questioned her about the property and when it was stolen and then "pored awhile over several mysterious books" but decided he was too busy getting in his harvest to help just then, but agreed to meet her in Barnstaple a week later.

This he did, charging her 25p for the privilege although after some haggling this was reduced to 20p. At this second meeting he said he "had discovered the thieves." They were a dark haired man and a sandy haired woman. Hardly an amazing discovery but he went on to promise that the thieves would return their booty within a few days. Unfortunately the days lengthened into weeks but nothing happened. Being somewhat puzzled they eventually reapplied to Wheeler but he dismissed them saying he had done all he could and could do no more. Not content with this they summonsed him for fraud.

In court Wheeler denied the womens' statements but the evidence was all against him. The reporter was surprised that Wheeler was so ignorant not apparently even having "the common shrewdness of our rural population" and marvelled "how such a man could inspire the most ignorant" in his claimed powers.

The magistrates quickly found Wheeler guilty and sentenced him to a month's imprisonment under the Vagrancy Act for "having by subtle means, craft and device, imposed on the complainant."

One assumed that such a public exposure of his lack of magical powers destroyed any standing he had – though as I have written before such beliefs continued well into this century and even exist today.

North Devon Journal 24.1.1991

3. OLD VICTORIAN CHARMER

The Victorians prided themselves on their solid, rational, no-nonsense approach to life – nowhere more than in the field of medicine.

Medical advances in the nineteenth century were spectacular and seemed to promise even greater discoveries based on technology and common sense. Imagine the disbelief when in August 1877 a so-called "white witch" appeared before a magistrate's court in South Molton to answer a possible charge of manslaughter through negligence in performing his 'alternative medicine'.

The man was John Harper, an octogenarian of West Down, who was apparently known as 'Dr' Harper. He was an ex-miner who had 'practised' his own brand of health care for over 30 years in the area. The charge was that on August 4 at Bishops Nympton he "did use certain subtle craft, means and devices by palmistry and otherwise, to deceive and impose upon certain of Her Majesty's subjects, contrary to the statute made and provided." The case followed "certain disclosures made at a coroner's inquest." The inquest was on a Mrs Sanders of Bishops Nympton who had been ill for many weeks. Her two doctors had given up her case as "beyond human aid" and her relatives had called in 'Dr' Harper as a last resort. Unfortunately she died a few days after he visited her.

It took the prosecuting lawyer a long time to drag out the details of the visit from the woman's relatives as they were afraid of what Harper might, or could, do to them. On his arrival Harper had asked for the exact date and hour of Mrs Sanders' birth. He then gave her a series of metal rods, wrapped at one end in parchment, bearing the names of the planets, which she struck against a stone held in her other hand. Whilst she was doing this Harper muttered some "charm or incantation." He also gave her some powder and "physic" and received 25s. (£1.25) for his trouble.

At his trial Harper's solicitor argued that the rods represented "a rough form of using electricity!" and he offered to call over a hundred witnesses who had been cured by this treatment. They included John Garnsey, a local ostler, who had been crippled for three years and had been advised by local doctors to have his leg amputated. Harper had cured him in six weeks. Another was Charles Lewis, a West Down shoemaker whose inflamed elbow had been cured in only three minutes!

Notwithstanding these successes Harper was found guilty and sentenced to a month in gaol. He was bailed out on £40 and took his case to appeal at Exeter in October. By this time Harper's powders and 'physic' had been analysed and found merely to consist of a herbal extraction from the centuary plant. This finding destroyed any last lingering doubts that the 'Doctor' may have poisoned his patients. The case was actually dismissed on a technicality – there was a mistake in the wording of the charge. One senses, however, that the magistrates were only too happy to wash their hands of the whole affair – superstition in the materialistic Victorian age was not to be taken seriously and was best ignored.

North Devon Journal 2.5.1985

4. WOMAN WHO DIED FROM A WIZARD'S AID

In an earlier article I referred to John Harper, a mining agent who set himself up as a local practitioner of 'alternative' medicine back in the mid-nineteenth century. Known in his own day as a 'white wizard' he is a fascinating character. Another event in which he featured has now come to my attention. It occurred in November 1851 at Braunton where a woman who had just had a baby and was feeling ill was told by friends attending her that she was "suffering beneath the spell of the enchanter" – that she was bewitched. This, not unnaturally, worried her intensely and she became fevered and then passed into a "fearful delirium." This, however, was merely taken as a sign that she was truly bewitched.

Her friends sent for Harper, who was then living in Union Street, Barnstaple, to lift the "curse" and cure her. Harper's actions are described in some detail. Arriving at the woman's home he commanded that one of the women present read the Bible – Deuteronomy chapter 30, verses 1 to 14.

Unfortunately the woman doing the reading went past the fourteenth verse. This slip threw Harper into an "aghast" rage and he declared "that by this accident the foul fiend had power to do his work, and all their efforts could not now save the afflicted person." The 'wizard' left immediately, though he advised calling in a proper doctor. The ill woman heard all this and the report on the case I have read reckoned she died of "fright", which isn't surprising. The writer ended his piece with a call "to place the individual who by the propagation of this superstitious dogma has sacrificed life" before a law court. Harper was stung into replying but the editor of the local paper disdained to publish his letter.

The editor returned to the story the following week describing Harper as "the great North Devon Star of witchcraft." Harper's letter apparently had denied responsibility for the woman's death and alleged that the poor woman had been delirious for months prior to his being called in, and that she was a hopeless case. A local doctor, however, said he had been called in ten days before she died and found her suffering from "milk fever" with no signs of delirium. He left her some medicine and on visiting her the next day found her much better. Several days later he again attended her and found that Harper had been and that she was much worse. He tried to argue with the women there but they maintained their patient was "witched". Within days she was dead "in most painful circumstances" having screamed out for Harper's magical help in her last paroxysms.

The article closed by pointing out that belief in witchcraft was not "confined to the lower class" but was said to "inflict all classes of society." The best preventative was "an intelligent investigation."

North Devon Journal 6.8.1987

5. LAST WITCH IN BIDEFORD LIVED TO 105

Every ten years in Britain the census is taken. These records are open to the public once over a hundred years old, though the first surviving ones date from 1841. In the past the census form was much less cumbersome than today but the results make fascinating reading. I have recently completed a copy of the Bideford census for 1851 and if one looks at the typical street one gets an intriguing view of Victorian North Devon.

Meddon Street is a long steep hill where 723 people lived in 1851. It was dominated by the town's workhouse (now an old peoples' hospital) where 139 inmates were listed. These included the Master – James Stevenson, a 42 year old ex-Colour Sergeant of the Coldstream Guards, whose wife Ann acted as Matron. They were helped by a schoolmaster and mistress who taught the large number of children in the Workhouse who were mixed indiscriminately with the old, the sick and the destitute.

Many of the children were in fact illegitimate – ten unmarried mothers are listed, their presence in the Workhouse grim evidence of the nineteenth century harshness towards such unfortunates. Amongst the sick were Mary Lee, a blind 80 year old widow and 70 year old Abraham Williams listed simply as 'idiot.'

All the inmates are listed as 'paupers' but the street could boast many occupations. Fourteen agricultural labourers appear, evidence that Bideford was still surrounded by farms. Culm miners from the famous Bideford paint mines appear, as do several potters and many masons. Some professional men were also listed – a vet, an auctioneer and three Inland Revenue officers. More unusual occupations were a clay pipe maker, an omnibus driver, an umbrella maker and a "knitster."

The commonest job was the mainly female one of "servant." This was the period when even humble artisans could afford a 'skivvy' – a very necessary help in that age of unremitting, hard, domestic work. These women varied from governess to parlour maid, but all were underpaid.

The oldest resident of the street was Martha Lee, aged 98, who was a Workhouse inmate. She died in 1853 and the *Journal* noted that she was the last witch in Bideford – and gave her age as 105!

Most of the street's residents were either Bideford born or else came from nearby villages. Only a few came from further afield. Bristol and London were the commonest birthplaces outside of Devon though a few came form South Wales and Cornwall. The most travelled were three children of a Wesleyan minister who had been born in Jamaica.

North Devon Journal 14.4.1988

6. THAT WELL KNOWN CURE FOR SPOTS!

In 1879 one girl's zealous pursuit of beauty led to her agonising death and a bizarre inquest. The girl was Mary Perry, a 24 year old servant who lived and worked at a Mr Gottwaltz's house in Mill Street, Bideford. She was apparently subject to depression and also seems to have had a spotty complexion.

To alleviate this a fellow servant got her a small bottle of white arsenic – apparently Victorian women dabbed it on their faces to cleanse and whiten them. Mary, however, either in a fit of depression or as a desperate attempt to clear her spots took a teaspoonful of the poison spread on a piece of bread and butter. The outcome was obvious – within a few hours she had died in agony and her body was removed by two council men "in a common hand cart."

The inquest was held the next day at the Dispensary on the Quay (the Portman Building Society now stands there). The 12 jurymen heard the evidence which seemed to point to temporary insanity and adjourned to a small room to make their decision. Unfortunately eight of them wanted a simple statement of death by arsenic whilst the other four insisted on a suicide verdict. Majority decisions weren't allowable and so the jury remained in discussion for the next 10 hours! The room this was taking place in was described as "a small ill-ventilated room without a fire." The coroner wouldn't even allow them to smoke to keep warm, though when he left at 1 a.m. the next morning they soon filled the room with smoke – thus adding to their discomfort.

The coroner returned at 3 a.m. and found the jury "almost despaired of ever agreeing". He then ordered the local Police Superintendent to lock them into the room without any food, drink or heat until they reached a decision. Even this didn't help and at 10 a.m. that morning the long suffering coroner reconvened the inquest and reviewed the evidence as well as accepting a new statement from the girl's employer Mrs Gottwaltz. After hearing this the exhausted jurors took just minutes to return their verdict, "That the deceased died by an overdose of arsenic."

With this rather obvious phrase the jurors took leave of their temporary jail though one was heard complaining that his wife would never believe him when he told her where he had been all night. Poor Mary was buried – a dramatic example to other girls not to take the pursuit of beauty too far.

North Devon Journal 29.9.1988

7. BRIDE'S LUCKY ESCAPE AT THE RECEPTION

"...Let him speak now or forever hold his peace"– a phrase that has doubtless caused many a bride or groom's heart to skip a beat as they stood before the altar praying no one would say a word! In Bideford in 1821, however, a bride's worst fears came true, not in church but at the reception afterwards. In December of that year a man calling himself Mr Sargent, described as "a dashing blade" who claimed to be "a man of fortune", came to Bideford and hired some rooms at an inn in the town. Here he "soon won the affections of one of the landlord's daughters."

Mr Sargent must have been seen as a fine catch, for the girl in question cast caution to the wind and allowed herself to be caught up in a real whirlwind romance. After only a few days she agreed to marry him and so the event took place. All was happiness until the reception. While the couple and their guests were eating their wedding breakfast "a relation of the gentleman made his appearance" and, as the wonderfully rounded language of the contemporary Press puts it, "not being acquainted with the occasion that brought the party together, without hesitation exclaimed, loud enough to be heard by all in the room, 'Well, brother, you are a lucky fellow. The business about Sal is all settled to our satisfaction and you may return home'."

The effect of this cryptic statement was immediate. The bride fainted, the groom swore and "the company stood aghast". On an explanation being demanded the groom admitted he was already married and in fact had two children at home as well as a wife. Indeed, he had come to Bideford only to avoid a paternity suit being brought against him by the woman called Sal! Needless to say, these revelations caused complete chaos and during this, Mr Sargent, or whoever he really was, made good his escape with his brother "and has not been heard of since", which isn't very surprising.

What is slightly puzzling about this case is that there is no entry in the Bideford parish register for this marriage. Possibly the vicar heard of the debacle before he entered the fact of the marriage in the register – or, if it was ever entered, removed it. Whatever the truth, one has to pity the poor innkeeper's daughter who no doubt became the laughing stock of the town for a while following her "marriage".

North Devon Journal 24.8.1989

8. RARE SHOTGUN WEDDING . . . AT THE AGE OF 80

Today the majority of our senior citizens are women...simply due to the workings of Mother Nature. On average more males than females are born but they die at a faster rate than females. In the past this imbalance was often overcome by the high death rate among women going through childbirth and its associated dangers from the lack of medical knowledge and general hygiene. This state of affairs led to men often marrying two or three wives during their life. One odd example of this occurred in Marwood in the late eighteenth and early nineteenth century.

In December 1824, William Gould, a sprightly 80 year old, married his third wife – 25 year old Jane Huxtable of that parish. Such an event would cause raised eyebrows even today, but at that time it was extremely unusual. A contemporary newspaper report, after noting that this was "the third time the venerable bridegroom has paid his devotions to the Shrine of Hymen", went on to detail William's personal history.

In his "youthful days" he had married a girl of his own age but she soon died – possibly in childbirth, but this isn't stated. He subsequently married again though this time his wife was "thirty years older than himself" – clearly William had different tastes to most men. The bride would appear from the Marwood parish register to be one Agnes Gubb who married William in March, 1812, and who died just two years later aged 80!

In a wonderful example of male chauvinism the newspaper stated that "death having released him of this antiquated dame, he has now again ventured on a blooming damsel." This marriage is recorded in the parish register without any other comment. This record may be silent – though the newspaper isn't – about the birth two weeks earlier of "a pair of chopping boys" to Jane and William! An octogenarian 'having to get married' in the early nineteenth century equivalent of a 'shotgun marriage' must have set the local tongues wagging for many months afterwards. William lived another nine years dying in January 1833 when his age was recorded, for some reason, as just 84. As if to redress the balance somewhat his widow Jane was remarried just over a year later to one William Wybron who, as far as I know, was about her own age.

As the saying goes, 'they did things differently in the past'. But just how differently is sometimes hard to believe.

North Devon Journal 5.1.1989

9. COUPLES WHO WERE MARCHED TO THE ALTAR

On December 30th 1828, St. Peter's Church in the centre of Barnstaple was host to a wedding service between John Gibbins and Maria Couch. They were married by the vicar, the Rev H Luxmoore, and like any other couple they retired after the service to the vestry to sign the parish register. John firmly wrote his name but his new wife could sign only with a cross. The witnesses were William Cousins and John Kempland.

An ordinary marriage perhaps but one with something of a story behind it. Maria came from Braunton and had apparently met John some months previously. Nature had taken its course and Maria had become pregnant or, as a contemporary newspaper report put it "exhibited prognostications of increasing the population of Braunton". Nothing unusual in this at that date but unfortunately

John had decided that he wasn't ready to settle down and had gone home to Bampton.

At this date the law was that pregnant spinsters had to inform the authorities who was the father of the unborn child. If the woman proved reluctant she could be taken before a magistrate and compelled to give the name under threat of imprisonment. A threat, incidentally, that was sometimes carried out. It seems barbaric to us today but family historians at least are thankful as it allows them to find out the fathers of illegitimate children! The authorities could force the man to pay maintenance, the reluctant father might run away and join the Army or Navy (a good source of recruits in those days) or the hapless couple could take their chances and get married.

In this case the Overseers of the Poor of Barnstaple – the men who looked after the town's poor – sent one of their number to Bampton "to conduct John to the arms of his longing bride". John came to Barnstaple under escort and in a lovely phrase it was noted that "to give him a higher zest for the pleasures of a wedding-day, he was not suffered to be at large, till the reverend clergyman had pronounced him and his blushing bride inseparably one". Poor John seems to have been confined in the town lock-up overnight, just in case he had second (or in this case third) thoughts.

There was one other small detail that needed clearing up – the question of the banns which legally had to be called for three weeks prior to the ceremony. The Overseers, however, were so keen to see Maria married that they paid for a special licence which allowed her to have an immediate wedding. As one last check one of the Overseers actually accompanied John and Maria right to the altar!

The reason for all this heavy-handed civic action was quite simple – money. Unmarried mothers and their children had to be looked after at the expense of the parish in which they lived. Parish officials, keen to keep their rate payments low, took every opportunity to rid themselves of unwanted charges such as illegitimate children – so explaining their dedication to duty in this case.

What happened to John and Maria I do not know. They presumably went to live in Bampton but unfortunately the parish registers for the mid-nineteenth century are lost so we cannot tell if

Maria ever had her child and whether she and John managed to settle down after their rather unusual beginning to married life.

North Devon Journal 27.7.1989

10. LONELY HEARTS ADVERT FROM A 'GENTLEMAN'

Most of us cannot resist reading the personal column in the advertising pages of our newspapers. One never knows what is going to be there, though more often than not, there are appeals for friendship from both sexes. Such adverts might be thought to be the result of our 'anonymous' society where people appear to find it so difficult to meet. But we would be wrong.

In reading the files of the *Journal* I was surprised to come across just such a lonely hearts advertisement – in 1828. Couched in the beautifully rounded phrases of Regency England it makes fascinating reading. It appears in the issue for November 13 1828, on the front page – for many years the standard place for all advertising.

Headed in bold capitals "MATRIMONY" it begins, "A Gentleman who has not by many years attained the middle age, whose height of ambition is to enter the marriage state in the hope that fortune may choose more auspiciously for him than himself, adopts this method as that most likely to interest the Ladies of North of Devon in his behalf".

That wonderful phrase about "fortune" seems to indicate a romantic spirit, but as we read on the more hard-headed qualities of that age become evident. The man, who remains anonymous, continues. "He is of a respectable family and possesses a comfortable independence". No fortune hunter he, or so we are led to believe. After getting the economic side of marriage out of the way he continues, "as for person, he merely mentions that his has been laughed at by many, approved of by some and even admired by a few; his health is good, figure robust and constitution vigorous." To add to this pleasing description, which conjures up a picture of a rosy-cheeked, Old English yeoman, it is noted that "he has acquired many accomplishments, but most especially that of a yielding disposition". One wonders whether his women readers found this attractive or not.

What sort of woman was being sought is then spelled out. "Any lady of agreeable person, domestic habits and moderate fortune, will, it is hoped, find in this advertisement a husband consonant to her wishes". Notice the reference to money; presumably poor women, however "agreeable" their person and accomplished their "domestic habits" needn't have bothered to apply.

Those who thought they met the requirements were asked to send a letter "post paid" which contained their "real name and address" to Barnstaple Post Office to be collected. For any that caught the gentleman's attention "an interview" would be "appointed". Because the advert is unsigned we can never know whether this lovelorn gentleman found a true love from his advertising.

North Devon Journal 11.5.1989

11. FOR SALE: A WIFE HE DIDN'T WANT

Divorce is common today, being no respecter of class or age; in the past, however, things were very different. Until 1857 and the first 'Matrimonial Causes Act' the only way of obtaining a divorce in England was to obtain a private Act of Parliament. Such Acts were very few in number and ruinously expensive, thus confining divorce entirely to the aristocracy.

What then did the working classes do when their marriages broke down? One simple and fairly widespread expedient was just to walk out and leave their partners. Unfortunately any remarriage in such a case always carried the threat of a bigamy charge and severe penalties for the people involved.

One other way was 'wife selling.' It was the accepted folk-lore (or folk-law) of England that a man who put his wife up for sale in a public market was instantly and legally separated from her if another man purchased her – no matter how little the price! The last recorded case happened only just over a hundred years ago in Northern Ireland.

I have only come across one case in North Devon and that occurred in March 1834. The story is reported in the *North Devon Journal* which called it, "One of those disgraceful scenes which have occasionally been exhibited, to the outrage of social order, and the degradation of human kind."

Apparently one Christopher Lock set out from Braunton with his wife to travel to Barnstaple one Friday market day. He was a stone-mason from Marwood "between whom and his wife much unhappiness had for a long time prevailed." He came to market "with the professed intention of selling her." The unhappiness referred to came from both parties – Lock was brutal and domineering but his wife had "formed an illicit connection with another man, a tangible proof of which has been produced" (i.e. a child). We are not told which came first, Lock's brutality or his cuckolding.

They must have talked over what course of action to take and decided that public sale would be suitable as, when they arrived in Barnstaple, "the wife with her paramour were in attendance at the same public house with the husband." Also there were "a crowd of curious to witness the proposed transfer." Presumably the plan was to offer the wife for sale with her lover being the purchaser – thus satisfying everyone involved.

Unfortunately for both, however, "a constable put an end to the drama, by taking the husband before the Mayor, who ordered him to be put in the constable's prison till the next morning." The wife, robbed of both husband and lover was taken "to the extremity of the parish" and "sent about her business."

One can only assume that the couple then merely separated and went differing ways without any recourse to this curious (and illegal) form of divorce.

I think it goes without saying in today's world that no woman would ever allow herself willingly to be exhibited for public sale – no matter how desired a divorce might be.

North Devon Journal 17.4.1986

12. DIVORCE MORE LIKE A GAME OF CALL MY BLUFF

In a previous article I wrote about the bizarre practice of 'wife-selling' and commented that this was a recognised, if illegal, method of divorce among the working classes in previous centuries. I have recently come across an equally unusual method of 'divorce' – again illegal – though this one actually ended up in a court of law.

At the Devon County Assizes in March 1851 the case of Kingdon versus Kingdon appeared under the ominous heading of "Bigamy". Denis Kingdon "an attorney formerly in practice at Hatherleigh, but lately resident at Torrington, was indicted for having married Anne Shear, his first wife being alive."

The first witness called was the Rev Samuel Raymond of Swindon who alleged that Kingdon had married Anne Caroline Kiddell Stock at Cheltenham on March 30 1831. He also identified Anne as being in court. His evidence was buttressed by the Cheltenham parish clerk who produced the marriage register signed by the Kingdons as proof. Two women, Mary Balkwill of St. Petrock and Sarah Anne Prust of Bideford, then appeared and swore that the Kingdons had lived as man and wife at Hatherleigh until they separated, apparently by mutual consent, in 1837.

The Torrington policeman, John Fussell, then entered the witness box and produced a copy of the registration of Kingdon's second marriage at Beaford on September 21 1840. A local farmer, Mr Judd, identified Kingdon as the man who signed the register.

The case appeared watertight and indeed Kingdon did not deny the facts. He did, however, produce "letters in mitigation of punishment" and alleged that he "had been persecuted by his wife (Anne) for years past." She had continually threatened to reveal his secret unless he paid her £10. Every time he paid, she signed an agreement not to charge him – but every time she broke it and demanded more. This time he had called her bluff.

The jury found him guilty as charged but the judge added "this was not an honest prosecution" but merely "an attempt by the first wife to extort money, which he could not countenance." So saying he sentenced Kingdon to pay one shilling (5p) fine and be discharged. Bearing in mind how difficult a Victorian divorce was, one is left wondering just how many bigamists there were in nineteenth-century Britain? If this case is anything to go by the answer would be many!

North Devon Journal 31.3.1988

13.THE SHAMING OF AN ADULTERER

Imagine, if you will, a sleepy, sun-drenched Devon village around the middle of the nineteenth century. Its roads are covered with white dust, its tranquillity unbroken by the noise of engines and its appearance unchanged in centuries. Imagine further then the shock of having this silence shattered by the tantivy of hunting horns, the staccato fire of muskets and shotguns and the excited shouts of a frenzied mob as they chase and bring to bay a stag. This, however, is no ordinary stag. This beast is two-legged and man-shaped, its antlers tied on above a face painted a hideous red. What on earth could be happening? Simply an age-old folk custom aimed at shaming an adulterer or would-be gigolo. Unbelievable as this sounds at first hearing, such events are well attested in the old files of local newspapers.

In 1854 for example a Mr Spear who was a tailor at Shebbear undertook a court case charging some men who had organised a 'stag-hunt' against him. The journalist who reported the case explained that such a hunt "is a farce wherein a man, disguised as a stag, with branching horns, is hunted through the parish by the rabble who, with guns and sticks, represent the hounds."

Such a hunt occurred when a man or woman was suspected of moral laxitude, the idea of the 'hunters' being to embarrass or shame them back on the road of righteousness. In Mr Spear's case even though he barricaded his doors they were smashed down and he was dragged out and kicked to the ground. But the defendants in this case were only fined one shilling each as they were "only following an old custom, intended to ridicule those who went astray."

In the April of the following year James Draydon, John Dunken, William Taylor and Philip Tucker were brought before the magistrates at Torrington for inciting a 'stag-hunt.' In this case their anger was directed against "a married man and a spruce young widow (who) had been seen walking together very lovingly." A mob of 200 collected and chased one of their number dressed as a stag through the streets of Torrington. In this case, as in the last, the bench took a lenient view as they decided "it was more for fun than any intention to break the peace," and only fined the four ringleaders four shillings each.

In January 1859 St. Giles-in-the-Wood was the scene of yet another 'stag-hunt' although in this case the 'hunters' over-reached themselves. The object of the mob's irritation was a Pc Sprague whose official position did not save him from such public censure. The 'stag' in this hunt wore antlers, had a painted face and wore a sheepskin. The policeman was surrounded by the jeering crowd but stalked off. On the same evening, however, with two fellow constables, he waited outside the local pub and when two of the 'hunt' ringleaders emerged arrested them for obstructing the police in the course of their duty. Once again the bench took a lenient view of the case and levied fines of one shilling each plus costs of 7s 6d. A note in the original report added that this amount was soon collected from the waiting crowd outside the court room.

The last local case I have come across occurred in Heanton Punchardon in 1928.

Bideford Gazette 15.7.1983

14. WHEN THEY CARPETED A ROAD FOR A BRIDE

Survivals of folk customs are now rare in England, but in the past every small locality seems to have had its own customs and traditions. In North Devon in the last century we had the village revels, 'stag hunts' of adulterers and the election of sham Mayors in Bideford and Barnstaple.

In Barnstaple the 'alternative' Mayor came from the Derby area where the poor, working class residents had other customs as well. One of these was reported in some detail in the *North Devon Journal* in April 1881. On a Saturday morning the peaceable and respectable inhabitants of Derby "were rudely disturbed from their slumbers" about 7 a.m. by some unusual marriage celebrations.

The couple were "well known in that quarter" and they had spread the news far and wide and hundreds of friends and acquaintances had come to witness the ceremony. The day had been chosen apparently because "it was a general holiday at the lace factory" which was then the main employer in Derby. The bride was 18 and "resided in Boden's Row – a street famous for its rows at all times", as the reporter jocularly remarked. The bridegroom "a spruce young man of about 20" lived "in an equally 'respectable' quarter – Princes Street."

All the bride's neighbours had "utilised their upholstery resources to the fullest possible extent" and "carpeted" the whole road. The bride thus walked to church without dirtying her feet – presumably this was a local marriage custom. The large bridal party "showed their pleasure by emitting a noise which would have done credit to a menagerie."

The groom left his house dressed in an antiquated top-hat, long tail-coat and white waistcoat. His party met the bride's party at the gate of St. Mary Magdalene Church but found it locked. The crowd, now numbering 500, marched up Vicarage Street and along Bear Street to the other entrance of the church which was open. So many crowded into the church that the poor vicar, the Rev Bull, couldn't get in.

No doubt he wondered what on earth was going on for a number of people had brought hand-bells with them "by no means of a musical nature" and were ringing these in the church. Another guest had "hit upon the happy thought of giving a peal upon the solitary bell in the steeple, which he did right lustily, to the great indignation of the clerk.

The vicar threatened to call the police whereupon the crowd (one can hardly call them a congregation) burst out laughing "and at once proceeded to throw rice – of which there seemed to be an unlimited supply – at one another, and thus created a tremendous din." The Rev Bull finally completed the ceremony and the happy couple "Left the sacred edifice, amidst great confusion and an overwhelming uproar above which would sometimes rise the screams of women and children for help."

On the way home both the groom and his 'best man' had their top-hats jammed down over their eyes by the crowd. Arriving home at 8.30 a.m., the crowd settled down to a day-long party at which vast quantities of beer were drunk. A day to remember certainly.

No names were given in the original report but two marriages are recorded in the register for that day and the couple concerned appear to have been William Turner and Mary Elizabeth Mock. Does anyone claim them as ancestors?

North Devon Journal 1.8.1985

15. THE CASE OF THE LODGER'S SURPRISE

The 'lodger' was for many years a stock figure of fun in British comedy – always a rogue, often a cheat and usually an enemy to husbands. With this in mind the spectators at Barnstaple Police

Court on May 4 1896, must have had all their ideas about lodgers reinforced when they heard the case of Jane Jones and George Larcomb who were charged with the theft of clothes worth £2.

The proceedings began simply enough. John Jones a local railwayman and husband of Jane recounted how he had married his wife, then a widow, nine years previously. They had "lived together peaceably and comfortably until the prisoner Larcomb came to the house." From that moment his home "became a perfect wreck." Jane had bumped into Larcomb in Barnstaple High Street one day in April, he being her late husband's brother whom she hadn't seen for ten years. He asked her if he could lodge in their house and John and Jane agreed. Poor John "gave his consent quite unsuspectingly." He also "had no intimation from either party of their intentions to run away" which they proceeded to do just a short while later.

Jane took with her one of their three children plus a box containing her clothes. John in desperation when he returned to find his wife gone asked the police to arrest her as a thief – though to be accused of stealing one's own clothes is a bit unfair! The eloping couple were arrested at Teignmouth and the box found at the left luggage office of the local railway station where it had been deposited under an assumed name. The pair were brought back to Barnstaple to answer their accuser.

Rather a sordid and not especially interesting tale one might think. It was at this point, however, that a sensation occurred in the court. Larcomb stood up and announced that he was in fact Jane's husband, not her brother-in-law. He had married her twelve years ago at Bristol when she was very young – "about fifteen or sixteen years of age." Shortly after their marriage, however, "there was a little disagreement between them and they parted." When he met her again in Barnstaple in April it was the first time they had seen each other in those twelve years.

Poor John was thunderstruck. He had always believed his wife to have been a widow – indeed he had seen the mourning cards issued at the time of the funeral of her first husband. Jane was forced to admit that "she had it printed at Mr Jones's, Boutport Street," in order to fool him. The court reporter noted that "Jones (who was greatly affected) here stated amid much sensation, that he was quite willing to take his wife back again if the magistrates would dismiss her, she had been a good wife, industrious and true, and had behaved as a wife should" – one might have doubts about the last sentiment!

The poor magistrates faced with a simple theft case that had suddenly turned into one of bigamy and deception could only ask whether Jane wanted to be tried as Mrs Larcomb or Mrs Jones – she chose the latter. After careful, and no doubt perplexed, thought the magistrates concluded "that Larcomb had exercised undue influence in order to get her away from her home and family." Because, however, she had pleaded guilty to theft they were forced to fine her 5s (25p) which John immediately paid. Larcomb received fourteen days gaol with hard labour and was taken away to cries of "shame" from spectators.

One can only hope that John and Jane lived happily ever after – but one wonders why the court took no notice of their bigamous condition. Perhaps a case of turning a blind eye and being pragmatic.

North Devon Journal 10.4.1986

16. MOCKING THE OLD MAYORS

Amongst the odd folklore of our ancestors were the 'mock Mayors'. I have dealt with the 'mock Mayors' of Bideford, Buckland Brewer and Derby in Barnstaple before, but two more of these strange functionaries have now come to light – at Goose Green, in Torrington, and at Parracombe. In June 1827 the *Journal* reported the election of the Parracombe 'Mayor' – an event that, according to the reporter, occurred every Whit Tuesday. At this particular election two candidates were standing, which seems to have been an unusual event and perhaps explains the newspaper coverage.

A public meeting was held in the open air where both candidates announced "that should he be so happy as to become the object of their choice he would perform the important duties of the office fearlessly, faithfully, impartially, etc."

Voting took place in public – no secret ballots then – with the result that the previous year's 'Mayor', W. Lovering, won again. After the announcement of the results the winner went to the Fox and Goose public house and "ascended a triumphal car" (i.e. a cart) decorated with evergreen boughs and ribbons. This was hauled through the village to the cheers of the crowd.

On his return the "returning officer" made a speech in which he attacked taxes of all kinds, "very gallantly addressed the ladies" and reminded the new 'Mayor' of the great importance of his office. The group then disappeared into the Fox and Goose for the rest of the day.

Further evidence about the Parracombe 'Mayors' comes from a manuscript in the North Devon Athenaeum, written by a villager, Arthur Smyth, which covers his memories of the years 1851-1935. He notes that the ceremony of 'mayor making' continued until the early years of this century, based on the Royal Hotel (previously the London Inn). Apparently it began on each occasion only after the participants had "got decently drunk". A wheelbarrow was used to transport the newly elected 'Mayor' and, by tradition, he was tipped into the Mill Pond at the end of the day!

Smyth also notes the existence of a man who "died not many years ago" who was always known as the "town clerk" in the village. He was a tailor by trade and apparently acted as 'returning officer' and speechmaker on these occasions. The ceremony came to an end only when one man who had been elected 'Mayor' for many years running died...and the ceremony died with him.

Such 'mock mayors' were, of course, just an excuse for a day of jollity and drinking, though they probably originated in our ancestors' love of puncturing pomposity wherever it occurred – and our early real mayors were nothing if not pompous! Perhaps it is a pity such harmless ceremonies have been allowed to lapse.

North Devon Journal 9.3.1989

17. DAY THE DEVIL APPEARED AT MARWOOD

A little time ago I wrote about the time the devil appeared at Marwood – since then I have discovered three letters in the 1896 file of the *North Devon Journal* which add to our knowledge of folklore and belief at Marwood and in North Devon generally.

They were all written by one Zachariah Smyth who clearly knew his informants well. He began, "North Devon has been distinguished for its belief in ghosts, pixies, Jack o'Lanterns and witchcraft," and then launches into a discussion of ghosts in Marwood.

A story handed down from generation to generation concerned the tower at the parish church. Apparently a laundress who lived at Westcott, a local hamlet, was visited on several occasions by a ghost who told her it wanted a tower added to the church. To achieve its end the ghost told the poor woman where to find a box of treasure carved on one side with a woman's head and on the other with the shape of an iron. She found the box and thus paid for the tower's erection.

Another ghost was that of "Squire Roberts" who haunted and hunted the area on a fire-spitting horse with a pack of spectral and headless hounds. He so troubled the parish that the local parson exorcised him to Saunton Burrows. Here the unfortunate "squire" was set to work to bundle up the sand "but as he could get no material to make the binds he was doomed to perpetual failure."

Smyth then moved on to pixies. In the evening of Midsummer Day the young men and women of Marwood assembled in the church porch to stage a night-long vigil. The pixies would then come and cause those doomed to die within a year to fall asleep!

A happier ceremony also happened on this night. Young girls would sow a bed of hemp-seed and chant the following verse at midnight, "Hemp-seed I sow, Hemp-seed I grow! Let my true love that is to be Rake this same seed now after me." The pixies were expected to send each girl's true lover with a rake – obviously an outcome that could be surreptitiously 'fixed' beforehand. It was probably the same girls who ensured that all the water pitchers in a house were full of fresh water and the fire laid each night – otherwise "the pixies would come and pinch them black and blue during the night."

Smyth then named two famous local witches – Will Groves of Mare, who "was considered to be a very wicked wizard" and Sal Ley of Middle Marwood "who kept a staneful of toads, and mused and fed them on her lap".

If they bewitched you one way of getting your own back was to insert a gimlet into the base of a chair and then get the witch or wizard to sit on it. Once on they could only escape by touching a living animal – while trapped you moved the chair near the fire and roasted them until they removed the spell! Another antidote to witchcraft was to find a horseshoe which "had been cast from the hoof will all its nails perfect." This was hung up above the door and would prove a very powerful charm. Many people still do this today though any old shoe is now used.

From these fairly exotic subjects Smyth went on to discuss other folk beliefs beginning with Christmas festivities. In Marwood on December 24 an ash shoot was felled and its branches bound to the trunk with withies. Ten to twelve men carried this into the house where it was ceremoniously burnt in the fireplace whilst hot spiced cider was drunk. On this evening also the local choir would sing their way around the whole parish. At the sound of "Hark, hear what news the hang-jels bring" each householder was expected to come out and offer hot drinks or cakes to the singers.

On Good Friday, the "barmless cake" was prepared being an inch thick and a foot in diameter. This had a hole in the centre through which a piece of string was threaded, it being hung from the kitchen ceiling until the next year. The old cake was "considered to be a perfect cure for 'skate' in calves."

Just after Whitsun Marwood Revel was held with its side-shows and wrestling matches with silver spoons as prizes. The fights took place on the bowling green "about ten feet below and adjoining the west end of the churchyard." A ring of men would form and the challenger would literally throw his hat into the middle shouting "A man! A man!" To take up the challenge another hat was thrown in and the two wrestlers would strip to the waist and put on loose jackets of coarse material to fight in. The matches were extremely bloody, kicking (in hob-nailed boots) was allowed and broken limbs weren't uncommon. Apparently though "It was not unusual for the parson and his daughters" to view the event. All this was accompanied with heavy drinking but if "revellers" got too "happy" the stocks were next to the churchyard wall.

Corn harvest was the busiest time of the year when wages were highest and food most plentiful. In the last field to be harvested a 'corn dolly' (a very old fertility symbol) was made and the farmer, surrounded by his men, would lift and drop the 'dolly' all crying "we have, we have, we have!" until he finally lifted it above his head to shouts of "the neck, the neck, the neck." The 'dolly' was then scrambled for and whoever captured it took it to the farmhouse in secret as the maids waited to throw buckets of water over the bearer if they could discover him. The "dolly" was added to the barmless cake on the ceiling until next year.

After the harvest "taty hacking" started so long as the potato crop hadn't been attacked by some of the diseases then common. A successful potato crop gave rise to a "taty cake feast", it being followed by the sowing of next years crops. After this bout of concentrated work, a "seed cake feast" was held by the farmer to which all the workers came.

Mr Smyth finished his memories with a long paragraph in praise of the modern advances over the 60 years or so of his life – the old flint and tinder-box had given way to matches, the rush-light to "the illuminating benzoline". Ignorance had been defeated by the parish school and even "the farm labourer is now enabled to vote for the Member of Parliament."

Great and good changes but one cannot help but mourn the passing of so many colourful beliefs and simple ceremonies that enlivened the lives of our ancestors.

North Devon Journal 2.4.1987 and 9.4.1987

18. WORKHOUSE GOVERNOR DISMISSED

I have written before about the birth of the workhouse system in 1834 following a revision of the laws relating to the poor and their care. Their creation was not without incident to judge from available evidence and they quickly gained an unenviable reputation for harshness and severity. This reputation was deliberately aimed at by heartless parish officials called Guardians of the Poor who hoped to keep the workhouse empty and thus save rates money.

In April 1840 a small news item in the *Journal* claimed that, "Since the new governor has been appointed at the Union Workhouse in this town, the number of inmates has been greatly reduced; no less than 23 left voluntarily on Monday last." The town in question was South Molton and the new governor was a Mr Leach who was clearly a hard man. His employers might have liked what he was doing but a reaction wasn't long in coming.

A fortnight after this news item the *Journal* carried a report detailing how Leach had gone out shopping and been trapped in Mr Chant's shop in King Street by a large mob baying for his blood. He had apparently "severely punished a poor child about four-years-old, in the union workhouse, with a cane on the bare back while in bed." Two constables had to fight their way though the crowd and escort the governor. Even so, "he was stoned, hissed and assailed with various missiles" on his journey back to the workhouse.

Several days later the governor was summoned before the local magistrates' bench but they deferred judgement until the Guardians of the Poor had met to decide their actions over the case. As he left the court Leach was pelted with "stones, eggs and all sorts of filth" even though he was surrounded by a posse of special constables.

In the evening a barn belonging to the family of the lawyer who represented Leach in court was set on fire and someone shot out the workhouse windows. In a marvellous example of stating the obvious the account of these occurrences in the *Journal* said, "There is no doubt that these outrages arose out of the general indignation which the conduct of the governor had called forth."

This was all the more surprising to the journalist as apparently Leach had come to the job "most highly recommended" – though by whom is not stated.

There is no further mention of the case in the local papers, but Leach does appear. In February 1841 the *Journal* announces his dismissal for "gross misconduct." He had in fact had an affair with one of the inmates Elizabeth Holmes and got her pregnant. In addition "rumour attributes to him several other similar cases of disgusting misbehaviour." Leach refused to go so local magistrates ordered constables to eject him.

From such stories as this came the harrowing reputation of the workhouse as a place of degradation and violence – thank goodness they have gone.

North Devon Journal 5.12.1991

19. WHAT'S IN A NAME?

All of us are born and all of us die and many of us are married at some time between these two events. Since 1538 the Church of England has kept records concerning these three events in the lives of its members. These records are contained in the parish registers which have details of baptisms, marriages and burials – Bideford's surviving registers date from 1561.

As part of my researches into the town's history I have been transcribing entries. By careful examination a whole range of fascinating data on our predecessors can be obtained. Taking a few years at the beginning of the nineteenth century I hope to show the variety of this information.

The baptismal entries seem a natural starting point and we can see, for example, that the number of baptisms averaged about 100 a year. This figure does not, of course, include non-conformists, always a sizeable group in Bideford, who were not members of the Established Church. The most popular month for the ceremony was April or May suggesting that conceptions were concentrated around August or September. This would reflect the agricultural rhythm of the year. With harvest in, a man could marry and in those pre-birth control days children soon followed.

Many of the actual entries in the baptismal registers are interesting in themselves. Thus in 1807 the melodiously named Ethy Squire M'Kay was christened. In 1809 a child was named Nelson Collingwood Robins – clearly the parents were patriotic. Similar things are seen today when football fanatics saddle their infants with the names of all the members of a favourite team.

An unusual even occurred in 1811 when John Lewis Walkey was baptised. A note in the register tells us that he was "an East Indian of Colour whose Father's nor Mother's name is not known." Presumably he had arrived in Bideford aboard a ship and had possibly settled here.

In 1812 a child was given the names Thomas Sierraleone Prince. In other entries for this family the name is rendered Prince-Sierra-Leone. Was he another member of the negro race or did his father have some other connection, perhaps through trading, with the African state whose name his child bore?

The year 1813 produced a whole crop of odd names, amongst them two mothers, Izekiah Branch and Peternell Camp; a father Briant Bartlett; and a solicitor's child Hinton Castle Smith. In the last instance the parents were obviously making sure that their child emphatically would have a set of unusual Christian names even though his surname was common. In 1815 there was Tamsilia Johnson, and the following year saw Sibella Taylor, the former the wife of a baker and the latter the daughter of a shipwright. Just to finish this look at baptismal entries I might mention Athanasius

Nagle who appeared in 1816 and Benhadhad Phillips in 1817 – two very rare names!

Some entries are noted as being 'base' or illegitimate and in such cases the father's name is usually absent although this can be found from other records. The average rate of illegitimacy over these years was about 5% – compare this figure with that for today which is about 25%.

From 1812 onwards the baptismal entries include the occupation of the father and help show the economic base of the town, centred as it was on shipping and general crafts. In addition eleven potters are named over just the five year period 1812-17, plus, interestingly enough, five schoolmasters. Amongst other rare occupations are a surgeon, butler, watchmaker, basket maker, stonecutter, peltmonger and druggist. The last was called Hogg and for many years his shop was on the corner site now occupied by Bideford Town Hall at the end of the Bridge.

The most unusual entry must, however, be that of Thomas Moore who, when his child was christened in March 1815 described himself as "comedian." There was almost certainly a theatre of some sort in Bideford at this time and perhaps Thomas was appearing there when his wife gave birth?

Moving on to examine the marriage entries, the first thing to strike one is the variety of places the grooms came from. Most of course were local or from surrounding villages but occasionally a man (or woman in some cases) gave as their home parish a place far removed from North Devon. Thus over the years 1803-12 there were men from Westminster, Battersea, Lostwithiel, Bristol and Sussex. Most of these places were coastal towns or areas and we would probably be right in guessing that trade had brought these men to Bideford and their brides. One or two entries, however, are puzzling. What can we make of the man from Reading and another, John Boyce Woods, from Wangford in Suffolk – both places far removed from the sea?

The months of October and November were the most popular for marrying – again, note, just after the harvest had been gathered in. The least popular month was February – still today one of the most unpopular months for weddings. A fairly cursory check of marriage date against the baptismal date for the first child shows that of fifty local couples married between 1806 and 1808 ten of the brides were already pregnant when they went to the altar. This figure is actually fairly low compared to other areas and appears to show the survival of the old tradition that a man would only marry a woman who could bear his children. After all, at this period, children were often a vital part of a family's economy in terms of earning power. Lack of offspring could seriously damage the family fortune. 'Trial' marriages are nothing new!

Although the baptismal registers lack non-conformist entries it is almost certain that virtually all Bideford marriages are in the marriage register. This was because from 1754 until 1812 any marriage that took place outside of the Church of England unless it was a Jewish or Quaker one, was automatically void and the children of such a marriage were illegitimate. Clearly it was in the non-conformists' own interests to marry in the Established Church, if only to secure inheritance rights.

We come finally to the burial entries. Again these are likely to be virtually complete for Bideford if only because the non-conformists had no large burial ground of their own at this date. From 1805 onwards the age at death is given in nearly every case and an analysis of these reveals interesting patterns. Of 468 burials over the years 1805-12 some 133 or just under 30% were of children aged under five. Indeed 72 were of children who never reached their first birthday. Such a child mortality rate is staggering to us today and was probably the result of insanitary conditions, bad eating habits and lack of medical knowledge. Virtually every family must have known the tragedy of a child's death though familiarity with such events would not have blunted the individual heartbreak.

Turning to the other end of the age scale some 157, or about 33% of the burials, were of people over 60 years of age. The oldest was Margaret Harris who was buried in September 1807, aged 98. The general rule would appear to be that if you were lucky enough to survive past the age of five you were all set for a long life. Presumably this was on the basis that having got through the dangerous first few years nothing much else could kill you!

Deaths do not appear to be clustered in any particular month though March, with its biting winds and showers seems to have had more than the usual monthly total of burials. Bideford's growth can be seen over the years 1808-12 when we compare the 296 burials with the 485 baptisms. This gives an average of an additional 38 inhabitants per year – almost exactly the same number recorded over the years 1971-81 – though much of this modern growth was due to outsiders moving into the area.

From the foregoing I hope I have shown just how much of interest is contained in what, at first sight, might seem fairly dry records. By careful use and imaginative reconstruction we can recreate a small piece of Bideford's past.

Bideford Gazette 3.2.1984

20. WOODEN COMPUTER INVENTED IN NORTH DEVON

There is no technology in the world today that has developed so rapidly as the computer. The first giant-sized electronic computers of 30 years ago have now been replaced by pocket-sized marvels of complexity and power. It is fascinating, therefore, to know that one of the original pioneers of the computer was a self-taught bookseller and printer of Torrington who was born over 200 years ago.

His name was Thomas Fowler and we owe our knowledge of him to a biographical sketch written by his son, the Rev Hugh Fowler, which was published in the *North Devon Journal* of August 1875. He tells how his father was born in 1777, the son of a Torrington cooper. He spent all his spare time reading and re-reading the only book he could find – one on mathematics. Mastering this he moved on to build himself a printing press and set up in trade as a jobbing printer. Flourishing in this business he helped fund and eventually ran the local bank, as well as becoming organist in St. Michael's church in the town. His inventiveness didn't stop at printing for in 1828 he patented a device known as the 'thermosiphon' which was the basis of all modern central heating systems using radiators. Unfortunately the patent laws were very weak and his work was pirated, he receiving no royalties or recognition for his invention.

In 1840 when he was 63 years old, and after many years of effort, he finally completed his 'calculating machine.' This was made of wood and measured five feet high, four feet wide and four feet long. It was apparently capable of working out complex multiplications and divisions – down to a millionth of a farthing! Thomas took his machine to King's College at London University and many leading scientists were impressed with its efficiency. Whilst there, however, Thomas died and the machine was taken to pieces and sent back to his son Hugh, who admitted he didn't know how to put it back together again.

He did inherit a set of printed instructions but apparently he hadn't bothered to try and follow them. One of these, says Hugh, was "dictated to my sister by my father whilst lying on his death-bed in great suffering from the disease of which he soon after died."

During his lifetime many had urged Thomas to make the machine in metal and thus improve its efficiency and robustness. Poor Thomas, however, could never afford this and so his creation remained in wooden form only. This 'calculating machine' and others made in the nineteenth century were the direct forerunners of our pocket calculators and home computers of today – and Torrington has every right to be proud of its inventive son.

One wonders if the descendants of Thomas and Hugh Fowler still have the 'machine' packed away somewhere forgotten and uncared for? What a wonderful exhibit it would make in Torrington museum today!

North Devon Journal 14.3.1985

21. MUSICAL 'TONIC'

Anyone who has ever studied any musical instrument will have come across the tonic sol-fa system. This easy to learn system was invented by one John Curwen who was a famous writer on music.

He was born in Yorkshire in 1816 where his father was a non-conformist clergyman. He decided to follow his father into the ministry when he was 16. After training he took up his first post at Barnstaple Independent Chapel in Cross Street. Some of his letters to friends have survived from this period and they give intriguing glimpses of North Devonian non-conformism and how his tonic sol-fa system grew out of his love for children and his interest in Sunday Schools.

The most interesting letter dates from March 1838 and concerns the leaving of his congregation at Bishops Tawton. It begins by noting that the village had a great number of children living in it but "since there is a good day school there, the children are more than usually intelligent and attentive." The Sunday School, however, when he arrived was "languishing" so Curwen began a weekly series of "Children's Own Services" held in the hour before the regular service. In order to teach them the hymns he experimented with different methods and hit upon the system that later made him famous. So good was he that soon he had a hundred children coming every week, indeed he noted that "the children could not be kept at home."

So successful was he that Curwen didn't want to tell them when eventually he got a post elsewhere but somehow the news leaked out. On his last Sunday, the woman who taught the day school asked him to come just once more and he agreed. On turning up he found a chapel crowded with children and their parents. The service that followed was conducted by the children themselves. They sang the hymns he had taught them and with the final prayer they all began "weeping bitterly" – in which they were joined by their parents. The service ended, Curwen shaking hands with everyone present, swearing he would never forget them.

He went on to various other ministries where he refined and adapted his system of teaching music. His first published article on the system appeared in the *Independent Magazine* for 1842 and within ten years had been adopted by nearly 200,000 people. Indeed so popular did it become that Curwen began his own magazine in 1852 to teach it. Within 50 years it was being taught to one-and-a-half million children in primary schools in Britain. Curwen died in 1880 much admired and respected for his contribution to the world of music – a contribution that first saw light here in North Devon.

North Devon Journal 21.3.1991

22. LOCAL ADVENTURES OF JEROME C. JEROME

One of the funniest books in the English language is *Three Men in a Boat* by Jerome K. Jerome. In North Devon we have a link with the author through his father Jerome Clapp Jerome, generally known simply as Jerome Clapp. In early 1840 Mr Clapp was offered the ministry of the Congregational chapel in Appledore. He was 33 when he moved to the village and, using his wife's inherited money, built a house he called 'Milton' and bought a farm known as the 'Berners estate' which extended from Bloody Corner to the New Quay.

The Clapp family seemed set for a long stay and it is clear that the young parson was popular to begin with. He often gave well-received lectures and was one of the first clergymen to officiate at the then newly-opened non-conformist cemetery in Bideford. As a landowner he appears in the columns of the local paper. In June 1850 he sued Sam Sheere "a well known offender" for poaching, and eleven months later it was reported that one of Clapp's cows had fallen over a cliff into the Torridge.

December 1851 saw a short notice which reads. "The Mine at Hupplestone – The reports from the above are still very encouraging. In the words of those engaged 'they never saw a speculation look more kindly'. We congratulate the Rev Jerome Clapp, the owner of the land, on his very good fortune; and trust that such a mine will be discovered as shall not only benefit the proprietors of the soil and company engaged but the neighbourhood generally." A year later we read that the "silver and lead mine at Ubbastone" has been suspended. Poor Clapp had, in fact, been cheated by a glib con-man into spending a large sum on this 'wild goose' chase. In his autobiography his famous son says of this episode that his father, "started a stone quarry"!

In September 1854 the parson appeared at Bideford Court to fight a case against Thomas Cook sen. and jun. of Appledore. The Cooks were members of Clapp's congregation and the senior Cook had, "thought proper...to post a notice on the chapel door, calling a meeting of the congregation to take place...for the purpose of choosing trustees for the said Independent chapel to take care of some £280 South Sea Stock, and £100 three per cent consols lying in various names, and also of the property of Mrs Betty White, with which that place is endowed."

Clapp was on his way to preach when he saw the notice and immediately pulled it down. Events then became confused. Clapp alleged that Cook tried to strangle him and only let go when Mrs Clapp shouted "You dare to strike him," though whether this was a warning or an exclamation isn't stated. Cook then said "Hell was too good" for the parson. His son got into a fighting stance saying "Shall I strike him father?" His father replied, "I am man enough for that, and for two pins I would kick him down the steps." Another young Cook began shouting "Go it father! go it, father!"

As if this wasn't enough, Clapp appeared only a week later in another court action. This time he was the defendant in a civil action brought by his neighbour, Mr Thorold of 'Bidna,' over a disputed boundary. Clapp again won his case but these two court appearances set him at odds both with his congregation and his neighbours.

It was probably not surprising, therefore, to see an advertisement in October 1855 offering Clapp's 'Milton Farm' for sale. Lot 16 included a quarry – probably the ill-fated silver mine. In July 1856 Odun House, now the Maritime Museum but then "lately occupied by the Rev J Clapp" was also offered for sale. In 1859 his famous son was born and it is recorded that he came back with his family for holidays in Appledore so clearly his father bore no lasting grudge towards the place.

North Devon Journal 11.7.1985

23. SAD CASE OF A VICTORIAN POOR 'LUNATIC'

Today mental illness is seen as just that – an illness. Our ancestors, however, regarded people suffering from such sickness as 'lunatics' or 'imbeciles' and treated them harshly. One of the saddest of these cases came to court in Barnstaple in May 1855, when one Edward Lancey, a 45-year old from Bratton Fleming, was presented as being in need of care.

His poverty-stricken parents had both suffered from some form of mental derangement and he seemed to have inherited some genetic disorder. He was 26 when his mind gave way and his mother, both bewildered as to what to do with him and ashamed of his strange behaviour locked him away in a room 7 feet by 6.5 feet wide and 7 feet high. He was kept in this prison-like cell for 18 months until, in 1846, he was transferred to the keeping of his sister and her husband Anthony Huxtable. This brother-in-law built a special room 8 feet by 6 feet, with just one window 12" square, in which to house poor Edward.

A neighbouring clergyman heard about Lancey's incarceration and got the local Relieving Officer to visit the farm and as a result of this Lancey was transferred to the 'Devon Lunatic Pauper Asylum'. Huxtable was then brought to court to answer charges of abusing, ill-treating and wilfully neglecting the person in his care.

At court a whole succession of witnesses appeared, though they can be classified into two groups – the first could be labelled 'horrified professionals', while the other might be called 'sympathetic locals'. Typical of the former was the Relieving Officer James Richards, who described finding Lancey in his locked room amid a "great stench". The 'lunatic' was lying on a straw bed wearing only a long shirt and having only a rug to cover himself. Richards had been accompanied by the Rev John Carwithen, of Challacombe, who reckoned the room "not a place fit to keep a dog in." Another visitor had been Mr Torr, a Barnstaple surgeon, who found Lancey speaking "gibberish" and very dirty and emaciated. His legs had doubled up and the surgeon judged him a cripple – partly because his left leg was broken. Torr reckoned he had never seen so bad a place as Lancey's cell, notwithstanding many years work among the poor.

These witnesses for the prosecution were followed by various locals and neighbours of Huxtable. William Blackmore was a Bratton Fleming mason who had known Lancey from childhood. He recalled that Huxtable always washed his brother-in-law as "he was so dirty that the women would have nothing to do with him." Blackmore was often called in to whitewash Lancey's room. A cousin of Lancey called Harriet Gubb then appeared to praise Huxtable's treatment of her relative, reckoning that he was as well-fed as Huxtable's own family. Another witness was the village carpenter, William Gill, who had been to school with Lancey where "he had been a capital reader, and kept good accounts." He had never seen Lancey ill-treated.

At the end of this Huxtable was sent for trial at the County Assizes in Exeter. Here, in August 1855 the evidence was re-presented and all the arguments rehearsed again. This time, however, the judge and jury found Huxtable not guilty of any crime and acquitted the Exmoor farmer – a telling indictment of Victorian ideas about mental illness.

North Devon Journal 15.10.1987

24. THE GIRL WHO DIDN'T EAT FOR SIX MONTHS
On February 2 1865 newspaper readers of Bideford would have been intrigued to read the headline. "Extraordinary case of

abstinence from food." Intrigue would have turned to amazement and then probably disbelief as they read the accompanying story. In the best journalistic traditions a reporter had followed up rumours concerning a young girl, ill with a mysterious disease. Bideford at that date was, of course, much smaller than today and tracking down rumours was no doubt easier. The gossip had led to a 14-year-old East-the-Water girl, daughter of Mr Mock, foreman at the shipbuilding yard of Mr Johnson. She was under the care of Dr Thompson, a local GP. The girl's name is never stated but if one examines the census returns for 1861 one finds James Mock a 39-year-old shipwright living in Torridge Street. Amongst his three children is Susan aged 10.

Her illness began, as we are told "on the most reliable authority" in February 1864, when the girl was "affected with symptoms that were believed to be rheumatic" – a not uncommon affliction in damp and poorly-ventilated nineteenth-century houses. Added to this, the girl's "stomach became very irritable" – and she found difficulty in retaining food. As her illness developed her spine became sensitive and her voice began to resemble a hiccoughing noise whilst her neck shook constantly. Two doctors prescribed various medicines and a diet but "the patient did not seem at all benefited." The medical men suggested she be moved to a fresher and more breezy area, and this was done. Her voice returned, albeit in a whisper, and the shaking ceased.

At the same time "her sense of hearing was at this time acute" but unfortunately she was still afflicted with vomiting every time she ate. The doctors stopped giving medicines, but the vomiting became so bad that they were forced to give her injections of broth or milk. The horror of this can be well imagined but what do we make of the next statement, "at length the girl objected so strongly that (the injections) were omitted occasionally and at length discontinued"?

The doctor still retained by the family expressed his fear of certain and rapid death and announced his "complete abandonment of the case" believing that hunger pains would compel his young patient to eat. In this, however, he was disappointed and (remembering this report was in February) "she has now been over six months without being known to take a morsel of food or to retain any fluid in the stomach." She was described as being in a sort of hibernation, lying on her bed breathing slowly and taking no interest in the world, although at times she was given to hysterical fits. As one might imagine the girl was described as "greatly emaciated, her spine being particularly distinct and every bone in it defined" – an horrific picture is conjured up.

The reaction of any sensible Victorian reader would probably have been disbelief but a note at the end of the report states, "extraordinary as the case may appear, the known truthfulness and integrity of the friends seem to preclude even the suspicion of collusion."

Long hunger fasts have been known but one of six months seems out of the question especially where no liquids are taken. What happened I have not been able to find out. The Old Town Cemetery register has no entry listing her burial over the years 1865-70 so presumably she survived and returned to a normal diet.

In other cases like this fraud has been shown to exist but the motive for such a painful and protracted deception must remain in the realms of abnormal psychology. One thing is certain, however, the word "extraordinary" in the title of the newspaper report is certainly true!

North Devon Journal 28.8.1986

25. TORRINGTON'S ELECTION SCANDAL 1869

I have written previously that electioneering in the past was a more robust undertaking than it is today. Certainly violence appears to have been the order of the day in the early nineteenth-century. With the introduction of a professional police force from the 1830's onwards, however, overt violence and intimidation died out – to be replaced by fraud, as occurred in November 1869 at Torrington.

A town council election which was hard fought was followed by the Conservative Association taking "a respectable tradesman", who was also "an active member of the Liberal Association," to court on charges of "having induced a young woman to personate a voter" at the polling booth.

The case was heard by five magistrates which indicates how important it was seen to be. William Toms was the defendant and the fraudulent voter was a Miss Mary Ann Thorne of New Street, Torrington. It was alleged that Toms had gone to 23-year-old Mary on election day and told her she had a vote – she said she hadn't but he produced a voters list where the name Mary Thorne appeared under New Street. Convinced by this Mary went off, voted, and as was then the rule, signed her name on the ballot paper.

Unfortunately the Mary Thorne on the list was a very well-known Torrington inhabitant being the postmistress and "a widow of advanced age" – points known to the polling station clerks! This Mary Thorne turned up in court and stated that she had had no intention of voting; had never voted and never intended to vote, which clearly established fraud on the part of the other Mary. Young Mary then cross-examined said, "I was frightened but I knew that I had not knowingly done anything wrong" adding "This is William Toms' fault."

The case put by Mr Rooker, a local solicitor, for William Toms rested on his ignorance of the details of the voters' lists – i.e. he truly thought the two Marys were one and the same. Rooker entered a long rambling explanation of how this happened and added that the local Liberal Association actually instructed Toms to "get you Mary Thorne to the poll." Mr Chappell, chairman of the Association appeared and agreed that this had occurred and that no mention had been made of "Mrs Thorne the postmistress".

The magistrates retired to give the case "their serious and anxious consideration." Deliberations over they returned and went through the case minutely but ended by giving Toms "the benefit of the doubt which arises", adding "we think Mr Toms has had a very narrow escape" – a statement which led to their being "hooted" as they left.

The Liberals celebrated their victory throughout the evening with a band which went to every party councillor's house and played "lively tunes...amidst cheering."

One wonders, however, if after this close shave they ever tried impersonation of voters again!

North Devon Journal 30.6.1988

26. STRONG ARM STUFF AT A BARUM FUNERAL

The Victorians loved a good funeral...and their newspapers are packed with lengthy obituaries of upstanding dignitaries and detailed descriptions of elaborate interments. It comes as a shock, therefore, to read a headline that appeared in August 1875 – "Disgraceful scene in churchyard" – above an article dealing with the funeral of a noted Barnstaple worthy.

Mr John Parminter "the oldest freeman of the borough" had died aged 78 and was being buried in the churchyard of St Mary Magdalene. Apparently he had made his will five years previously leaving his property divided equally between his wife and six children. For some strange reason, however, he had made a new will just two weeks before his death in which he left all his property to his only son John, landlord of the George Inn in the town. Each daughter received only £5 under this new will.

When the old man died the daughters turned up to pay their respects and begin the sharing out (as they expected) of the property. When the heir told them about the changed circumstances they, rather naturally, grew angry, and "declined to join the mourners at the house" only joining the funeral cortege on its way to the churchyard.

At church they refused to sit with their brother and after the service was over and the coffin was being lowered into the grave began abusing their brother and his wife "with such vehemence as to interrupt the solemn service." Indeed one of the sisters "from Swansea" was "so indecorous in her conduct" that the poor vicar taking the service "was compelled to stop and order her to be removed." Strong arm tactics over an open grave! The woman was hysterical by this time and "prayed aloud to the Almighty for vengeance on her brother and his family." One of the bearers was an off-duty policeman, Pc Jones, and he threatened to arrest her if she didn't keep quiet. This caused the "shrieking sister" to draw back and the service "was concluded peacefully."

As the cortege reassembled, however, abuse broke out again. By this time a crowd had collected and "called shame upon them for their unseemly conduct." The party somehow managed to get back to the dead man's house and the will was read. This caused further angry scenes and then "very grave charges" were levelled against the brother by his sisters "as to the cause of their father's death."

This, though, was as far as the case went. The sisters could not substantiate their allegations and so departed, still feeling cheated and angry – leaving poor old John, their father, to finally 'Rest in Peace.'

North Devon Journal 4.11.1985

27. THE MAN WHO LIVED IN AN OLD CHIMNEY

Researching the past is usually a matter of recording the activities of our ancestors – most of whom lived stable, normal, uneventful lives. Every now and again, however, one comes across a true eccentric – and North Devon had its fair share of such people. One of my favourites is Joseph Becalick or Becklake of Woolsery.

Joseph was a local farmer in a small way in the late nineteenth century. He began life as a humble farm labourer but was filled with that good Victorian ambition – the urge to 'improve' himself – to which end he attended evening classes run by the Vicar of Woolsery.

With his hard won education he secured a part-time job as rate-collector for his district and purchased a small farm at Cranford in his home parish. He evidently prospered as within a few years he was employing two servants to help him work the farm and look after his domestic needs (he never married).

All appeared well until about 1885, (the records are unclear,) when he was on a visit to Bideford market on agricultural business. Whilst he was gone a fire broke out in his farmhouse and it was almost completely burnt to the ground – a not unusual occurrence. Joseph's reaction, however, was anything but usual. Arriving back he found the only part of the building to be left standing was one wall supported by an old-fashioned chimney with its huge fireplace. This fireplace was about four feet by six feet and into this "amid the ruin of his home, the poor man crept, and lay down to sleep."

One sympathises with him in his adversity but his next step strikes one as bizarre. He found his fireplace home so congenial that he proceeded to live there for the next 20 odd years – "through storm and sunshine, in spite of wind, rain, hail or snow!" He cooked his meals over a log fire and slept in a "deal box."

In April 1908, however, neighbour Mrs Andrews noticed that he was looking ill. She kindly offered him a cup of coffee "which he eagerly accepted and asked for more." The next day she visited him and found him "in a state of collapse." She called the vicar, there being no doctor, and the two of them managed to wrap poor Joseph in blankets and drive him by cart to Bideford Hospital. Unfortunately he was so weak that he died two days later.

His obituary, which gave his age as "about seventy" noted that although he lived "under indescribably squalid conditions" he was rumoured to have been "possessed of ample means." Proof of this was offered by the fact that a few years before he had begun building a new house but, for some unexplained reason, had abandoned it only half completed. Such stories of secret wealth are often told about eccentric, lonely people, of course, but in this case they may well have been true. In the month following his death Joseph's farm was auctioned at the New Inn in Bideford and the five lots made £572 – a very respectable sum at that date.

So perished the "chimney dweller" of North Devon – surely a man with few competitors where oddity of habitation are concerned!

North Devon Journal 7.5.1987

28. GREGORY: THE LOST POET OF NORTH DEVON

Asked to name the poets and writers of North Devon one would be hard put to think of many – perhaps Gay, Kingsley, Williamson, Capern and Ted Hughes would exhaust the memory.

There is, however, another we might claim – John Gregory. He was born in Bideford in 1831 into a poor family who could afford to give him only a few years of schooling before apprenticing him, aged just 11, to a local cobbler. His apprenticeship lasted seven years and "at the close of the long working day, he devoted what leisure he had to study, and learnt to regard all books as foot-notes to the Book of Nature."

His hard town life was somewhat tempered by the long walks he took in the countryside around Bideford with its dusty white lanes and hedgerows festooned with wild flowers – one wonders if he ever came across Bideford's postman poet Edward Capern as he went his rounds?

At the completion of his time as an apprentice Gregory went to Bristol to gain fame and fortune but times were hard and in 1856 he was forced to tramp the roads of South Wales looking for casual work. After four years he returned to Bristol where he settled down and married, eventually becoming "boot-repairer" to Clifton College.

From his earliest days in Bideford he had been writing poetry but he didn't publish anything until he was 40 years old. Publication then only came because he paid to have his first volume printed. Called *Idylls of labour* it reflected his working class background – an interview with him published in 1911 says he was "an avowed Socialist" who could trace his political beliefs back to "when a lad he came under the sway of the Chartist agitation" in Bideford.

One reviewer was on record as saying of his work, "there is much inspiration in it for the social reformer" – presumably Gregory was drawing on the hard lessons learnt in mid-19th century Bideford for his verse. Certainly he was closely involved in early trade union movements in Bristol and was an active radical organiser.

He published three more volumes of poetry – *Song Streams* (1877), *Murmurs and Melodies* (1884) and *My Garden* (1907) as well as hundreds of single poems in newspapers and magazines. Reviewers were kind to him, comparing him favourably with Robert Bloomfield, John Clare and even Robert Burns – especially in regard to his treatment of nature themes and his overwhelming love of the countryside. His verse is now all out of print and seems to be forgotten by everyone in his birthplace. Perhaps a revival is due – though if it is as good as Capern's perhaps it is better left undisturbed!

North Devon Journal 27.8.1987

29. FIRST PENSION DAY OF THE WELFARE STATE

We take much for granted – perhaps nothing more so than pensions – yet they only date from January 1st. 1909. On that day the first State pensions of 25p a week were paid out to a select few – the idea of 'retirement age' hadn't yet come in and only certain people were eligible.

The occasion was marked locally by public meetings, speeches and celebration. In Bideford a huge public tea was held where nearly 1,000 people heard the local MP Mr Soares reckon that "many would remember that occasion as a great birthday – the birth of a new era in social reform." Pensions "would, he firmly believed, bring peace and contentment in many a home where otherwise there would be poverty and despair."

In Barnstaple nearly 300 qualified for pensions and the first to be paid was to George Heayel who went to the old Post Office in Cross Street to get it. He was later followed by one of the elderly women from Horwood Almshouses who had been living on 12½p a week and who was reported as saying of her pension "twill be a great benefit to me." Another old man told anyone who would listen, "It is the first sum I have ever received in my life without working for it."

At Summerland Street Post Office postmaster J R Gent gave each pensioner a card inscribed, "To commemorate the nation's gift of an honorable pension to the veterans of industry, January 1st. 1909. With every good wish for the coming year from Mr and Mrs J R Gent."

In the Bideford area nearly 400 pensions were paid out, the oldest recipient being a 99-year-old Parkham man. It was noted in the paper, "At Bideford Post Office one assistant was practically occupied the whole day in paying the money." Some might say nothing much changes!

At Ilfracombe 108 pensioners collected their money. A blind 95-year-old reckoned, "This is the best day I've had for many a long day, thank God for it." South Molton saw 55 pensions paid out with another 35 at Combe Martin. At Clovelly the new pensioners were so grateful they clubbed together to send a telegram to the MP.

One pensioner, however, missed this first payout. He lived at Chittlehampton and, in a wonderful piece of dialect, told all his friends, "E nawed twaden that day ta begin to dra. Tha pensions begin ta-day, bet us shan't git the fust week avore nex Vriday." He may not have received his but everyone else eligible did. So began the first real Government-inspired social payments that, over the years, have grown into the Welfare State we have today.

North Devon Journal 11.6.1987

30. TOWN CRIER A 'COLOURFUL CHARACTER'

The traditional post of Town Crier is happily still with us. Today it is usually only a ceremonial post, although the Bideford one still occasionally 'cries' events through the streets. Around the turn of the century the most famous of these men, probably in the whole of Britain, was the 'Mounted Crier' of Ilfracombe, one Robert Martin. He featured on countless tourist postcards and made quite a living out of 'crying' events and lost property.

In September 1913, however, Robert was charged by the Ilfracombe police with "being drunk while in charge of a horse on the highway." He and his pony had been arrested in Market Square, Ilfracombe by Pc Bedford. At the court case the policeman said his attention had been drawn to the defendant by the way in which he was swaying in the saddle and the manner in which he was shouting. He went up to him and asked him to dismount "as he was not in a fit state to be in charge of the pony."

Robert refused and had to be pulled off by the constable and Sergeant Woolacott who had also arrived. The two then took the 'crier' home and handed him over to his wife, Pc Bedford saying. "Missus, if Robert comes out any more, I shall lock him up." Robert's only comment was "You have been trying to have me for a long time, and now you have got me" – a comment ignored by the police.

At court Robert conducted his own case and cross-examined the policemen at length but they stuck to their evidence although they admitted that neither had seen Robert enter or leave a public house – though, of course, this was no evidence as to his drunkenness or not.

One witness was Mr F Lord who, when asked by the magistrate, "Could you hear distinctly what he said?" answered "Not so well as usual. Towards the conclusion of the 'crying' his head gradually fell forward on to the horse's mane, and he mumbled something nobody could understand." Robert admitted this was true but blamed it on the fact that the message he had been paid to cry was written in pencil and he "could not read it very well."

After this not very convincing explanation Robert launched into a curious rigmarole claiming, amongst other things, "I dismounted like a man" and "one man saw him drinking a glass of soda and milk outside Mr Blackmore's shop" but he couldn't remember the man's name – a statement greeted with laughter in the court. He concluded his 'case' by stating, "His opinion was that the police wanted to do away with the mounted bell business. He was now able to hold a thousand or two thousand people, and they thought he was creating an obstruction."

The Crier then sat down and awaited the verdict – which wasn't long in coming. Fined £1 plus costs. Robert asked for a fortnight to pay, but this was refused so he paid up and left. One wonders how the case affected his 'professional' duties. I am unsure when he gave up his post but he certainly sounds a very colourful character.

North Devon Journal 28.4.1988

31. TASKMASTER LOST OUT IN LOVE STAKES

Memories of schooldays usually make for good reading – the more so when they extend back to the beginning of the nineteenth-century. In 1849 the *Journal* carried a series of reminiscences by 'Vindex' who had gone to Bideford School in the early years of that century – and very revealing they are.

The writer never gives the full name of his teacher but he was the Rev Thomas Ebrey master of the school from 1803 to 1812. Described as "at least six foot high and of goodly proportions" he had a florid complexion and "good features." 'Vindex' was his youngest boarder and unfortunately arrived "when the school was on the decline." This decline could be traced directly to "a too rigid system of economy."

Meals consisted of huge helpings of suet pudding followed by scraps of meat – a cheap way of filling young stomachs. Come Autumn "a large store of herrings were salted in" and a third of a herring plus three large potatoes "which were very cheap in those days" provided the main Winter meals. Each Saturday the boarders got boiled veal followed at Sunday breakfast by a soup of the water it was cooked in.

If the food was bad the teaching was worse. Ebrey is described as being "a continuously sullen and hard taskmaster" who could on occasions give way to "ungovernable fits of passion." His normal punishment to any student was to take a book and "thrusting it violently into the unfortunate victim's face, and making his nose as flat as a pancake, he would exclaim, with great vehemence – "Can you see it? you stupid ass!!". This led more often than not to "a most violent bleeding at the nose" – which isn't surprising.

This reverend gentleman apparently never bothered much with the Bible merely allowing one of the pupils to read a prayer aloud at meal times. This was the pupil's first training session for "the public recital."

Once a year the students appeared before the Mayor and Corporation to recite a Latin passage. Such a public occasion was important to Ebrey and he made sure the boys were word-perfect by constant repetition.

One of Ebrey's affectations was noted by 'Vindex' who wrote of his master's "beautifully regular and even set of small teeth" which were meticulously cared for – even to the extent of drinking nothing hot. In church each week he would look at the various rich widows and spinsters when "his face would be all radiant with the most bewitching smiles."

'Vindex' said he only did this in order to obtain legacies – which often happened.

North Devon Journal 21.4.1988

32. WHEN ELECTIONS WERE FOUGHT WITH FISTS

Through the use of written records a historian can go back a thousand years in Britain but, as with all such sources, their usage is restricted to what was actually written down or what has survived. This is why oral history, or the recording of people's memories on tape, is so important today

Recently I was privileged to record several hours conversation with Bill Tithecott who was born in Myrtle Grove, Bideford in 1902. His birthplace had been bought that year for £225 by his grandfather, W Giddy, who was an old sailor. Some of Bill's earliest memories are of his grandfather's stories about sailing voyages out from Appledore which lasted up to 2½ years!

As a boy Bill helped in his grandfather's sail-making business situated in an old sail loft at the end of the old man's garden next to the cattle market in Meddon Street. Often he was enlisted to pull canvas through a foot-operated sewing machine – the material was too stiff to push. This home work was carried on after a 12-hour working day which began with Mr Giddy walking to Cox's yard at Northam at 6 a.m.

Various items were turned out in this home industry including most of the sailcloth blinds used in the High Street shops as well as tents for gypsies – apparently there were large numbers of 'travellers' in North Devon at this date. Sometimes young Bill accompanied his grandfather on board the many ships moored along Bideford Quay to repair their sails on site and swap sea stories with the salty old captains.

All of this of course was carried on out of school time. Bill was only three-and-a-half when he first attended the East-the-Water Primary school in Torrington Lane where a Mrs Leonard taught him. It was her husband who kept the coal cellars in the yard on which the present-day police station now stands. When his family moved he changed to Geneva Place Primary School ending up finally at Old Town School.

As well as helping his grandfather he also did a series of part-time jobs before and after school. He delivered milk, cleaned houses and worked for Dr Cook the dentist, who lived in Tower House on the Strand. After leaving school at 13 he went straight to full-time work to help the family income. He went to Mr Pearse the printer and then to his father's workplace. His father was a foreman shoe-maker for Titus Burrow in Allhalland Street with four men under him and young Bill joined them as a shop boy. This was during the First World War and Bill says "Anyone who had a business in Bideford had to go in front of a tribunal", the idea being that the tribunal members assessed whether you should or should not be conscripted. His employer went and was excused conscription as long as he worked 3 days a week on a local farm – which meant that 14 year old Bill became temporary manager on those days. The best selling line at this time was the 'Dartmoor Boot' which was a very hardwearing labourer's boot.

The shop's shoemakers worked until Saturday afternoon and then went home only to return at 6 p.m. to collect their week's wages – a common practice in many trades. This meant that the womenfolk only had money to do their shopping at this time and apparently many shops in the town stayed open to 8 p.m. on a Saturday night to cater for them.

When he was old enough Bill joined the Church Lads Brigade as a drummer with the full knowledge that he would soon be conscripted if the war continued. Before he was called up however, peace was declared. Bideford first heard the news when a lorry load of airmen from the Westward Ho! airfield drove into town. The official declaration was given by the Mayor from the steps of the old Post Office in High Street (now the TSB) and the town was certainly lively that night.

At this time Bill was living in Silver Street and well remembers when the present Scout headquarters was Dingle's grocery shop where you could get a jar of treacle for 1d. Dingle's stables and stores were in Silver Street where the garage now stands. Another local shop was Friendship's confectionery shop in Honestone Street where 1d bought a basin of beef dripping.

A few events stand out clearly in Bill's memory from these years. In 1915 he was taken seriously ill with peritonitis and had to be carried to the Meddon Street hospital on a stretcher. He spent 13 weeks in hospital after being operated on by well-known Dr Toye. His bed was the 'Hamlyn' one – Mrs Hamlyn of Clovelly Court provided all the linen and once a month came in to check that it was all clean and woe betide if it was not!

To stay in hospital cost money unless you could collect four 'recommends' a month. Every January books of 'recommendation' slips were purchased by various benefactors, and bodies such as the church, chapels and mayor. They then gave them out to 'deserving' cases on application and Bill remembers chapelgoers being refused a 'recommend' by the church authorities and vice-versa.

Another notable event was an election. Bill can recall two rival groups collecting and marching towards each other – the Tories along Mill Street and the Liberals down High Street. Meeting at the road junction they would then stage a pitched battle. One time a baton wielding mounted policeman tried to keep the groups apart but, for his pains, was taken and nearly thrown over the Quay into the river! Hustings were held in the Market Hall and fights involving up to 40 men were common. As Bill remarked, with some understatement, "They took their politics seriously then."

One other memory concerns his late wife. She was working at the collar factory in Rope Walk, the very large building that still stands, until it closed due to rising transport costs. Some 200 girls were made redundant and the employment exchange, then in the front room of one of Queen Anne's Buildings in High Street, could not cope. In order to have enough room the Market was used temporarily as the exchange though the sheer numbers involved meant that unemployment was the fate of many.

In his adult life Mr Tithecott went on to help build many of the buildings we see today in the town as well as helping during the Second World War to construct Winkleigh airbase and the Mulberry Harbours. Now aged 81 he still looks extremely fit and has a very agile mind – a splendid example of a true Bidefordian.

Bideford Gazette 10.2.1984

33. THE 'BAD OLD DAYS' FONDLY REMEMBERED

Now in his 80th year, Frank Garnsey is a living treasure-house of Bideford stories and history. Known to many as the founder of Kingsley Decorators, he was born in 1905 in Honestone Street into an old Bideford family. His grandfather, William, was a currier or leather-dresser in the Westcombe Tannery. This stood on the site now occupied by the council depot and produced tanned skins for local shoe and harness makers. His own father, also called William, was a blacksmith and used to work for Priscott's behind the shop now occupied by Blanchards in Mill Street. Here he hammered out ornamental iron work for gates though, in the First World War, he put his skills to another use by building two concrete barges at Barnstaple.

Frank recalls Honestone Street as "quite a lively sort of street" with herds of horned cattle being regularly driven down it to the cattle market there. He went to Old Town School and clearly remembers all the town's scholars being marshalled in Victoria Park and then marched up to a meal in the Pannier Market to celebrate the coronation of George V.

Another memory of food concerns the weekly trip to Ashton's grocery shop at the top of Meddon Street (now an off-licence) to collect barm, or brewer's yeast, brought over from Barrow's brewery at East-the-Water. This was used to produce the family bread dough, which was packed into tins borrowed from Friendship the baker who then baked them in his large oven for a small fee. His shop later became a cafe and now houses the Moose Hall flats.

Around this time, women were campaigning for the vote and even Bideford had its own Suffragettes. They heard that Lord

Asquith, the Prime Minister, and his second wife were coming to spend some time at Clovelly Court. Asquith managed to elude their reception committee at the railway station, but the women then festooned the drive to Clovelly Court with their banners. Stirring stuff indeed!

In 1913, Admiral Dowell, who lived at Ford House, died and his coffin was placed on a gun carriage and hauled by a team of 'bluejackets' across the bridge to East-the-Water cemetery. Frank and his fellow pupils were thrilled to see such an unusual sight.

This was also the time when the streets of Bideford echoed to hawkers' cries such as "Clovelly Herrings," "Sweep" and "Rags and bones and rabbit skins – bring 'em out and I'll buy 'em." Another was "Pitchers and Pans" and this heralded a man and cart laden with earthenware from the East-the-Water potteries in Torrington Lane.

While at school the war broke out and one of the Frank's teachers became a Conscientious Objector. He was regularly mobbed and jeered by the children at the instigation of the parents and at one time the poor man had to be rescued by the Baptist minister but, as Frank says, "he was the bravest man in Bideford in sticking up for his principles."

Owing to the shortage of men, Frank left school aged 13 and went to work in John How's building and wharfage concern along New Road (where Wickham's now is) as a clerk at 5/- (25p) a week. After a time he asked for a rise – a request met with horror by his employers – though he did get a shilling (5p) extra for his ten hour a day, six day week!

Frank's three brothers all joined up and one was in the Seaforth Highlanders. Wounded in 1915, he returned to convalesce in Bideford and caused a sensation in his kilt – the first seen in the town. When the war ended at last the streets of Bideford were full of people wandering around in a daze not knowing quite what to do or think.

In 1923 Frank left How's and went to work for Dingle's the grocers at their shop in Buttgarden Street (opposite Tower Street) under Harry Dingle whom he described as "a real old beauty" famous for his colourful language!

Even more colourful, perhaps, were the old style elections Frank remembers. Violence between the Tories and the Liberals was the order of the day. At one meeting in the Pannier Market, Lord

Salisbury was pelted with potatoes and, at another, rotten eggs greeted the Tories at their Bridgeland Street headquarters.

During one campaign, one unfortunate candidate was in his open-top carriage turning into High Street from Grenville Street when an assailant rammed his top-hat down over his eyes! In another contest, the entire populace of Providence Row (now a car park) voted Liberal in support of a proposed budget change and strung a huge banner reading "Budget Street" across the entrance to their Row.

In 1930 Frank was elected secretary to the Ancient Order of Foresters. His election took place in the Pannier Market before most of the 2,000 local members who flocked in from the surrounding area. His office was in the Bridge Buildings and his main job was collecting subscriptions and paying out sick pay in those pre-social security days. He remained there until the Second World War and then founded Kingsley Decorators in 1946.

He is still hale and hearty today with a wonderful fruity laugh, though he is sad as he says that Bideford has changed beyond all recognition since he was a boy – and although much that was bad has gone, some of the good seems to have gone with it.

Bideford Gazette 25.4.1985

34. EIGHTY YEARS ON: CHILDHOOD REMEMBERED

Writing these articles does lead to pleasant surprises – recently I was loaned a typescript dealing with the reminiscences of one William Lynch who comes from Muddiford hamlet in Marwood. Now living in Sussex William has recalled all the many details of life in North Devon before and after the First World War.

He was born in 1905 into a large family which included a grandfather 'King' Lynch and a grandmother both of whose memories stretched back into the mid-nineteenth century. Grandmother's earliest memory was of living on a farm near Mortehoe where "the fishermen used to row up from Ilfracombe and shoot any sheep that were browsing near the edge – the sheep tumbled down and they whipped them into their boat and away."

William's birth and those of his contemporaries was welcomed with much jollification. On one such occasion William's father and a friend "charged up an old cannon to fire off and celebrate."

Unfortunately it blew up though no-one was injured – a big piece was left in the garden of 'Sunset' at the top of Playford Mills Lane.

His childhood was idyllic – schooling at the village school and learning his trade with his father. On his first day at school he experienced a flush toilet for the first time. It was nearly his last as when he pulled the chain and saw water pouring down "I ran for dear life, thought I'd flooded the place." He walked three miles to school every day and often spent a morning sitting miserable in wet clothes. His teacher, a Mr Pill, was respected and, unusually for the time, used the cane very sparingly – mainly because it upset him so much.

The stream that flowed through Muddiford was the centre of his childhood life. In it he tickled trout – once taking 69 in 3 days – and caught eels using entrails threaded with worsted wool – when the eels took the bait they couldn't free their mouths from the wool. Eelskin cut in strips provided him with his shoelaces. An uncle used to cut his hair – "he'd drop a basin over our heads and clip around with sheep shears and that was it."

At times the old steam engines would halt outside his parents' cottage to take on water from the stream – and William always had to go out and check that sparks from their chimneys hadn't set the thatch on fire. The stream was also where the women cleaned the carcass of the family pig. On one occasion the Cheriton Otter Hounds picked up the scent and followed the bloody water right up to the women.

The hamlet was served by travelling salesmen from Barnstaple including 'Cock' Robins the baker – "he and grandfather used to attend Tory meetings, and, although he was as deaf as a post every so often during the Tory speechmaking he would shout 'liar'!" These salesmen came by cart and it wasn't until 1910 that William saw his first car. It was driven by his uncle Jim Scott who was chauffeur to General Scott of Marwood House.

Aged 11, William travelled to Barnstaple in a horse-drawn coach from Combe Martin alighting at the Barley Mow in Boutport Street. He recalls that during the journey "the woman sitting beside me felt faint and had to slacken her stays." The journey was a rough one on crushed-stone roads steam rolled into a hard surface. William remembers men using sledgehammers and hand hammers "with whippy handles" cracking stone for the roads. The surface was durable but the white dust was inches thick in summer.

William began working with his father after the First World War but he had itchy feet and eventually migrated to Canada where he spent most of his life. His reminiscences cover many more topics than I have dealt with here – the full set can be found in the North Devon Athenaeum.

TOWN AND LANDSCAPE

35. WATER, WATER EVERYWHERE

Water rates bills aren't exactly welcome and many people find cause for complaint with their supply – but we must be thankful that our Victorian forefathers had the inspiration and energy to create our present water supply system. Most of us take running water for granted and it is only a freak occasion like the 1976 drought that brings home to us how reliant we are on our usually inexhaustible taps. Yet what came before the Victorians? Country districts, of course, used wells, but what of a town like Barnstaple where demand was so much greater? The history of the water supply in Barnstaple can be traced back nearly 300 years.

On August 30 1698 an agreement was drawn up between the Mayor, alderman and burgesses (leading citizens) of the town on one part with a group of four men on the other. The men were Daniel Dowell and Edward Dyson, gentlemen, and Ambrose Crowley and Richard Loubridge, ironmongers – none of whom were local. Clearly the gentlemen were the capitalists and the tradesmen were the practical engineers.

Not only did the men get permission to lay pipes, they were also allowed to site a "cistern" or reservoir tank on land "at the western end of the church" (St Peter's). As part of their agreement the four men promised to provide "an engine to extinguish fire at any house in the borough" – possibly this was Barnstaple's first fire engine? Within eight months another agreement was struck by the four men – this time with Arthur Champneys, one of the two Barnstaple Members of Parliament at the time. He owned the rights over the stream at Rawleigh and these he leased to the company. The rent was £2.13.4d (£2.66p) a year.

By July 1700 water pipes from the Rawleigh site had been laid, but the site of the "cistern" had been found to be unsuitable and so the Corporation leased another site to the company. This was a "plot of ground in and being in a certain street of Barnstaple called Birdport (presumably Boutport) containing 28 feet in length and 14 feet in breadth". This land was evidently at the junction of Joy Street and Boutport Street near where the East Gate used to stand.

The "cistern" evidently wasn't that large, but this was Barnstaple's first piped water supply. These original pipes were of elm, each stretch being bored with a three-inch hole and then joined to its neighbour. Leakage and contamination must have been excessive. In 1887 a 5ft length of this original piping was excavated at the Boutport Street end of Bear Street and found to be lined "with a slimy substance" but otherwise extremely well-preserved. As the wooden pipes became unserviceable they were replaced by lead ones. The final removal of all wooden ones may have occurred in 1724 when a new contract between the suppliers and the corporation was signed. The new metal ones were only 1¼" in diameter, but they probably didn't leak as much as their predecessors!

In 1859 these lead ones were themselves replaced by 9" iron piping, the contractor making, so it was said, some £2,000 on the sale of the scrap lead. This was done by the Barnstaple Water Company which survived until nationalisation of all the old water authorities.

Barnstaple residents may also be pleased to think of all this history as they next go to pay their water rates. Perhaps not so happily, they might also like to ponder on the cost of a year's water rates in 1830 – they averaged in total just 18/- (90p)! Happy days.

North Devon Gazette 2.1.1987

36. BIDEFORD ... 'REMARKABLY FORBIDDING'

Bideford has attracted many visitors over the years and many have left their impressions of the town to posterity. Some have expressed their delight in our buildings and bridge whilst others have been less than complimentary about certain aspects of the town and neighbourhood. One of these visitors was William Marshall, a Yorkshire man who was a famous eighteenth-century writer on agricultural matters. In 1796 he published his *Rural Economy of the West of England* in which he recorded a long horseback journey he took through Devon, Cornwall and Somerset.

He approached Torridgeside, according to his account, from the south coming through Torrington which he describes as being "proudly situated" although he adds, "There is no posting inn in the place and only one chaise kept for hire." He leaves the town with the slightly ambiguous comment, "Nevertheless the town is neat and the people alive."

Riding along the Torridge valley he observes "a lovely wooded valley, thriving oak timber; well thinned and set out" and he meets "strings of lime horses, with pack saddles and bags of lime. Also two-horse carts, with lime and sea sand." These materials were, of course, to be spread on the land in order to increase its fertility – a natural dressing in the days before chemicals.

Coming into Bideford Marshall states bluntly, "the town ... is remarkably forbidding. The houses are meanly built of timber, brick and mud covered with bad slates or bad thatch. The streets are awkward and narrow and everywhere there are immense piles of furze faggots." Marshall remarks of the furze, "These dangerous piles of fuel are for the use of the pottery, for which only, I believe, this town is celebrated: chiefly, or wholly, the coarser kinds of earthenware." In the town itself he notes "in every vacant corner ... composts of earth, mud, ashes etc. are seen."

Clearly he didn't think much of the town and he had even worse things to say about some of the inhabitants. Thus he describes some labourers he sees at work on embanking the Pill stream (probably where the Park now is) in the following terms, "If the men who are employed upon it may be considered a sample of the labourers of N. Devon, they exceed in idleness their countrymen of the West." The bank these men were working (or idling!) on gives, the writer noted, a suitable site for the tide mill that he saw at one end, but which has now disappeared. Not content with berating the labourers he then turned his attention to the middle classes and found them wanting in manners, which he blamed on the coarsening nature of all seaport towns.

After these harsh words it comes as a relief to read his comments on Bideford Market. He describes the animals set out for sale and enthuses over "The heifers ... with remarkably fine bags! – the most promising appearance of milk that I have observed in the Devonshire breed of cattle." The corn market was full and the shambles or butchery "full of good mutton" whilst there was also a good display of river fish. He also notes "Cart loads of country bread, exposed in the market place for sale. A market article this, which I have not before observed." One wonders what country bread was and how it differed, if at all, from the home-made town variety. He ends with the comment "Upon the whole, the market of Bideford may be set down as very respectable."

After this brief inspection of Bideford he rides off to Barnstaple – evidently at low tide for he observes "The tide out; many men employed in loading pack-horses with sand left in the bed of the river."

As far as I know William Marshall never returned to Bideford and from reading his journal of his only visit one can only presume that he was not well-pleased with the town at all. Certainly the picture he conjures up is not very attractive, though it must be added in Bideford's defence that Marshall was noted for his virulent pen and scathing comments. An irascible observer at the best of times, it needed some very particular sight or clear sign of agricultural improvement to impress him and bring out his praise. Perhaps eighteenth century Bidefordians were not so bad after all.

Bideford Gazette 15.1.1982

37. A HAPPY ENDING FOR GEORGE

In March 1862 "an old inhabitant" of Bideford (his own description) sat down and penned a long article for the local paper on his reminiscences of the town over 50 years. Most of this fascinating piece was taken up with the history of one building, that on the corner of Mill Street and High Street. Today it houses shops: but the "old inhabitant" takes us back to 1810.

At that date it was the property of "a maiden lady by the name of Banbury". Reference to a record called the Bideford Land Tax listing for 1810, now in the Devon Record Office, shows this lady to have been Miss Catherine Banbury. She had apparently let it out as a shop for some years but in 1810 George Staveley, an auctioneer and ironmonger, had approached her with a view to purchasing it for his business. George offered the spinster "a stated sum to be paid down, and forty pounds per annum for as long as the invalided proprietress should live." The Land Tax returns for 1811 show Mr Staveley as the owner so clearly the offer was accepted.

Happily for Miss Banbury and unhappily for the auctioneer she "took to sea bathing and, ... used to hire Molly Hookway's black mare ... and ride to Abbotsham cliffs ... winter and summer, thereby, through salt-water immersion in a flannel dress, took a fresh lease of her life" and lived another twenty years!

As if this wasn't bad enough worse was to follow. George began making large alterations to the somewhat ancient structure and, when taking up some flagging in a passage his two labourers came across a hundredweight of "ancient silver coins." Temptation proved too much for the labourers and they scooped up as many of the coins as they could carry and started off for Plymouth. After three months 'spree' one, Joe Northcote, returned. The second one was never head of again. George, however, still had the major part of the find and must have been well-pleased with his unexpected windfall. Clearly George did not, unfortunately, know the law on treasure trove.

At that time John Clevland of Tapely in Westleigh was the Lord of the Manor of Bideford and was the rightful owner of all such 'treasure trove.' He demonstrated this in rather an abrupt way when he came into George's shop and said "Sir, you have found some curious coins, I presume; I should like to see them." George obliged and set them out on his counter whereupon Clevland's butler "swept them all into a basket he was carrying," Clevland adding by way of explanation "I am Lord of the Manor, and this treasure trove is my property. Good morning sir."

As in all the best stories though, everything came right in the end for George. Among his other jobs he also ran an agency for lottery tickets. He was a member of a group that purchased a £20 ticket which went on to win £20,000 of which George received a thousand pounds.

On his retirement in the 1830s he held an auction of his ironmongery goods but being dissatisfied at the prices being realised called off the sale eventually selling the whole lot for £600 to some dealers from Barnstaple. These gentlemen, in clearing out the huge accumulation of goods, found in the cellar a "pavement of massive iron backs for grates being placed along edge to edge." At their auction the Barnstaple men made a very large profit – no doubt much to George's chagrin!

George died in 1837 and his will survives. In it he leaves goods to four of his five children, a step-daughter and a grandson. remarkably (and uniquely in my experience) the first legacy to be mentioned is where he leaves "all the liquors and other consumable household provisions" to his wife Ann. This very strange and rather pointed wish suggests a further unhappiness in George's life, in this case with his marriage.

The building in High Street was sold, as his will stipulated, being purchased by John Lee, another auctioneer, who also undertook cabinet making and house decoration, was postmaster of Bideford for about 20 years and in addition a town councillor. It was apparently this busy gentleman who remodelled the building into the shape we see today. He was one of the last to introduce plate glass into his shop – not through innate conservatism but rather with an eye to getting the best available. When his fellow tradesmen asked when he was going to modernise his premises he always replied, "I shall bide my time, I have my drawings and designs all ready, and when they have finished, I shall commence and cap them all." This he did in about 1858-9 building a verandah at the first-floor level (now gone) and inserting many more windows and new rooms, as well as plate glass.

As postmaster, John Lee would have used his own house for postal business purposes from 1840, when the 'Penny Post' was first introduced into Britain. No doubt the citizens of Bideford would have been very proud of their new ornate and imposing Post Office. Poor John did not live very long after his rebuilding schemes were finished as he died on April 1st 1860 aged 60, being buried in the Old Town Cemetery.

He was succeeded by his son Frederick Lee who expanded the furnishing side of the business giving up the postal work to a Mr Cadd further up High Street (in what is now the TSB building.) The writer of the reminiscences waxes lyrical about Frederick's shop saying it was "daily visited by the elite" and noting "a tastefully laid-out office, with desks, lamps of the first fashion, and altogether assuming a degree of comfort, with alphabetical pigeon-holes for papers; stands for ledgers etc.; and an elegant boudoir for ladies and gentlemen adjoining, wherein to receive orders. A long flight of stairs and balustrade lead to an upper comprehensive showroom stored with the superabundant stock, from which a side viaduct guides to the long workshops and double tier of benches, where carving is done and costly furniture is manufactured." At the top of the building a new showroom had been made out of what was once the Oddfellows Lodge whilst behind was "ample stabling and timber stores".

The newspaper article only takes the story up until 1862 but the building later became the Kingsley Hotel with the shop on the corner being a fish and game merchants. Both had several other uses before being taken over by Currys after the last war. Hodges are relative newcomers but the buildings are much as John Lee left them in 1860 – a monument to the Victorian merchant spirit of Bideford.

Bideford Gazette 17.8.1984

38. WHEN WAS NEW ROAD NEW?

People in Bideford may sometimes wonder why the section of road from the bottom of Torridge Hill to the Library is called New Road. When was it new? The story is well worth telling.

Before 1825 the only road from Bideford to Torrington was via Gammaton – one had to go through East-the-Water and Weare Giffard. In 1824 it was suggested that a new road should be constructed on the West bank of the Torridge via Landcross and this came into being as a turnpike road in 1825. When it reached Bideford, however, instead of being carried along the Quay as one might expect it was routed up Torridge Hill and along Buttgarden Street. This odd route was justified by saying that most traffic along the road came to Bideford Market and thus this was the quickest route.

Not everyone, though, accepted this assurance. In a short-lived publication entitled the *North Devon Miscellany* a letter appeared on June 1 1824 which set out a different view. Writing of the proposed route the correspondent said, "It is a subject of almost universal regret that when it leaves Holliclew Wood, instead of preserving its level, and view of the river, by entering the town by the Bridge, it is most strangely determined to cross the valley by a dry bridge or raised causeway, and to enter the town by Buttgarden Street. To effect this, an immense valley must be filled up, a hill lowered, and, after its completion, the ascent will be sufficient to extract a puff from a tolerably strong winded west countryman."

The letter-writer hints very strongly at what he calls "private reasons" for this route being taken – one which a later writer calls "the Alps of the Town." These private reasons were the desire of the owner of the New Inn to have all the coach and pedestrian traffic pass by his hostelry. The New Inn had long been a centre of the transport network of North Devon with many coaches using it as a base, especially the very profitable mail coaches. The thought that all this lucrative traffic could disappear presumably caused the innkeeper to pull all the strings he could – with great success as we can see from our road pattern today.

When the road was being built there were rumours that large burial pits – said to date from the plague years in the seventeenth-century – were disturbed, although their proximity to the town would seem to rule this out.

After this road was built those who had wanted it to follow the riverside route did not sit back and accept the situation. Instead they got together and subscribed up to £5 each towards the construction of a toll-free road along their chosen route. This collection, however, was insufficient even though one of the collectors organised an amateur troupe of comedians whose shows raised some cash for the cause. The alternative road was begun but it appears that the group behind its construction had insufficient finance to finish it and thus they were forced to hand over the half-completed road to the Trustees of Turnpikes who eventually opened it but charged tolls – the opposite result the original group had looked for. The road rapidly became known as New Road at this date.

Bidefordians had to wait until 1876 for the removal of the turnpike tolls. By this date the road had become the major route-way into the town and indeed was widened at a later date to accommodate the increased traffic flow. Today, now some 170 years old, it is still called New Road.

Bideford Gazette 5.2.1982

39. AND THEN THERE WAS LIGHT

Travel towards Barnstaple from any direction at night and you will be greeted by a blaze of light. This is something we take for granted today but it would have amazed our ancestors. The first street lighting of Barnstaple dates back to 1826 when, "All the principal streets, and a considerable part of the outskirts of the town, were lit by oil lamps." These primitive contrivances were actually paid for by public subscription. But the money raised, unfortunately, didn't cover the costs of the necessary oil!

This was highlighted in January 1827 when Abraham Aaron, a well-known local Jew, fell over Barnstaple Quay and drowned in the dark. Amongst the calls for the unlit lamps to be used was one from the *Journal* editor who wrote, "For the credit of the town, for the comfort and safety of those whose pursuits call them in the streets after the light of day is withdrawn, for the prevention of vice and immorality we sincerely hope this great desideratum will ere long be effected."

The outcry was successful – the lights were lit during the summer – but they weren't very effective. It wasn't until 1838 that the newly reformed Council voted to light the town by gas out of the rates. The Mayor and two councillors were sent to survey the town and they reported that a total of 65 lamps were needed although some of these were already in place. The council rapidly agreed to this and by May 1839 the lamps were illuminating the town – though still for only 100 nights a year.

In July of 1839 however, a London policeman who had come down to report on crime in the town called for continuous lighting as, "In the dark state, and from the extent of ground with so few men to go over, it is almost impossible, even with the utmost vigilance of the Police, wholly to prevent Robberies." This swayed the council and they offered to spend more in order that the lights be lit every night – "omitting the Night of the full Moon and two nights before and two nights after."

As the years went by so the number of lights also rose – to 142 in 1869 and 280 in 1897. Electric lights made their first appearance in Barnstaple in 1887 but that is another story for another time. Suffice to say on the next occasion you are out after dark in Barnstaple think of the long history of those everyday objects – the street lights.

North Devon Journal 15.12.1988

40. NEW 'GARDENS' FOR THE POOR

In the early decades of the nineteenth century there was much public debate about the rising costs of looking after the poor. The great number of disbanded soldiers and sailors after the

Napoleonic War were added to those made redundant by the introduction of new machinery. One answer was to give the poor some way of helping themselves through the provision of allotments and Combe Martin seems to have been well in the van of this movement. In a letter to the *Journal* in December 1835 one John Ridd, who claimed to be the originator of the scheme, detailed the development of the idea.

In 1832 he was reading the *Journal* when an article about a new Act of Parliament caught his eye. The new legislation allowed the churchwardens and Overseers of the Poor of any parish to get together with the Lord of the Manor, plus the majority of landowners, to enclose up to 50 acres of common land as allotments for the poor.

Ridd was "strongly persuaded in my own mind of the benefit that would accrue to the inhabitants of Combe Martin from such an enclosure". Obtaining the support of Sir Charles Watson who was Lord of the Manor he went ahead, only to clash with "a host of narrow minded prejudiced individuals" who "sprang up in opposition to the measure and continued to oppose the proceeding at every step."

Overcoming all obstacles the first allotments were hired out in spring 1833. Some 96 "industrious cottagers" were thus given half an acre each at a rent of 2p a year for the first two years, so long as they fenced their own areas. After this the rent rose to 50p a year.

The net result of this scheme was that demands for parish relief (the dole) had fallen some 50 percent, income had risen and the labourers and their families were no longer hungry. In addition John claimed that the poor were now better mannered, more sober, frugal and independent than ever before. His only regret was "that the benefits of the allotment system have not, as yet, been more duly appreciated."

North Devon Journal 23.8.90

41. HOW A POOR POEM REACHED POSTERITY

In my researches into local history some of the most interesting things have been found totally by accident. While searching for something else in a box of old pamphlets I came across a booklet, worn with age but carefully repaired, entitled *Barum or North Devonshire – a poem by Henry Miles Staveley.*

The pamphlet contains about 330 lines of rather poor poetry that would deserve to be forgotten but for the local references it contains. It was printed by J Wilson of Bideford in 1860 and seems to have been inspired by the Great Exhibition of the Bath & West of England Agricultural Society which was held at Barnstaple in 1859.

The author begins his verses by looking at Barnstaple – "the Metropolis of the North" – and then moves on to survey the whole of "Devon's Northern beauties." Thus we read,

"Newport and Pilton, with their flowery vale
And genial breezes which you thence inhale"

Bideford, Torrington, Combe Martin and Lynton are quickly sketched in with rather stodgy phrases and we,

"Return to Barnstaple, whose tide we meet,
Bearing Taw's Commerce and the lighter fleet,
Conveying such commodities on shore
As fill each warehouse and the bonded store."

From here Staveley deals in more detail with the Taw and Torridge writing as he 'moves' down the Torridge,

"View the gay landscapes spread on every hand,
The mile long promenade by the river's strand,
Meadows and Orchard Hill behind the same,
Studded with Villas bearing each its name,
And gorgeous Mansions built by Mayor White,
Give the admirer's gaze untired delight."

Mayor White of Bideford was a local builder who evidently was responsible for developing the Orchard Hill area – still noted today for its detached 'villas' and large houses.

Crossing Northam Ridge the poet came to Northam Burrows where, as might be expected, the pebble ridge was described at length. Of more interest are the four lines concerning Sandymere and Goosey Pool,

"Noted in Winter for its ice-clad lake,
Whereon good skaters much enjoyment take,
And soldiers with their cued and hob-nailed shoes,

Dart o'er the ice themselves to amuse."

When was the last time people went skating there I wonder?
Moving around the coast we read about the "lock and shipwrights' yards" at Appledore. From here Staveley takes, in a figurative sense, the ferry to Instow which he somewhat oddly terms "Barum's Brighton." Landing on Instow beach he turns and 'sees' Lundy. With a couplet worthy of McGonagall he talks about the seals on the island
"...Davis George, by aid of lantern-light
Would kill these creatures for their oil at night."

After this he goes into a long and very outspoken attack on his old school teachers. He seems to have attended the old Bideford Grammar School – then housed on the site now occupied by the Torridge Council buildings. His bitter commentary is summed up by the lines
"Pedantic learning without reason fraught
And Greek and Latin by the birch-rod taught."

adding,
"How long shall youth endure the rigid rules
And brook the tyranny of Grammar Schools?"

After venting his obviously keenly felt spleen on his old teachers he turns to happier thoughts writing about
"The Cider-press with its crude apple cheese
The rustic youths amuse themselves to squeeze."

The highpoint of the poem, however, is where he describes the girls of Devon in ringing terms,
"Of Britain's Isle, her votaries may declare,
Devonia's Belles are 'Fairest of the Fair'."

Who am I to disagree? To our ears the poem reads somewhat clumsily yet the mixture of romanticism and ordinariness is oddly pleasing – and one thing is for sure – no-one writes poems like this any more.

North Devon Journal 6.6.1985

42. VICTORIAN SENTIMENTS FOR OLD BRAUNTON

Some months ago I wrote about a local descriptive poem written in the 1860's. Another poem has now been brought to my attention from about the same time...this time about Braunton. It was published in 1856 from the offices of the *North Devon Journal* by Thomas Mortimer and runs to several hundred lines. It begins in typical Victorian style,

"Braunton! I've lov'd thee long and well.
Still on thy varied charms delighted dwell;
For here contented with a humble lot,
I early built myself a lowly cot."

Evidently Mortimer was a local and, to judge by later lines, a good gardener. His garden and greenhouse produced,

"Quinces – medlars – mulberries are there
The luscious green gage and the melting pear."
as well as *"grapes, chestnuts, walnuts and filberts."*

He next described the view form his windows including 'Chanter's Tower,' built by an Appledore merchant as a look-out. Mortimer speaks of Chanter as "My schoolfellow" – presumably at Bideford Grammar School. Bideford itself gets a mixed compliment,

"A town endow'd with nature's riches.
Of old renown'd for burning witches."

Another section on Instow also reads somewhat oddly,

"Omitting Instow, I were much to blame,
So justly prized for sanitary fame."

Its sanitary fame rested on its benefits for invalids.

His poetic view carried on round the coast taking in Clovelly court "in all its beauty drest" and on to Hartland Point and Lundy. After this panoramic view he returned to Braunton talking of its "far-fam'd field" and the local iron ore mines found by a local geologist named Symonds. He also mentions two of the village's famous "epicurean" products – "Our priz'd dried apples and delicious laver", Laver yes, but why "dried apples"?

Braunton Burrows is a nature reserve today but even in the mid-nineteenth century it was obviously an attraction for naturalists. Mortimer writes that they,

"...may pass the longest Summer's day,
In seeking insect myriads strange and gay."

So far his poem had been one of praise for North Devon but in describing Braunton he writes,

"The village straggling and not overclean
And all unworthy of each neighb'ring scene."

Not the sort of sentiment to endear him to his friends one would have thought. The poet apparently blamed the large number of public houses,

"Where signs of beasts still selfish hearts entice
To wallow in the mire of sensual vice."

- a not too subtle attack on the Red Lion and Black Horse which then existed in the village. He moves on to the "ancient grand and gothic pile" of the church and mentions the chapel of St. Brannock. Viewing the Barnstaple turnpike road he writes of – "...the new road mail coach with goodly team." Braunton's postal link was important both to the tradesmen and also as a mark of growth and development in Victorian Britain. Next to the new-built vicarage was the similarly new school room of which Mortimer had high hopes.

His last section describes Braunton as the sun set and he goes into raptures over the beauty of the Taw and the loveliness of the famous Braunton orchards. The last couplet sums up his wishes for the future of the village – that all the inhabitants,

"Helping to form a loving, lov'd community -
The people and the place in perfect unity."

It is a pity that people do not write such poems today – they probably just take photographs and videos instead.

North Devon Journal 30.1.1986

43. THE BEGINNING AND END OF THE VICTORIAN PIER

The story of how Westward Ho! took its name from a Charles Kingsley book is well-known. The developers of the resort decided that the name had just the right hint of romantic Englishness they needed to sell their new village.

Less well-known is the story of another of the developers' companies – the Northam Burrows and Landing Pier Co. Established in 1864, the company was set up to raise funds to build a pier. The plans called for a 600-foot long promenade with a cafe and bandstand at the pierhead. At this date J Pine-Coffin was the company chairman with Captain Molesworth and Colonel Wheller as the principal shareholders. An Act of Parliament and sufficient funds were needed before building could start. The company finally got going in February 1870. In that month a contract was signed with a Mr Gooch, who had been responsible for Bognor pier.

Building however was slow and in October 1871, a massive storm inflicted severe damage on the unfinished structure. Only 150 feet of the pier was left standing and the damage was put at £1,300. The contract with Gooch was declared void and a new one signed with W & J Abbott of Bideford. At the same time, the design length of the pier was shortened, presumably in an effort to get it built quickly and get it earning back some of its cost. The pier opened for business in July 1873.

However at an annual meeting in February 1874 the chairman had to report that only 80 out of the 150 shares had been sold and that some £5,141 was owing to various creditors. The only way of meeting this debt was to sell the pier. It was offered to the developers of Westward Ho! who seem to have bought it at a knock-down price.

A few years of good weather seem to have helped the pier's fortunes along with some 'special events' organised by the operators. In 1875 for example, a 'Monster Picnic' was held on the pier when some 1,000 people sat down to lunch. Westward Ho! pier, however, gradually became shabby and less inviting. The end came in February 1880 when a storm hit and broke off two legs. In fact just three months later, the owners began dismantling the pier as it had "become dangerous as well as unsightly." So ended the very short life of North Devon's only Victorian pier – a victim of both the natural elements and, perhaps, the economic incompetence of its owners. All that remain today are a few corroded stumps revealed at low tide, the rusting remnants of a once proud Victorian amusement.

North Devon Journal 17.5.1990

44. HOW BIDEFORD WON ITS FREE LIBRARY

One of the busiest buildings in Bideford must be the library. At any time on any day there are customers coming and going. Yet until 1877 there was no library in the town and if you weren't well off – and most people weren't – books were a luxury beyond your reach.

In March 1877 a public meeting was held at the Town Hall to consider whether Bideford should adopt the Public Libraries Act passed 22 years earlier. Adoption would mean rates being used to set up and fund a Free Library for the townspeople. On the night of the meeting it was clear that there were two groups present. Those "known amongst us to move with the times, in accordance with the spirit of the age" and the others "who were evidently opposed to the contemplated measure" as the local reporter put it.

The supporters of the measure were led by Mr Narraway (who later became Mayor) who said such a building would benefit all and "would be a place of resort for apprentices and young men, after leaving their shops and their counting houses and would not only prevent them to a certain extent from getting into evil company, but would be a resort for relaxation and recreation which would benefit them morally, intellectually and physically."

The 'antis' didn't dispute this but suggested firstly, that the rates couldn't bear the cost and secondly, that more money would be generated if subscriptions were called for. Mr Clements said that the fact that so few of the 'working class' had bothered to attend the meeting showed there was little real demand. Snidely he went on to say that they would have got more support if the 'pro' lobby had provided "an old fiddle and a barrel of beer" to attract the 'working class' to the meeting. When the vote was taken, however, there was an overwhelming majority for the library.

This was only the first skirmish of a long battle. In April a concert was put on to raise initial funds but wasn't very successful.

In May, at the Town Council, Mr Narraway produced a list of people willing to subscribe £50 between them to help launch the project. One name notable by its absence from this list was that of the Mayor, Thomas Trewin, who bluntly said that he "did not believe it."

The one concrete result of this meeting was the setting up of a provisional library committee whose first job was to find rooms in which to house their scheme. One sign of the prevailing attitudes was the suggestion that more than one room was needed as the social classes would refuse to mix. It was also seriously suggested that the 'rich' would use it during the day, whilst the 'poor' would come in at night.

In August the council met with the Bridge Trust and Mr Narraway asked for a £50 donation towards the library. Dr Thomson of the Trust "quite concurred in this, for a more important movement than that of the Free Library had not been set on foot during the many years he had been in the town." Notwithstanding this the Trustees only voted to give £25. At the same meeting £25 was also given to help buy a new church clock, one member saying that he thought the clock "of far more importance to them than a public library."

With this grant, the promised subscriptions and support from the rates the library was soon established in its first home – in Bridgeland Street in the building now used by the Freemasons next to Lavington church. For £30 rent per annum it occupied the back room on the ground floor whilst the 'Reading Room' of the 'Bideford and Westward Ho! Art and Science Class' was at the front. At long last Bideford had a public library.

All was well until May 1878 when the property was put up for sale at £400. Mr Narraway pressed the Council to buy the building outright but no decision was reached and the building was sold. The library's lease ran out at Christmas but it seems to have remained in being as in August 1882 it was ceremonially rehoused in the newly erected Bridge Buildings – site of the present-day Torridge District Council offices.

The library finally came to its present home in 1906 when Andrew Carnegie gave a large sum to the town to establish a permanent and purpose-built home for the collections. Two years later a museum was opened within the library building and although this has now gone we still have our 'Free Public Library'

– a wonderful living monument to the actions of Mr Narraway and his supporters over a century ago.

North Devon Journal 24.10.1985

45. A GIFT THAT GAVE NORTHAM ITS MEN'S CLUB

Visitors to Northam cannot miss the solid stone buildings on the main road that houses a launderette and chandlery ... looking much as they did when built over 110 years ago, but now with a greatly changed role. The block began life in July 1880 as a working men's club erected under the auspices of the Church of England temperance movement and the story behind its construction is of some interest.

In 1878, the vicar, the Rev Dimon Churchward, was offered the site free of charge by a former vicar and "immediately set to work" to raise the money to build a clubhouse. Circulars requesting donations were issued and he called in the help of the ladies, who "worked so assiduously that in the course of a few months they had collected together sufficient articles to hold a bazaar whereby they raised more than £300" – a huge sum in those days.

Unfortunately the vicar required double this amount and, as if in answer to his prayers, a £300 cheque arrived from a Mr Allen, a rich Liverpool merchant, whose father then lived in Northam. His gift came with two conditions – the building was to be non-sectarian and had to be completed by July 1880.

With the money available work rapidly began. An architect, J R Bryden, was appointed and, "Stones for the erection of the clubhouse were offered gratuitously by Dr Heyward Smith and also A Wren." Other parishioners freely loaned horses and carts to move the stone. Tenders for the building were invited and one of £627 from Messrs Lock and Cook was accepted. Work was completed by July 1880 as Mr Allen had specified and a report of the opening ceremony describes the building as "being in the Gothic style" with a hall 20 feet by 30 feet, a reading room 22 feet by 16 feet and a smoking room of the same size.

The building was inaugurated on July 2, with a public tea where 240 people had cake, buns and strawberries, followed by hymns and prayers. The speeches seem to have gone on for some time to judge by contemporary newspaper reports. The vicar said he hoped the "working men would come forward in great numbers and join" as membership was not confined to teetotallers but "would be open to moderate drinkers as well." He did, however, add sternly that "only confirmed drunkards would be refused admission" – one wonders how many Northam residents that ruled out!

Some of the speeches were slightly odd. A Dr Bulteel of Plymouth said he was a "strong supporter of institutions of this kind, because they promote social intercourse without Republican tendencies" – whatever that meant. A local magistrate Henry Tardew "drew an effective contrast between the states of Northam when he was a boy, and its present condition." He didn't elaborate but reckoned that the improvement "religiously, morally, and socially" was due to the Temperance movement and the work of the clergy.

After the speeches the audience sang 'Abide with me' and Northam officially had its first public meeting place which still today is a handsome building.

North Devon Journal 15.5.85

46. HOW BIDEFORD'S MARKET HALL WAS BORN

The year 1984 saw the centenary of Bideford Pannier Market. In 1881 the Town Council purchased the Lordship of the Manor of Bideford and so acquired responsibility for the market. At this time Bideford Market was a run-down and dirty collection of stalls and sheds that had developed over the previous two centuries on a site at the top of Bridge Street. The Council decided in 1883 to replace the old-fashioned 'shambles' with the magnificent stone structure we see today. Building this replacement, however, took time and obviously the market traders had to go somewhere else during demolition and construction.

The councillors met in May 1883 to consider a temporary market and various proposals were made. The first suggestions were on the Quay or at 'Ascotts Green' in Buttgarden Street which was then "the present site of the sheep pens." I am unsure where this actually was – possibly next to the present modern hotel. Other suggested sites included the upper part of High Street where "some sixty years ago a large cattle market was held on a field "below the factory" entered from Pitt Lane – presumably this was the collar factory at Westcombe.

The most favoured site though appeared to be the Quay and one councillor, Mr Braund, produced a petition from the market butchers supporting this site. Another councillor, however, suggested that "they would sign anything if they could thereby sell a small joint of meat." Mr Braund hotly repudiated this – though as he himself was a butcher one would expect it of him! In the end the council voted for the Quay to be used.

Only a week later the council met again and, incredibly, rescinded their previous motion on the grounds that it was apparently illegal to site anything on the Quay as it contravened an Act of Parliament. A suggestion was then made to site the butcher's stalls along the pavement in front of the Farmer's Exchange pub (next to the present-day Joiner's Arms) but this was turned down as the building contractor for the new market reckoned there wouldn't be enough room for them. The meeting broke up in acrimony with no decision having been reached.

Two weeks later they met again and a suggestion that the temporary market be set up behind the Ring of Bells in Honestone Street and next to 'Highfield' was popular. The newspaper report of this meeting is headed "Lively meeting of the town council" and not without reason. One councillor, Mr Dawe, began by saying that "he never saw a more dilapidated place, or a worse one for the purpose of a market, than the Ring of Bells." Other councillors joined in saying that they wouldn't dream of letting their wives and daughters go near the Ring of Bells – one does wonder what sort of reputation the pub had.

Other councillors spoke in favour of the pub site, one adding that there was an old "barn there available for a corn market." Mr Dawe, however, "characterised the remarks as rubbish." This meeting also broke up in disarray though they did agree to set up a committee to look into the whole question. The exasperated Mayor was quoted as muttering "We shall never agree."

This unsatisfactory state of affairs dragged on for another two months until at last, in August, the council reached a compromise decision. The temporary market was to be held in two places – the butcher's market to be in "the space below the Torridge Inn", (the sheds still survive today), and the other traders were to be allowed to erect stalls at the bottom of Meddon Street opposite the old

Torridge Inn. The old market ceased trading on August 7 1883, and the traders moved en bloc to their new home.

North Devon Journal 9.1.1986

47. WHEN A TOWN'S BEST HOTEL STAYED DRY

Barnstaple High Street has its fair share of impressive buildings. The most imposing of these is Victoria Chambers – a marvellous multi-storied late Victorian extravaganza with a huge tower. It is a building which can boast a century of history.

In late April 1887 the newly-formed Victoria Temperance Hotel Company Ltd. publicly announced their intention to raise £5,000 to build a new hotel – the sum to be raised with 900 £5 shares and 500 £1 shares. The first chairman of its directors was William Philip Hiern of The Castle in Barnstaple, supported by nine other directors (all honorary) including N Chammings of Stoke Rivers, and William Passmore of Heanton Court.

The announcement was accompanied by a prospectus which clearly set out the company's intentions. These were "to establish in Barnstaple a first-class temperance hotel and hostelry at which no wine, ale, spiritous or intoxicating liquors are to be sold." The site at the corner of Gammon Lane and High Street, was owned by the Hon Mark Rolle who had "kindly intimated his willingness to grant to the company a reversionary lease at a moderate annual ground rent."

The site was already occupied by two old-established businesses but these were given their marching orders. One was run by Zachariah Smyth who described himself as "coach builder, auctioneer, mining and estate agent, manure merchant and district manager for the Gt Britain Insurance Company." His neighbours were W B and T Joce, "wine, spirit, ale and porter merchants" – doubtless the teetotallers chortled to think of this concern giving way to a temperance hotel!

The sort of customer the new business hoped to attract was clearly stated in the prospectus, "It is proposed to rebuild and adapt the premises to make them suitable for a first-class hotel, with good accommodation for the clergy, gentry, farmers, and commercial men, and generally to fit up and furnish the house in such a manner as shall prove conducive to the comfort and convenience of all classes of temperance customers."

The directors advertised that they "offered a premium of £20 for the best plans to carry out this scheme" – a prize won by an architect T King James. By September 1887 the required capital had been secured and a notice appeared, "Tenders are required for the first section of the work to be done in the erection of the Victoria Temperance Hotel in High Street, Barnstaple."

Building proceeded quickly and the hotel appears to have opened early in 1888. The final development came with an advertisement in April when "G H Vicary begs to announce that on May 1 next, he will open the extensive stabling attached to the New Victoria Temperance Hotel, High Street, and will be able to give first-rate accommodation for upwards of one hundred horses. Farmers and others attending market will find this stabling most convenient, and a staff of horse-keepers always in attendance."

Thus was the building constructed, though within a mere 10 years it had fallen into financial trouble being sold by the company in 1896 to Edward Chanter from Torquay. He kept it up for a short time and always advertised it as the "best and most modern hotel in the town." Sometime after the First World War it dropped "temperance" from its title and became just an ordinary hotel – a reflection of changing social values and behaviour. Eventually it was used by the North Devon education department and today it houses Fosters' Menswear Shop.

North Devon Journal 21.8.1986

48. CASTING LIGHT ON THE PAST

Anyone entering Bideford or Barnstaple at night is greeted with a blaze of light from the street lamps, the brightly illuminated shops and the advertising hoardings. Yet this sparkling display of lights is only a recent innovation. Indeed, we can trace its beginning back over 100 years ago to February 1887. Before this date paraffin, gas and candles had been used to provide a warm but relatively feeble light.

In that February, however, one resident of Barnstaple took the plunge and provided himself with some of the new-fangled electric lights. So novel was this that his experiment merited the headline,

"The Electric Light in Barnstaple." The report which accompanied this began, "The establishment of Mr George Sloman, baker and confectioner, of Joy Street, was last evening lighted by electricity, this being the first time the 'new illuminant' has been used for such a purpose in the North of Devon. The dynamo used is of the Siemen's type, and is capable of lighting fifteen lamps of sixteen nominal candle power each."

This first experiment actually used thirteen "incandescent or glow lamps, which were of quite 20 candle power." This is the rough equivalent of just four modern 60 watt bulbs – hardly excessive for a shop one would have thought! The system was powered by a gas engine though the reporter was forced to add, "Engines of this class, however, are not absolutely steady in running, and this causes a slight wavering of the light. This was very evident last evening." The whole apparatus was put in place by Mr A Gay, who proudly described himself as "electrician" – North Devon's first – who confidently predicted that he could overcome the flickering effect of the new lights. Needless to say "Mr Sloman's brilliantly lighted shop attracted general attention last evening." As far as I can tell the shop was at the corner of Green Lane and Joy Street.

The newspaper returned to the subject the following week commenting that this new lighting "had been much commented on during the past week, and some hundreds of persons have visited Mr Sloman's shop." This gentleman was obviously of an adventurous nature as he told the reporter that he "intends lighting the whole of his house by means of electricity, and that a large dynamo will forthwith be obtained to replace the comparatively small one now in use."

Where one shopkeeper went, of course, others were sure to follow and it was reported that, "it is rumoured that some of the tradesmen in High-street are likely to follow Mr Sloman's example – at all events, so far as using the electric light for business purposes is concerned."

I like that last phrase about "business purposes." Clearly the hard-headed tradesmen did not envisage anything so extraordinary as lighting their houses with this new energy! A hundred years later and it is hard to think of how we would manage without the ubiquitous electric light.

North Devon Gazette 9.5.1986

49. THE HISTORY OF A BUILDING

Bideford is a town rich in historic buildings – it has been spared the wholesale civic destruction that has occurred in Barnstaple and the wartime damage of Exeter and Plymouth – yet very little has been done to study this building heritage. Recently I became interested in the area around the Pannier Market and this article is the first fruit of that interest.

The building housing John Brown's carpet and hardware shop is a striking one, standing as it does on the brow of the hill that is Grenville Street. It is clear that the building at one time consisted of both the present day shop and the adjoining Radio Lantern building.

Mr Brown took over the premises a decade ago from Messrs Wickham's who were using it as a store. They in turn had taken it over from the World's Stores group, who had run it as a retail grocery – their name is still present, worked in mosaic on the front door step. Many will remember this store and some older Bidefordians can remember Messrs Tattersills who owned the shop until about 1924/5.

Tattersills also ran it as a grocery and were renowned for their widespread advertising. Their business was well run and at one time they had four branches in the town. Mr E J Tattersill was Mayor for three years running over the years 1901-3. They took over the premises in 1895 when they were known as Tattersill, Newhead and Snow and one of the first things they did was to sell a large area of their frontage to the council and begin rebuilding. It is difficult to believe now, but the building at that date extended out half-way across Grenville Street, making the entrance to the Market Place very narrow. The council took the opportunity that came with the rebuilding plans to buy about 1,000 square feet of land – at 92½p a square foot, to widen the road.

On March 15 1895 the foundation stone of the new premises was laid by Miss Violet Tattersill, and we read that "Mr Tattersill addressed a few cheery and complimentary words to the men, and expressed a hope that the work would proceed without hindrance or accident, and would, when completed, be a source of satisfaction to all concerned." The contract was to be completed within six months. The builders were Cock and Lamerton and the cost was approximately £2,000.

The new building replaced one that already had a long history of selling groceries. In an 1889 directory one Henry Ackland is listed as the proprietor running the grandly named Bideford and North Devon General Grocery and Provision Supply Stores. By this date he had already been there for ten years.

In the 1871 Census, however, another name is listed at this address. This was Charles Henry Octavius Sellick, who ran his business as a wholesale grocery. A news item from the local paper in September 1875 shows that he also ran an off-licence as he successfully applied for a wine and spirit licence at this date.

Sellick appears to have been the purchaser when the shop was advertised for sale in March 1862. Then it was described as a "Shop and premises, with the gardens and greenhouse and detached warehouses thereunto belonging, and now and for some years past in the occupation of Mr Thomas Trewin, grocer." It was "at the bottom of the marketplace in the most eligible part of the thriving seaport and market town of Bideford."

Thomas Trewin first took up residence in 1845, but his years at the shop were not without incident. He appears many times in local court reports, suing suppliers for bad goods or debt, although several times he was sued for short weights. Thomas went on to become Overseer of the Poor and later Mayor in 1876.

As I said, Trewin took over the shop in 1845 when he purchased it from Thomas Chope, described at the time as a "Whole and Retail Grocer, Tea Dealer, etc." When the changeover took place the old and new owners took a joint advertisement to announce the fact in the local paper. Chope thanked "the gentry, clergy and inhabitants generally" for "the very liberal support he has received." Trewin noted that "the principles upon which their trade will be conducted is that of real quality, small profits and quick returns."

A fascinating story has come down to us about Thomas Chope. He was a Wesleyan Methodist and when chosen to serve as one of the 12 voluntary constables of the town, refused to follow the custom of attending the Mayor and Corporation to church each

Sunday. He was summoned by the local magistrates, with the Mayor as chairman, and fined 5/- (25p) which he only paid under threat of being put in the stocks for four hours. He brought a civil action against the magistrates and got a refund and in so doing effectively destroyed the old habit of compulsory church attendance for civic officials.

This Thomas Chope was the son of another Thomas who was the local tax collector for Bideford. It is from the tax listings that Thomas senior compiled that we can trace the history of the building back another 50 years. 'Grocer' Thomas appears in the Land Tax from 1824 to 1831 as the owner, but Thomas senior is given as the owner in 1823 – presumably he gave or willed the property to his son in that year. Thomas senior paid the tax due from 1804 to 1823, but the actual building was apparently let to various tenants. It is interesting that, in the light of the present day situation, from 1794 to 1812 the building was divided into two.

Between 1801 and 1804 the building passed into the hands of Thomas, its previous owner apparently being Roger Chope who might have been the father of Thomas senior. He is listed as paying the tax from 1795 to 1801. He was a general merchant, but as yet I know little about him.

From 1780, when the tax lists begin, until 1794 ownership was in the hands of the executors of Thomas Coplestone. They let it to a whole succession of tenants about whom I know little more than their names. Coplestone himself was a mercer (or draper) of Bideford and with him my researches have, for the time being, halted.

Thus we have been through more than 200 years of the history of just one building – not very colourful it must be said – but still of interest to all students of the past history of the town.

Bideford Gazette 23.1.1987

50. BRIDGE MARVEL STOPS FLOODING

Car drivers take it for granted today but in 1928 the raised causeway across the Taw valley just outside Bishops Tawton was hailed as an "engineering marvel". Officially called the Newbridge Causeway it was ceremonially opened in May 1928. A long report in the *Journal* gave details of the six-hundred-foot-long causeway.

Apparently modelled on a much larger viaduct in the Lea Valley in Essex the causeway cost £8,000, took one-and-a-half-years to build and was designed to be at least two feet above the highest recorded floor mark. The support beams had been driven into solid rock some 30-feet down to give a solid foundation and because the "new fangled" reinforced concrete had been used, "more than 75 per cent of the whole cost" was spent in North Devon on local labour and locally produced materials.

The "impressive opening ceremony" saw a large gathering of county council officials, local councillors and spectators. The first speech was given by a Mr Higgs, the chairman of the grandly named North Devon Main Roads Committee of the Devon County Council. He gave especial thanks to Sir Bourchier Wrey who had given the necessary land, adding that the same gentleman had always been helpful in the past when the old road flooded.

He was followed by the Rev A B S Wrey, the rector of Bishops Tawton. In his speech he noted that crossing the Taw Valley at this point had been a problem for as long as anyone could remember. He reckoned that "many there present had seen that valley full of a raging torrent of water from bank to bank, causing great damage." He finished his talk by praising the wisdom of his fellow county councillors, a body "very often criticised for their extravagance and other sins." In this case they "were a body of excellent people and business-like in their methods" who had decided on a course of action to stop the inconvenience associated with the old road. With that he cut the ceremonial tape across the road and declared it open.

The wife of the chairman of the Barnstaple Rural District Council then unveiled two commemorative tablets listing the various people and groups involved in construction of the bridge. With that the party went off to lunch and a major engineering feat took its place as a feature of the North Devon road system still being valued today some 62 years later.

North Devon Journal 13.9.1990

OCCUPATIONS

51. MARIJUANA: AN OLD CROP FOR NORTH DEVON

In 1525 the surveyor employed by Cecily, Lady Harrington and Bonville drew up a list of the leaseholdings of his mistress. She had, by marriage and inheritance become a major landholder in the Westcountry and wished to know just what she owned. The record has survived and has now been published. Although most of her Devon lands were in the South of the county she also owned areas in North Devon – mostly in Ilfracombe though other parishes do appear.

The list might appear fairly dry but there are points of interest. Firstly the names of the farm tenants. In Barnstaple we find a Henry Orynge, in West Ashford the good Norman name of Fitzharberd and the odd female names Jaketta and Emota. At Ilfracombe there was Thomas Enkyldon – a name that still exists today as Incledon. In the same parish there was the melodically named Andrew Pyncowe. For family historians the survey is a goldmine predating the earliest parish registers by some 12 years. These names are listed next to particular properties many of which are named and can be traced, in mutated form, down to the present day.

In Barnstaple, for example, we find "Bare Street" and meadow called "Rakk Mede" – the names exist today as Bear Street and Rackfield. Ilfracombe which has fifty separate landholdings listed throws up a whole crop of names many of which are still recognisable. Thus there is "Chambercombe", "Est Bowden", "Hurne", "Horedown", "Culver Park", "Runyclyfe", "Shankdon" and "the Torres."

In addition to giving us information about the names we can see how large the farms were. In West Ashdown Richard Morrys farmed 36 acres, 20 arable and 16 pasture – a pattern repeated throughout the parish and indicating the subsistence nature of sixteenth century farming. No production of cash-income dairy goods then – after all there was no means of transporting dairy products. In Ilfracombe, on the other hand, there appears to have been more pasture than arable – indicating the poor nature of local soils.

In most of the North Devon places listed there are entries for "hempland". Small in area but valuable in production, hemp went to make rope and provide cattle food. Hemp isn't grown today – perhaps because it also produces marijuana – an interesting crop for North Devon!

North Devon Journal 19.5.1988

52. MILLING CORN BY STEAM

North Devon has never been a great industrial area yet one of the first specialised industrial buildings in the area is still standing today. Go to Bideford and you will find an undistinguished rather stark, three storey building standing behind a coal yard at Westcombe.

In January 1827 the *North Devon Journal* carried a paragraph from their Bideford correspondent who wrote, "Our extensive new corn mills are nearly finished, and will set to work shortly after the arrival of the steam engine, which is daily expected from London; this will be a great acquisition to this town; in consequence of the long drought last summer and the destruction of the tide mills, we were obliged to send all our corn to Torrington to be ground." The tide mills referred to appear to have been at Hallsannery and Cleavehouses on the Torridge estuary.

The builders of the new mill also constructed a square-shaped water reservoir – approximately where the entrance to the coal-yard is today – which was fed by the small Westcombe stream. This was to feed the steam engine which arrived soon after. By July 1827 it was in place and working under the two proprietors, Messrs Facey and Pugsley. Samuel Facey was the working half of the partnership and it was due to his energy that the newspaper could praise the "new steam mills" in September of that year.

Facey seemed to combine his milling activities with owning a public house and producing malt for brewing. He owned the aptly named Malt Scoop Inn in Cooper Street and ran a malting business in a special building at the rear.

The new venture flourished and Facey was soon advertising for another miller. At the same time his partner Pugsley was replaced by Charles Roe, a local corn merchant. It is all the sadder therefore that the same paper which carried the news of early success should have to announce in its issue of May 2 1833 that Mr Samuel Facey of "the steam mills" in Bideford had died aged 59. A month later an advertisement asked that outstanding claims against his estate be directed to the firm of Facey and Roe of Bideford. John Facey, presumably Samuel's son, also made clear that the business was to be continued.

Only a few months later in November a short paragraph in the 'Marriages' column announced that John Facey, maltster, had married a local girl, Miss Handford. This pattern of marriage after a father's death was usual. The heir found he had inherited enough to get married on and so he did – a case of father's misfortune being a son's gain.

John Facey, however, hit hard times. As the industrial revolution progressed during the nineteenth-century so corn milling became concentrated more and more in the hands of a few very large steam mills and the Bideford works could not compete. By July 1845 the mill was being offered for sale.

No buyer appears to have been found but sometime in 1848 John Facey died and the papers noted that a Liverpool company, Young & Co were to take over the "steam mills". This firm, however, disappointed the local community and within weeks of restarting operations in the Westcombe factory they left saying that the building was unsafe.

In November 1850 the "desirable extensive, long and well-established corn mill" at Westcombe was auctioned at the New Inn, Bideford, by Facey and Roe. The description comes from an advertisement which adds that the mills were "capable of manufacturing 150 sacks of flour per week". With the mill went a house of five bedrooms, two parlours, a kitchen, a pantry and a brewhouse. The buyer was apparently one Richard Pain but the business entered into a very lean period and around 1873 the old mill was turned over to the production of collars and this industry lasted there until the mid-1920s.

As I said it is hard to equate the building we see today with the thrusting nature of early nineteenth-century industrialism but there it is – a mute witness to a previous age.

North Devon Journal 3.4.1986

53. WHO INVENTED ESTATE AGENTS' JARGON?

Love them or hate them but estate agents are here to stay. Yet when did their profession begin? Naturally it is difficult to give an exact date, but here in North Devon we are on firmer ground. In March 1830 the *Journal* carried an advert giving information about the establishment of "Ormond's Registry for Servants and Apprentices and General Agency Office for Letting and Disposing of Houses, Lodgings; Furnished and Unfurnished; and Stock of every description."

This J Ormond was the first 'estate agent' I have come across and he backed up his advert by listing "14 sets of lodgings" to let, 10 houses to be sold "of various sizes and situations" as well as "several servants wanting situations". He was based in Barnstaple High Street and this "registry" appears to have been an offshoot from his main business of pottery selling.

The following month Mr Ormond advertised that "he intends to publish his first list" of houses for sale noting that "All persons having property to dispose of will find this to be far the cheapest and best method of publishing it." He struck a modern note when he added "no charge is made except the property is disposed of through the recommendation of the office." He also informed those "who may be pleased to honour him with their support, that no exertion of his shall be wanting to further their interest and to give satisfaction." Servants who wanted to register their availability were told not to bother applying "except they can produce unexceptionable characters" i.e. good testimonials.

The first property listing must have gone well as on May 31 1830 Ormond advertised that "1200 copies of the second list of all the property to be disposed of then on the register books" were to be published. These lists weren't only for locals; copies were sent to London, Exeter and Plymouth as well as "all the large inns, reading rooms, etc., in the principal towns in Devon and Cornwall." Outsiders being attracted in to North Devon are clearly nothing new. This second listing offered 29 houses and 19 sets of lodgings. In addition three servants were wanted by local employers.

Not content with apparently inventing estate agency in this area Ormond can also be blamed for introducing the hyperbole so much associated with the profession. This is clear from the same advert which he ends with this wonderfully bombastic statement, "The publicity given to all matters published in the list exceeds by far anything of the kind attempted in this part of the country; it is superfluous to say anything in its favour as the support it has already received bears ample testimony to its utility." The language may be more flowery than today but the basic style is still with us!

It should be added that Ormond's business disappeared after a few years – but he was to be followed by many, many others.

North Devon Journal 14.9.1989

54. DUMMETT: THE BLIND POSTMAN OF BRAUNTON

Most people reading this will have heard of Edward Capern the Victorian postman-poet of North Devon but how many have heard of his contemporary Robert Dummett the blind postman of Braunton? Dummett was born in Braunton about 1802 and lost his sight in early childhood. Facing up to harsh reality, however, he chose to ignore his disability as far as possible and became determined to earn his own living and not rely on others.

His extraordinary choice of career began almost accidentally. As a young boy he began "goods errands" and became noted for his total trustworthiness by "the respectable people of Braunton". They apparently had "perfect confidence in his correctness" while "his character afforded full assurance of his sobriety and fidelity." From running errands he progressed to taking and fetching letters and parcels to and from Barnstaple. This was pre-1840 in the days before the postal system as we know it today was set up and when the only local "posting point" was Barnstaple.

When Rowland Hill introduced his 'Penny Post' in 1840 Robert Dummett was the obvious choice as postman for Braunton. He became a celebrated character in the locality being noted for "his upright and rather tall person" as he "made his way with measured pace, keeping close by the wall as he came along the street, and tapping the ground with his walking stick. Before setting off each day his wife told him where each piece of mail was addressed to and "the nicety of his sense of touch, enabled him to deliver his various freight" correctly in every case.

Dummett was thought of so highly by the people of Braunton that when a post-office was eventually established in the village he was seriously put forward as a contender for the job of postmaster but "the unsuitability of making a blind man a postmaster was too obvious for the department to overcome."

In 1839 he and his wife had begun a small grocery and drapery shop in Braunton adding a malting business to it in 1849. At first things went well but in 1861 he was declared bankrupt to the tune of £2,286-odd. He had run up his largest debts to his wholesaler, a Pascal Widlake, of Barnstaple, and when his cheques were returned his creditors came clamouring for their money. He was forced to sell both his drapery and malting business along with the buildings to help satisfy these creditors. In addition Dummett owned the adjoining farm house, barn and stable, eight acres of Braunton Marsh and 12 acres of arable land in the Great Field. These raised £447 altogether and helped increase the dividend paid to the creditors to 4s 6d (23p) in the pound.

This was a major set-back and Dummett never seemed to recover his drive and self-confidence. Luckily the inhabitants of Braunton still respected their blind postman and they managed to obtain an annual income for him from "Day's Charity for the Blind" which helped him greatly in his last years.

His obituary closed by noting that he was "a shrewd and intelligent man, and was held in general esteem." He died after a long illness, aged 70, on May 23 1872, and was buried in Braunton.

North Devon Journal 22.1.1987

55. DESCRIPTION EXAGGERATES REALITY

Estate agent exaggeration has become a cliché today. We all know that "deceptively spacious" means there isn't room to swing a cat and that "outstanding views" actually refers to the pig farm next door. We might be forgiven for thinking that such hyperbole is a late twentieth century phenomenon but we would be wrong. Some 150 years ago an estate agent was producing descriptions of the property he was handling to rival even the most flamboyant practitioners today.

His name was George Robins and he lived in London although his business was based on selling properties throughout England. In July 1841 Robins advertised for sale three houses at Lynton. He began by describing Lynton as being just a "ten hours" ride from

London and set in countryside that "has powerful claims on the early attention of all those who would avoid the expense and fatigue of visiting Switzerland, and yet could delight in the opportunity of partaking of the SPLENDOUR OF ITS SCENERY IN ENGLAND." (capitals were one of his specialities.)

After setting the scene he dealt with his first property – a "splendid Swiss villa placed on a rock of fearful height" overlooking the Lyn river and surrounded by "the woods of paradise" – a setting which he describes as "the realms of fairy land."

After these flights of fancy he rather oddly limits his description of the house to merely pointing out that it has "hot and cold" baths with no mention of numbers of bedrooms etc. This lack of detail makes it virtually impossible to identify which building he was talking about, unlike his second which was a "Swiss Cottage" known as "Watersmeet." Now a National Trust property and visited annually by thousands Robins described it as "one of the prettiest things in Europe" although "very petite."

Access was by road between "the mountains where the hanging woods are clothed in verdure to the summit." The cottage was surrounded by "pleasure grounds" and next to a beautiful confluence of two rivers. In case a potential purchaser was worried that the rivers might be noisy Robins added that "the sound has a tranquillising rather than a startling effect." Again, unfortunately, he doesn't bother to describe the accommodation available at all.

His last property was the Combe Park Estate half a mile from Watersmeet. This consisted of 130 acres plus a half built "residence of some pretensions" which allowed a purchaser "of unexceptional taste to direct its completion." Unfortunately the buyer had to like "Gothic style" architecture because this was the style in which the house had been begun. An extra bonus for the hunting man was the presence of red deer, partridge and woodcock as well as some good fishing. Further details plus intriguingly, drawings of each property, were available from local libraries and hotels throughout Devon price 6d though no price for the properties are given.

One wonders who could resist Robins' golden prose and would

any estate agent today get away with describing Lynton as the "REALMS OF FAIRY LAND."?

North Devon Journal 28.5.1992

56. 19TH CENTURY LICENSEE WENT BUST OVER £255

The Victorian era is renowned for its solidity and stability when everything was fixed and sure. That this was not always so is proved by a box of parchment documents contained in the Devon Record Office at Exeter. These are the files of records dealing with those unfortunates who went bankrupt in nineteenth century Devon.

In one box there are a set of papers concerning one Roger Crocker, an innkeeper and commission agent who went bankrupt in 1846. He gave his address as the Castle Inn, Allhalland Street, Bideford where he had carried on business for nine months. This Inn was on the site of the present Torridge Council Offices and was notable for being the only public house in this road.

He was a well-travelled man, the record noting that he had previously been landlord of the Malt Scoop Inn in Cooper Street for 21 months and host of the New Ring of Bells in Honestone Lane for six and a half years. His debts were euphemistically referred to as his "present embarrassments".

The main bulk of the records concerns a listing of his earnings and expenses over the period February 1846 to April 1847. Thus on February 26 1846 he had about £10 in cash but "being pressed by my creditors" he had to sell the stock and furniture of the Malt Scoop Inn which realised £23.19.2d. It is rather surprising in the light of this that over the next month he "purchased small quantities of beer and spirits, and sold the same at a profit of about 15/- per week". One wonders what his customers thought of drinking in a pub with no furniture. Over the same period he earned £4.10.0 as a commission for measuring corn.

From March 25 to July 13 he was reduced to rather desperate straits. He notes, "I left the Malt Scoop Inn and rented a small cottage and worked as a labourer and earned about 12/- per week." Clearly Roger was unhappy about this and so on July 13 he attempted to retrieve his lost fortunes when he "took the Castle Inn, Bideford and...purchased for ready money 185 Bushels of

Malt and brewed the same which produced 1480 Gallons of Beer, and...sold the same at the profit of about 4d per Gallon" thus raising £24.13.0. He also made £9.18.0 by selling the "waste" products of this brewing venture.

He adds, "I have also sold on an average about 1 Gallon of spirits per Week at a profit of about 5/- per Gallon". Obviously Victorian tipplers were hard drinkers. His work as a commission agent for Thomas Norman of Buckland Brewer brought in nearly £12 whilst a further £16-odd came from 12 people who owed Crocker various small sums. He also made money by the speculative purchase and threshing of two ricks of barley. Crocker's total earnings over the 14 months were £221.19.10d – not bad for the period when labourers were receiving roughly £32 per year. His expenses however, were fairly hefty.

Thus the rent for the Malt Scoop Inn came to £8.15.0 plus another £1 in taxes. From February 26 to July 13 he "Expended in Maintainance of Myself, Wife and seven children...20 weeks at £1.5.0d. – £25". His cottage rent came to £3 whilst rent on the Castle Inn was £11.18.11d. On top of further maintenance expenses and rent charges later in the year he also spent 18/- on "Coach hire and Expenses to and from Exeter" – presumably his case was heard in Exeter and he had to pay his own travelling charges. Overall expenditure was £221.18.8d., that is ½d short of his income.

This nice balance was ruined when his creditors were listed. There were 30 of them to whom Crocker owed over £250. These were mainly farmers though the list also included a Mill Street surgeon, Mr Ackland, and a Landcross lime burner, William Partridge who was owed £6 for potatoes. A Mr Tucker, a farmer of Buckland Brewer, obviously had a flourishing cider press as the Bideford innkeeper had run up a bill with him for that drink.

Against these creditors were set the outstanding debts owed to Crocker. Seventeen people owed £306.8.7d; of these were 2 'good' debts, 3 'doubtful' and 12 'bad'. Amongst the latter was Robert Brooks, a Bideford butcher, who owed £38.2.0d. – a sum covering a large number of drinks if it was for alcohol. Two of the bad debts were obviously impossible to collect – Mr Trathen, farmer of Buckland Brewer, owed just over £4 but "was now in America", whilst William Sluman, grocer, was of "residence unknown". A surprising one was the near £30 owed by the Rev Mr Smythe whose whereabouts were again unknown.

The imbalance of debts and credits was the reason for Roger Crocker's bankruptcy proceedings. He was adjudged bankrupt in May 1847 and as far as I can see left Bideford, presumably to go back to labouring work and attempting to re-enter his old trade of innkeeping – no doubt as a wiser and more careful trader.

Bideford Gazette 6.5.1983

57. THE EARLY *GAZETTE*

At the time the *Gazette* became a tabloid in March 1983 I wrote a commemorative article about the early history of the paper. In that piece I admitted that, "the early history of newspapers in Bideford is complicated by missing files and past mistakes." I think I corrected some of the past mistakes in that article, and now I am very pleased to say that the problem of missing files has been overcome. The North Devon Reference Library has just taken delivery of a series of microfilms covering the whole run of the *Gazette* to date. These have been prepared from a master set at the British Library (formerly the British Museum Library) in London.

I was keen to see these but, when I first looked at them, I was puzzled to see that they gave the starting date as 1st January 1856. Yet, when I had written to the British Library in 1982, they gave the date of their earliest surviving copy as 10th June 1856. Had they discovered some earlier copies in the meantime, or what?

Excitedly, I sat at the microfilm reader and imagine my pleasure when I saw copy number 1 of the *Bideford Gazette* – only this number 1 didn't bear that name – no, it rejoiced in the resounding title of *Devon and East Cornwall Gazette and Commercial Advertiser*. It only became the more familiar *Bideford Gazette* six months later – thus indicating why the June date was given to me when I inquired.

The first issues were only four pages long and it was clear that three of these, containing national news, were purchased 'ready printed' and only the front page, bearing local items and adverts, was printed in Bideford. Such a system was common with provincial papers at this date as news-gathering services were still primitive and most papers were still printed as 'sidelines' by jobbing printers. The early title had a very attractive engraving of a bee-hive, which was soon changed to a royal coat of arms, though even this heraldic device was dropped when the name changed.

In the first edition the printer and editor Thomas Honey wrote, "On making our first appearance before the public, in this form, and on the very day when we pass from the old year to the new, we cannot but feel the responsibility that must attach itself to us; and in the arduous time that lies before us, we shall endeavour honestly to discharge our duties." The reference to "arduous time" was to the Crimean War then raging, which had already claimed several local lives.

On a more business-like note Honey also added, "To Correspondents – The Editor is not responsible for the Contents of Correspondent's letters" and "We cannot undertake to return rejected communications." Clearly, Thomas knew where his income was to come from for he also wrote, "Advertisers are respectfully reminded of the advantages of this Paper as an advertising medium. It is circulated widely in North Devon and East Cornwall. The terms for advertising are very low, and will receive prompt and careful attention on being sent to T Honey, Printer &c, Bideford."

The first number only boasted ten advertisements, but it did carry an original poem by Edward Capern, the local 'postman-poet' which, however, wasn't very good! Of particular interest to local historians was a list of 12 "agents" for the paper, i.e. local correspondents to whom both news and adverts could be given. Such lists are rare and this one is especially intriguing as it gives occupation as well as showing just how widely the fledgling *Gazette* was distributed. It reads as follows, "Mr Mules, Silver Street; Appledore – Mr Vinson, draper; Holsworthy – Ann Batten, ironmonger; Hatherleigh – T Hatch, shoemaker; Stratton – P W Bray, auctioneer; Beaford – J Luxton, harness maker; Hartland – Mr Trick, harness-maker; Northam – Miss Davidson; Clovelly – Mr Beer, grocer; Instow – Miss Sweet, draper, stationer etc.; Buckland Brewer – Mr Sanders, builder; Chulmleigh – Mr Woolf, draper." Notice that only three women are listed, though one of these was an ironmonger – an uncommon calling for a Victorian woman.

By the third issue there had been some changes in the agents. Mr Sanders at Buckland Brewer, had been replaced by a local shopkeeper, Miss Fulford, and Mr Ellis, a butcher at Monkleigh, had been added to the list. By issue four, a Mr Thorne, at Shebbear, had become an agent and by the fifth number even a tiny place like Parkham was represented by Mr Martin, the village schoolmaster. Clearly, with places like Holsworthy and Chulmleigh included, Thomas Honey was planning a large-scale circulation.

As I wrote in my earlier article, however, poor Thomas died only 11 months after starting his paper and it continued only due to the fortitude and persistence of his young wife, Eliza, who, though apparently pregnant at the time, took over the running (and writing) of the *Gazette*.

Why Thomas changed the paper's name is unstated – perhaps he realised his limitations and settled for a title that identified his publication more closely with its actual readership in Bideford. The truth will probably never be known.

North Devon Gazette 7.6.1985

58. FAMILIES IN DISTRESS AS SHIPYARD GOES UNDER

Imagine reading the heading "Appledore Shipbuilders go bankrupt!" – a frightening thought when one considers the numbers employed there, but an event similar in impact to this, did once happen. In February 1867 local newspaper readers were told, "Bideford certainly stands pre-eminent for the high class of vessels turned out from her yards as regards numbers and tonnage." Yet only seven moths later in the *Bideford Gazette* appeared the dramatic headline "A LOCK OUT." The accompanying paragraph told how the workers at the shipyard of Messrs George Cox and Son at Cleavehouses had been turned away from their work by the owners.

Some had "already left the town" to find other work and the writer supposed that the yard's surprise closure "will cause distress in several families and add to the financial crisis which has for some time existed in the neighbourhood." At this time Cox's were one of the largest firms on the Torridge and employed a very large workforce (150 in 1863 for example) so one can imagine the "distress" their closure caused.

Cleavehouses at Bank End had long been a major shipbuilding site with a history stretching back to 1805. George Cox had apparently gone into partnership with the then owner Thomas Evans while his son John Cox joined the company in 1858.

On September 26 1867 appeared an announcement that George and John Cox had been declared bankrupt and that their first financial examination would be in October. By the next month an official assignee had been appointed to work out the debts and assets of the firm. These were provisionally listed for the judge in the Exeter Bankruptcy Court where the case was heard. The detailed listing came in January 1868 when total liabilities were given as £16,261 5s 7d – a huge sum for Victorian Britain where wages for agricultural labourers were roughly 10/- (50p) a week. The breakdown of debts and credits are fascinating. Thus some £91 6s 10d was owed to the yard's workmen in unpaid wages and John Cox owed £375 to the local draper! One wonders how this bill was run up.

The largest creditor by far was the English Joint Stock Bank which was owed near £8,000. This bank had apparently got itself into difficulties and called in all its loans. Cox's had borrowed some £9,000 in 1864 and the sudden demand for return of the outstanding portion of the debt had dealt a mortal blow to the yard.

The reason for incurring such a large borrowing was given by George Cox. In 1864 his company had contracted with a Mr Batt of Swansea to build four ships for £46,000. At the time the yard also had orders for ships worth another £14,000. In order to increase the yard's efficiency and fulfil these orders much new machinery had been bought and this was paid for by the bank loan.

Other debts consisted of mortgages taken out on the Cox's property. Thus a Mr Bartlett of Newton Abbot had a mortgage on Clay Park House and 3 cottages at Northam worth £1,200, a Mr Buse of Bideford had the shipyard mortgage worth £4,000 and another Bideford man had a mortgage on the Chircombe estate (this house is, of course, still standing at Cleavehouses).

The assets of the yard came to £7,894 4s 7d thus leaving a very sizeable deficiency. Machinery and fixtures were valued at £3,500 and the "saw mills, smithery etc." at another £3,500 so clearly the yard was very much a self sufficient unit. Among cash in hand was £213 from the sale of John Cox's furniture – though as this was all sold to his uncle in Bridport it at least stayed in the family.

A moment of drama came during the proceedings when it was alleged that during the week previous to the collapse of the company, and on the very day itself, numerous waggon-loads of goods had been removed from the yard and secreted in Bideford to avoid their seizure by the creditors. Evidence to support this claim came from the toll-house keeper at Northam who said he saw at least 20 waggon-loads of copper and furniture go by his gate on the day of the bankruptcy. These were "driven very fast" and were taken to a warehouse in Bideford owned by a local merchant Mr Heard. A barge was also used to remove bulky goods.

The carter involved, Richard Kivell, was cross-examined about these loads but the court got very little from him. Mr Heard was also questioned but denied all knowledge of these activities. The evidence of the toll collector was never actually disproved but the Judge in his summing-up found there had been no impropriety in Cox's dealings and that there had been no concealment of assets.

Indeed it was the Judge's opinion that the bankrupts had "been sinned against rather than sinning themselves." This was presumably a reference to the bank whose problems had caused those of Cox's. Both George and John were then discharged from bankruptcy. The case had clearly been too much for George as he left the company but his son carried on working at Cleavehouses until 1877. In that year George died and John, who had been ill, had to give up the business. He died two years later and was buried with his father in a grave in Northam. So ended a famous Bideford shipbuilding enterprise.

Bideford Gazette 22.6.1984

59. TAKING STRIKE ACTION FOR A NINE HOUR DAY

ON STRIKE! An expression that produces strong feelings in most people, but they are not the invention of modern man. In 1872 Barnstaple was racked by a series of industrial disputes every inch as bitter as any we see today.

In February of that year readers of the *North Devon Journal* would have noticed a small advertisement on page one. "The Smiths, Plumbers, Tin Smiths and Machinists of Barnstaple ARE ON STRIKE FOR THE NINE HOUR SYSTEM". This was a basic working week of 54 hours – nine hours a day, six days a week. Compare this with the current average week of 35-40 hours. In the same edition was an article about the building workers of Torrington who had agreed to ask for 6d (2½p) a day extra instead of the 54 hour week, a decision praised by the editor.

During the next week the Barnstaple strikers met in the Guildhall. Some men were already on the 54 hour week and these 'lucky' ones agreed to support six striking men. A committee of 15 was formed to carry this out and amongst its members were George Viney of the Derby Lace Factory, Mr Coxten from the Railway Station and Henry Pearce from Westacott's shipyard.

The strikers were joined that week by carpenters and joiners who had asked for a pay increase but were offered it only if they accepted hourly rates – with no guarantee that earnings would match wages under the old weekly rate. Clearly Barnstaple men were made of tougher stuff than their fellows elsewhere for the *Journal* editor pointed out that the carpenters of Ilfracombe had already settled for the new hourly rates which had pushed their wages to a princely £1 for a 61 hour week!

It appears that the metal worker's strike ended very quickly for the same week a dinner was given to the proprietors of the Lace Factory by their workmen in gratitude for the new hours and wages. Mr Allen Trist, the senior foreman, advised the men to "make the best of the extra time they now had. They might enjoy the Saturday afternoons with their wives and children in little excursions, and so invigorate their health and make their children heartier." In fact the men developed the local football league.

But the carpenters still had a fight on their hands. Over 30 were on strike after their employers refused their demands saying that the men should bear in mind "the probable interference with building speculation if the price of labour should be greatly augmented". The employers added that they would carry on using their own labour and that of their apprentices, who were legally forbidden to strike.

The carpenters were joined by the Bideford "coal lumpers" who unloaded the coal boats for 3s a day plus 6d (17½p) for beer – but the beer money had to be spent in a certain pub. They demanded an extra 6d per day and the right to drink where they wished – and the demands were rapidly met.

By the end of February the master builders conceded the carpenters' point that hourly rates might lead to lower wages and said they would guarantee the number of hours to maintain the men's incomes. This didn't satisfy the men. The only response from the strikers was a letter saying, "We have told you once, and that is as good as a hundred times, that we shall not work by the hour at all." In an editorial comment the *Journal* added "we learn that the places of the old hands are becoming rapidly filled up."

By the middle of March, however, the strike collapsed with those few men who had not already left Barnstaple going back to work. The employers had added ¼d an hour to winter rates to compensate for shorter winter days. The *Journal* editor made a final comment, "We congratulate both on the settlement of their differences; and are glad to hear that there is abundant employment in the locality at present for all available hands and more."

No one could really claim victory, though this did not stop other groups striking later that year – amongst them the Barnstaple shoemakers and the charwomen of South Molton. In the next few years there was a boom in building in North Devon which helped both men and masters and helped push bitter strike memories into the past.

North Devon Journal 3.1.1985

60. WHEN TUPPENCE HA'PENNY WAS PAID FOR 1,000 BRICKS

Before the days of mass-production and easy transport, if a builder wanted a large quantity of bricks he looked around his local area for the nearest brickworks. Evidence of local bricks being used in Bideford is very common – the cream bricks from Peters Marland are an obvious example. Some 35 years ago during alterations at the Royal Hotel at East-the Water a chimney breast built of orange-red bricks stamped with the legend "Torridge Patent Co. Bideford" was found. These bricks came from a short-lived yet interesting little works at Cleavehouses alongside the Torridge.

This was begun in the 1870s by a Captain Molesworth whose family owned this land for many years. It is recorded that the operation was only in being for about ten years though even this short period of working has left its evidence in the landscape. If one visits the area today the most obvious thing is the large quarry behind the house known as 'Flag Staff.' From this, large quantities of shillet or rotten rock were dug out and loaded on to a light railway which ran down to the edge of the river bank and on to a turn-table which turned the waggons to run parallel with the bank. These loaded waggons were then hauled up a steep incline to the top of a platform about 60 feet high and there tipped out.

It was then mixed with clay and shovelled between two large revolving iron rollers which crushed the rock while a fine jet of water was sprayed on the mixture. After this the material was passed through a second series of rollers and possibly a third. By this time the material was back at ground-level and must have looked like a pebbly sludge.

As it reached ground level so it was forced into a honeycomb-like structure with sections the size of the required bricks. Whilst the mixture was being packed in so a revolving belt passed underneath removing the excess clay and stones. These moulds were then emptied by hand, each brick being sprinkled with fine sand by a boy in order to help handling – much like dusting pastry with flour. The unfired bricks were then loaded into wheelbarrows and taken to the kilns to be baked. These kilns are shown in an old photograph and were near where the 'Old Kiln House' now stands. Two tall chimneys can be seen plus a series of long, low buildings – presumably these were the drying and storage sheds.

The clay that went into these bricks came from two sources. One was from local pits in the valley that runs inland from the site. Most, however, would have been brought by barge from the pits at Fremington which had supplied most of the area's clay for several hundred years. Mixing it with the shillet helped 'bulk' it out and allowed cheaper bricks to be produced. The fuel for the kilns was probably coal from South Wales although it is just possible that local culm from the pits in Pitt Lane was used. The works were certainly in existence at this period and many people will remember the fine quality seam exposed when the Supreme Magic company's stores were built at the junction of High Street and Pitt Lane.

In 1948 an old man, then in his 80s, who had worked in this industry noted that the working day was 12 hours long from 6 a.m. to 6 p.m. and that the rate of pay for this lengthy day was on a piece rate of 2½d per 1,000 bricks! This man's average earnings, as a boy, varied between 2s and 3s (10p – 15p) a week – hardly excessive by any standards.

It is hard to visualise this hive of activity when one visits the site today. The clearest evidence, apart from the overgrown quarry is the large quantity of broken bricks scattered along the river's edge. These are coloured bright orange and have a crumbly texture owing to the fairly large pebbles included in them. None of the ones I could find were stamped – presumably the Royal Hotel bricks were imprinted as they were a special order and as such justified the extra hand labour required.

A stamped brick from these works is now held by the North Devon Museum Trust. Other local bricks are also held and I know they are always glad to receive new examples as well as show visitors around. I have not, as yet, been able to trace any close-up photographs of this local industry. I wonder if anyone has in their possession or can add to the rather scanty knowledge of this interesting Torridgeside undertaking.

Bideford Gazette 1.10.1982

61. WHEN SILVER WAS MINED

August 1907 was an exciting time at Landkey. Several months previously silver ore had been discovered at Newton and Broadmoor in the parish. A villager who was also a water diviner, J W Gabriel, became interested and searched the whole parish eventually announcing "that on about fifty acres of Harford, Landkey, there are heavy deposits of silver, which can probably be mined at a comparatively small cost."

The owner of Harford, G Dennis, was incredulous and demanded proof. This Gabriel gave him (and an interested group of spectators) using his 'apparatus' – a hazel twig plus some silver coins. The twig was held lightly by the diviner and first rotated and then became still "as he crossed the line (of the silver seam) at several points." At one stage the twig broke such was the force exerted by the ore. To test these responses Mr Dennis placed silver, gold and tin on the ground and Gabriel's accuracy in locating and identifying them completely satisfied the landowner. Indeed, at one point Gabriel even indicated the gold fillings in the teeth of one of the crowd!

Once news of the 'find' got out all sorts of people came forward to tell their stories. One old timer, a Mr Hopkins, recalled that silver ore had actually be found at Harford many years before whilst the owner of Tower Hamlets Quarry at Bishops Tawton announced that he had also found silver. Others remembered how a mine had been commercially worked a long time before in the adjoining parish of Swimbridge. An old silver miner from the well-known silver mines at Combe Martin, J Scoins, visited Harford and said the rock there "exactly resembled" that which "preceded the silver ore bearing deposits" he had worked in his youth – not you will note, the actual deposits themselves.

In the light of continuing local scepticism Gabriel was tested again at the site – and passed with flying colours even though he was watched by a group of cynical Pressmen. At one point he tied two stones, one of 1lb and the other 3lbs, to either end of his 'divining rod' but it still revolved in his hands when he crossed water. He even found silver and gold deliberately hidden when blindfolded. Interestingly "he attributes his ability to find water and minerals to a shock from lightning which he received whilst in the Metropolitan police many years ago."

A local, unnamed geologist came forward to list various earlier finds of silver, from Pickard's Down, Barnstaple, the Hannaford valley in Swimbridge and North Molton – this latter site even provided gold at one time. Unfortunately apart from the Combe Martin deposits most finds were, he said, too small to be worth working. Northing daunted Mr Dennis commissioned a Mr Oatway of Newport, Barnstaple, "to commence blasting operations" at Landkey. There were to take place on some waste land on his Harford estate. His confidence had been strengthened by "a mining expert from Plymouth, who has accompanied him over the land in question" and been optimistic.

The story then goes quiet – until some six months later when a paragraph appeared in the local papers that a trial pit had been sunk with "promising results" but unfortunately had been flooded. Work was "to immediately resume" but it seems never to have restarted. I have looked in vain for further references but there are none. Whatever did happen it seems that this is how, in a lame fashion, the great Landkey silver mining boom ended.

North Devon Journal 4.6.1987

62. A GARAGE THAT MADE CARS IN BARNSTAPLE

One of the oldest garage businesses in Barnstaple is Prideaux. Now based in Coney Avenue it began on the long thin site between Bear Street and Vicarage Street. The firm was established in 1884 when Richard Prideaux bought out his master William Gibbings who had first set the works up around 1845 to make coaches. Richard continued this coach-building tradition and took his son Harry on when he was old enough. Harry was keen to expand the business and after a course of training opened a "motor department" in 1907 which both sold and constructed cars from components. I wonder how many people realised that Barnstaple once had its own car plant?

In 1912, however, the company nearly disappeared. One night in late June the works were closed as usual. The gas and electricity were turned off and the men left for home and their evening meal. Within four hours, however, a "raging furnace" of a fire had broken out and gutted the main part of the buildings. The alarm was raised at 12.30 a.m. by a local journalist who rushed to the police station where they instantly telephoned the fire brigade. A Mr Westwood, one of the firm's employees and the then Mayor of Barnstaple, Dr Harper, rushed into the building and began driving cars out, whilst other members of the public helped remove more portable objects.

Morning revealed the true extent of the damage. The entire works, except for the section facing Bear Street and the blacksmith's shop, were smouldering ruins. Six cars had been destroyed with five "motor bodies, ready for mounting with chassis." In addition 25 carriages – horse coaches – were burned. The "expensive new machinery" installed just months previously had also been wrecked – and it was so new that it hadn't yet been insured.

The firm was nothing if not resilient and Harry Prideaux announced that the plant's 37 workers were to be moved to temporary workshops in the Square. It was to be "business as usual" whilst rebuilding went on as quickly as possible.

The report of the fire in the *Journal* was accompanied by a letter from the Mayor appealing for subscriptions to help replace the personal tools lost by the workmen. He listed the first nine subscribers and in the weeks that followed enough money flowed in to replace all the lost equipment. At the same time Harry

Prideaux pushed on with his rebuilding plans and within a relatively short time the business was back at full pace.

North Devon Journal 11.8.1988

63. ONE-MAN PAPER PRINTED IN THE LIVING ROOM

Many *Journal* readers write to me as a result of these articles, often adding details to stories I have written. In several instances their letters have led to new articles and I was pleased when a Bideford couple phoned me to offer me some odd copies of the *Hartland and West Country Chronicle* they had found when settling the estate of an old relative.

The *Chronicle* was started in 1896 by Thomas Cory Burrow and it lasted until May 1940. In one of the last issues is a reprint of an article headed "World's Strangest Newspaper" which appeared in *Tit Bits* magazine and gave the history of the *Chronicle*. This noted that Burrow was "editor, reporter, advertisement manager, printer and distributor". He first collected his news by cycling around the Hartland area and then "spends long hours setting up the type by hand in his attic office in the main street." The printing press "fills half his living accommodation." The paper, which was issued irregularly, was printed on A4 size paper and at its largest reached 32 pages and cost 3d.

Burrow actually printed news from an area extending from Bideford to Morwenstow although Hartland material predominated – indeed the *Chronicle* resembled a parish magazine more than a newspaper. The *Tit Bits* article says Burrow did everything, but he had an assistant from about 1918 to 1938 and in the earlier issues a long article on local history written by R Pearse Chope regularly appeared. As Burrow got older, he copied more and more local items from other North Devon papers.

Not only news was printed. Other fairly constant features included local births, marriages and deaths and a list of changes of address. In January 1910 is listed the birth of a daughter to Mr and Mrs George Clout of Lundy who was baptised Muriel Nellie Lundy Clout!

As with all newspapers, adverts appeared. In 1918 T Beer & Sons, the local blacksmiths, were advertising a "motor car" for hire as well as "ponies and jingles" (carts). In the same year W Jenkins advertised "try a pair of my breeches and convince yourself of Good Fit" – which can be taken in several ways. The year 1939 saw O'Donnel & Sons of the Shamrock Cafe offering lamp oil, stoves, china, brushes, seeds, fish and chips, groceries and fruit for sale. The cafe still exists with the same family running it.

The *Chronicle's* penultimate issue was in June 1939, eight months after its previous appearance. Burrow described this copy as "Largest Interval, Most Crowded, Record Size, Greatest Difficulty" adding "Help keep the old home paper on." Unfortunately, the previous issue had made a loss of £4 and its editor was 67 years old and evidently finding it hard to cope. Indeed, publication ceased after a last appearance in 1940 with Burrow himself dying aged 83 in Bideford in 1956.

An affectionate history of the paper and its editor was published in 1981 by Alan Vanstone. As *Journal* readers were told a few weeks ago the *Chronicle* has been revived in a very similar form to its predecessor under the title *Hartland Times*.

North Devon Journal 19.10.1989

RELIGION

64. THE MORALS OF 17TH CENTURY YEOMAN BEARE

Morality is seen very much as a personal affair today – but in the past moral behaviour was regulated by the church and enforced through a series of church-run courts known as Consistory Courts. Because of the cases they dealt with they were usually termed 'Bawdy Courts.' The records they created survive from an early period and make fascinating reading. One North Devon case comes from Chulmleigh in the 1680s.

In May 1682 a defendant described as a "yeoman" appeared before the Consistory Court at Exeter and was questioned about the marriage of Digory Beare and Elizabeth Hellyer, of Chulmleigh. He stated that they were married "about halfe a yeare since" by licence from the Bishop. Within "some few weekes of theire inter-marriage the said Elizabeth was delivered of a child." This was clear evidence of pre-marital sex.

A second witness then appeared – William Hellyer, a blacksmith of Chulmleigh and brother to Elizabeth. He related how Digory and his sister were married at Eggesford by the Reverend Laskey and how their child was born about six to eight weeks later. Clearly the couple had married away from their home parish to avoid scandal and gossip. William went on to say that Digory had lived with him for a year prior to the marriage and "did frequent the said Elizabeth's company" and "they were accompted (accounted) sweethearts and had a kindness for each other in ye way of marriage as it was generally reported in ye said towne and parish." Elizabeth had in fact admitted to her brother that she was pregnant by Digory Beare. William ended by saying that the child had lived but that his sister had died just two weeks later.

The court had little option in this instance but to drop the case. In other cases where the couple had been found guilty of 'incontinence,' as it was termed, they had to announce their guilt before the whole parish in church on Sunday – often wearing a white sheet to indicate their penitence.

The Consistory Court still exists today but is a pale shadow of its former self – the last notable local occasion it was in operation was during the dispute at Torrington church over a 'Black Madonna.' One might ask whether we need a morals court today or not – but human nature being what it is it almost certainly would not work!

North Devon Journal 5.11.1987

65. WHEN THE RECTOR SOLD PEWS BY THE YEAR

In April 1745 forty of the leading men of Bideford met and produced a 'terrier' ... not a dog, but a document based on the Latin term 'terra' meaning 'land'. It lists the possessions and rights of a church and was a vital document for a clergyman to have when any parishioners challenged these rights. The Bideford one began, by listing "furniture, utensils and ornaments of the church." The church silver is described, including two pattens or dishes given in 1675 and 1684. There was also "A large Sattin Carpet with a fringe of Gold and Silk and four Gold tassels" – presumably for the altar area.

At this period class distinctions were nowhere more evident than in the church and in "Mr Mayor's" pew there were "four cushions of crimson velvet, one bordered with gold lace and fringe, three others with golden fringe." No other cushions are listed for the rest of the congregation, so presumably they made do with sore knees.

Within the church building there were some 50 pews which literally belonged to the rector and which he sold or rented – at 6d (2½p) a year. Incredible as it seems, this selling of seats in church went on well into the nineteenth-century.

The parish clerk was said to receive 4d (2p) from every family who attended the church "by his own collection." Clearly he could have been very poor if his powers of persuasion were slight. The clerk at this date was George Donn – father of Benjamin the famous Devon mapmaker. Another church official, the sexton, was paid £2.6.8d (£2.34p) a year.

A long section of the 'terrier' dealt with the glebe land which went with the rectory. Some 47 acres were involved in seven fields, two at East-the-Water, and five on the western bank. This included land known as Middle and Western Catshole "now called Brickfield" which points to an interesting piece of industrial history. The land was near Ford and Bowden Green. Also listed was a two-and-a-half-acre field called Twinaways – still marked today by the Twinaways Store in Clovelly Road.

The rectory is described in detail, a valuable record as the building was completely rebuilt in the mid-nineteenth century. It consisted of "two piles of building joyned together from west to east by a passage" covered with "good slate or helling stone." The western section was known as "the old building" and had four rooms including a kitchen with ashen floor – the ash or cinders soaking up spilt liquids in those days before easy-to-clean floor coverings.

Next to this was a "brewhouse" where the servants would have brewed the rector's beer, important at a time when plain water was often contaminated. Above these two rooms were "two good chambers ... with good deal floors." In the eastern half were "two good parlours, two light closets, and a buttery to the north." There was a red-tiled cellar with two bedrooms and also two utility rooms. This section is stated to have been built in 1742 by the patron of the parish Lord John Gower "the most unblemish'd name of the present age" as the 'terrier' politically put it.

So ends this most interesting document which can be found in similar form for most parishes in North Devon – in many cases from an earlier date than this Bideford example.

North Devon Journal 12.12.1985

66. THE WOMAN PREACHER

The complete early history of non-conformity in North Devon has yet to be written. Any writer who takes on the task would be well advised to read an article that appeared in the *North Devon Journal* in April 1886. Written by one Roger Giles it deals at length with the life and times of Joanna Brooks alias Neale – an ardent feminist before the word became fashionable and a fascinating Georgian character.

She was born Joanna Prouse 200 years ago in 1786 in the hamlet of Dyke at Clovelly. Her father was a small-scale farmer with the usual large family and "to relieve her parents of some of the strain to which they were subjected, she chose to go to service." She did, in fact, become servant to a Bideford family and then moved with them to Morwenstow where she married George Brooks, a local carpenter.

She was noted as an ardent churchgoer – then apparently an unusual trait. Giles says that most people spent Sundays "cock-fighting, wrestling, wrecking, smuggling, poaching, badger-baiting, dog-fighting and drinking" and he blamed this on absentee vicars more interested in their tithes than their job. He also made reference to the "annual revel" with its wrestling matches for silver spoons.

One Sunday in 1815 Joanna was so overcome by religious zeal that she stood up in church and began preaching. Her remarks were cut short, however, "for she was speedily ejected...as it is part of the Church's discipline that women must keep silence therein." Nothing daunted she finished and harangued the congregation as they left – although apologising to the minister as she did so! The event soon brought her some notoriety and Mr O'Brien, one of the founders of the Bible Christians, came to see her and as he was all in favour of women preachers, enrolled Joanna into his sect.

Poor George, her husband, was annoyed at all this and "endeavoured to thrash the new religion, as it was called, out of her." When this didn't work he reckoned she must be "deranged" and "a medical man was procured to certify as to her mental condition." Joanna, however, was made of stronger stuff and she argued with him "so well that he declared her arguments were in accordance with the doctrines of the Church of England, and advised her friends (!) not to molest her."

A few years later George died leaving her with four young children, and one can believe Giles when he writes that "she had a struggle to support her little family on the proceeds of a small shop she ran." This was, of course, before social security and widows' pensions. Some years later she married James Neale a local preacher, and he helped her in her self-appointed position of itinerant preacher around Clovelly. She became very well known in the area always dressed in plain 'Quakeress' fashion.

After overcoming the problems already sketched out she had one more major fight. When Methodism was introduced into Clovelly the owners of the village, living at Clovelly Court, tried to stamp out the new sect. This they did by threatening to have any villagers who joined thrown out of their rented cottages. One man owned a freehold property and allowed the Methodist preachers to use his house and it was from here, with Joanna's active help, that the sect grew and prospered until at last even some of the Clovelly Court family came to join in worship.

Joanna died aged 71 in 1857 being survived by her husband who emigrated to New York State to join his son. So died a strong character – a woman perhaps many years ahead of her time who is especially worthy of note as the discussion about the ordination of women priests still continues.

North Devon Journal 15.5.1986

67. COLOURFUL CUSTOMS FROM OLD DEVON

In 1873 a local man, Mr C Wood, gave a well-attended lecture in the Baptist Church in Bideford entitled "Peeps into North Devon Towns and Villages from AD 1770 to 1870". His talk was well-reported even though it "dealt more especially with the dark side of North Devon life in the past century."

Mr Wood was clearly a deeply religious man and much of his talk was concerned with this aspect of local history. An old preacher once told him about the poor state of religious knowledge amongst the local labourers saying, "When I spoke to them of the Saviour they often startled me by saying that they had 'heerd of un, but had'n seed'n'." Of a hundred houses visited by this preacher only fourteen had bibles in them.

These statements run counter to the usual view of a North Devon full of chapels and religious fervour. Indeed about 1800 "to the West of Bideford there was not a single chapel or Sunday school for 20 miles." Also at this time a witch who openly attended Bideford market "was regularly supplied with commodities" by people eager for her services. It was also a common belief that a pigeon's feather in the bed of a dying person would prevent the release of the soul which "was thus held in irrepressible agony."

The irreligious state was tackled by men like John Rendle "one of the earliest Wesleyan local preachers at Bideford" who undertook incredible workloads to spread the gospel. He began each Sunday by walking to Putford to preach at the 9 o'clock service, then rode to Lane Mill in Woolsery for a service at 11 a.m., walked to Clovelly for two meetings in the afternoon and evening and walked back to Bideford – a dedicated man indeed!

If we are to believe Wood, however, they had to be dedicated. He recounts how the early non-conformist meetings were regularly disrupted. Drums were beaten outside chapels and doors were pelted with stones. In one instance a goose was pushed down a chimney bringing vast quantities of soot with it, whilst at another meeting house the rotting entrails of a pig were thrown over the congregation. At Torrington the chapel windows were smashed and the worshippers themselves stoned. Our ancestors certainly took their religion seriously.

At least they did in most cases. Rendle was once preaching at Parkham "when a stranger entered and whispered to those nearest the door. One after another left, until the preacher was left alone." Apparently "the pious owner of the preaching place had just returned from Peppercombe with his tubs of (smuggled) brandy and his neighbours had hurried out to assist him in putting them out of sight"! Other smuggling stories included one about the cargo brought ashore at Clovelly about 1825. Wood says "some of the brandy was taken through Bideford in a hearse to elude the town officials." Most of the smuggled material was carried on "small active horses" that had been "soaped and greased to slip out of any hostile grip."

His earlier reference to the absence of Sunday schools is interesting. Apparently any form of education for the poor was opposed as it "would make the children insolent to their superiors." Some went so far as to say "books, pens, ink and paper were never intended for such trash as they!"

The speaker's non-conformist leanings come out most strongly when he talks of some of the old church customs in the early years of the nineteenth century. At many churches after Sunday service the young men of the parish would play tennis in the church yard. The parish clerk would usually stand on a gravestone outside the church door and announce sales, lost and found goods, hunting appointments and forthcoming wrestling matches!

Clearly such goings-on angered the more pious and in the movement to stamp out such things the non-conformists were a major force. Indeed Mr Wood ended his lecture by saying that the "cross had gloriously triumphed" – though at the expense of some very colourful (and generally harmless to our way of thinking) old customs of North Devon.

North Devon Journal 14.11.1985

68. BOTHER AT THE CHAPEL

The year 1828 saw the opening of a Wesleyan Methodist chapel at West Buckland. This humble building "served a considerable portion of the parish" as a contemporary report put it – but "a few individuals have pursued the most unlawful and unjustifiable measures" to try and discredit this newly gathered congregation.

Apparently trouble had begun as soon as the chapel opened its doors for the first time. We know that "on almost every occasion that religious worship has been performed in the Chapel...a mob has collected around, and by every possible means disturbed the worshippers within." In order not to exacerbate the situation the Wesleyans met at different times to the local parish church but this had no effect on the mob.

The chapel-goers "turned the other cheek" and tried to ignore the hecklers but this only inflamed them to such a pitch that one Sunday in November 1828 the mob began stoning the chapel building. Indeed "a large stone was aimed at the preacher, and hurled through the window, which, had it taken the course intended, would, in all probability, have dispatched him to another and a better world." Luckily the stone missed the Reverend Mr Rees but it did cut through his hat which was hanging behind him.

The next night crowds prevented Mr Rees from even entering the building. The local constable, although present, did nothing to help. This proved too much for the congregation and they caught five of their tormentors. One was a boy whilst two of them were found to be servants of the Rev Blight, the rector of West Buckland. Clearly there was an obvious suggestion that this clergyman did not like competition in his parish!

The following day the five appeared before magistrates. All the bench were church of England men but notwithstanding this they found the five guilty. The maximum fine was £50 or gaol until the fine was paid – effectively life imprisonment – but the Wesleyans requested clemency and so the offenders were only fined £1 12s 6d (£1.62½p) between them. The fine money was spent on bread for the poor of the parish. In addition the five had to make a public apology to the minister and his congregation and "promise never to be guilty of a similar offence".

At this point in the proceedings Mr Rees stepped in and showing true Christian charity, paid the boy's fine himself as his parents were penniless. One magistrate, the Rev Fortescue "also expressed the extreme abhorrence he felt at the conduct they had pursued, and severely reprimanded the constable who had witnessed these tumultuous assemblies."

The report on the case in the *North Devon Journal* ends with the comment, "From a regard to their characters and their future pursuits in life, the names of the offenders are withheld." A charitable ending to an unpleasant case.

North Devon Journal 23.1.1986

69. A SPORT TOO 'RUDE' FOR A CHURCHYARD

Today our churchyards are havens of peace where the dead lie quietly. That this was not always so is shown by a dispute that occurred in 1836 between the parishioners of Berrynarbor and the local clergy. On July 4, the day following the village 'revel', the parishioners went to the Old Bowling Green on the north side of the churchyard to attend the annual wrestling match. This was a long-standing tradition, but on this occasion the churchwarden, on the orders of the Archdeacon of Barnstaple, refused them entry to the churchyard to protect "the vicinity of the church from being profaned by rude sports."

A local gentleman, Joseph Bassett of Watermouth Castle, was so incensed by this action that he put an advertisement in the newspaper saying that come what may the adjourned 'revel' would be held in September on the traditional site. He, and 200 others, also subscribed to a prize of £10 to be wrestled for on that day. He went further and wrote to the *Journal* setting out his case maintaining that the northern part of all churchyards was traditionally "a playground where the labouring classes enjoyed themselves after the toil of the day." The annual 'revel' as commonly held in Devon was a time when local people played host to their neighbours, he added, "The houses are white-washed, and "the young men take a turn at wrestling in the parish playground."

The Archdeacon, he reckoned, had acted in alarm at the growth of the non-conformist churches and rather than use persuasion to attract them back to the established Church had put on "a fanatical display of unwanted sanctity." This strong feeling against the Church of England wasn't unusual but it rarely found such clear expression.

When the new 'revel' day came it was "ushered in by the ringing of the bells and the firing of fowling pieces." Some 3,000 people turned up to see "jugglers, mountebanks, tumblers, puppet shows and every kind of rustic revelry" including, of course, the wrestling matches. That Bassett had made his point was clear and indeed the 'revel' day continued for many years unhindered by the clergy.

Just to drive his point home Bassett wrote in his letter to the paper, "Whatever influence a clergyman may in future possess over his parishioners, must be obtained by moderation, humility and other Christian duties...to fail in an attempt to do what is wrong, not only excited ridicule, but also contempt." Strong words that give us a rare insight into the feelings of those among our nineteenth century ancestors who were opposed to the Church of England.

North Devon Journal 13.12.1990

70. MASSIVE TOWN ROW OVER NEW CEMETERY

I wonder how many of us have visited the Old Town Cemetery in Bideford? For those seeking a spot with atmosphere of the past there is no more interesting place in the town. Now sadly vandalised and overgrown it is a treasure house of the town's history.

The area is now one of peace and tranquility but it was not always so. When it was first laid out the cemetery created a massive row and split the town into two warring and vituperative camps. The story, which went on for the best part of a year, can be pieced together from contemporary newspaper reports. In October 1841 a small article announced that "A new burying ground is to be enclosed in the higher part of the town near the National School." This being Victorian England, however, the cemetery was divided strictly into two – one part for members of the Church of England and the other for "Dissenters." There was to be no mixing between these two groups, not even in death.

It was agreed that the "dissenters should build the partition wall" and that the churchgoers should pay for the consecration of their half by the Bishop. This decision was arrived at "after some disputes" – an understatement as the following events were to show.

Things went smoothly for a while, the first burial occurring early in January 1842 even before the ground had been totally levelled. In early March of that year, however, the trouble began. A Vestry meeting was called and the chapelgoers were invited along. The 'vestry' at this time was a closed group of prominent local men (all members of the established church) who had the power to levy a rate on all the ratepayers of the town whatever their religious persuasion. The meeting had been called in order to set and collect a rate to pay for the consecration service and the construction of the dividing wall.

The dissenters would not accept this. Their spokesman, a leading Bideford solicitor named Rooker, announced that they were opposed to the rate as it meant them helping to pay for a church service that they could not, in conscience, accept. Mr Rooker went on to ask, acidly, why the rate was necessary – the chapelgoers had raised the £25 cost of the dividing wall voluntarily but apparently the church members had not been so forthcoming with regard to the consecration expenses of £22.10s.

A vote was called for and the rating suggestion heavily defeated. The vestry was not to be so easily defeated, however, and they announced that a poll of all ratepayers in the town would be held to decide the question. Interestingly the rate they were arguing over was 3d (1p) in the £ – hardly noticeable by today's rate standards!

The poll duly took place extending over a Saturday and Monday and the local papers reported the Saturday results as follows, "Against the rate 182, for it 107." The report continued, "On Monday the most strenuous exertions were used to get the parishioners to the poll by both parties...One old woman in particular, whom, had she not been escorted by two reverends in holy orders, it would have been terrible inhumanity to transport from the atmosphere of a bakehouse to the inclemency of March winds." Farmers from outlying areas of the parish were also dragged in, in some cases complaining bitterly of the waste of time and money.

After counting the result was announced to a crowded meeting in Bideford Town Hall – victory to the dissenters by 262 to 189 votes. The churchgoers, however, did not take the result well. Indeed "Captain Ellis avowed his conviction that the auditors must have been guilty of fraud, for he believed it impossible that such could be the result after so much trouble had been taken to bring the voters to the poll." Clearly Victorians believed in speaking their minds and didn't mince words! Colonel Bailey added, in an obvious expression of sour grapes, "that the church gave the dissenters the part which they occupy." This was strenuously denied by the dissenters and the meeting broke up in acrimony.

The end result was that the Church of England members had to raise the money for consecration of their part of the burial ground amongst themselves. This wasn't until July when the Bishop of Exeter came and held the service. The outcome was a great victory for the dissenters of Bideford and one which showed clearly the power of the 'chapel' in the town.

Interested visitors to the Old Town Cemetery today can still see the wall in question although the Church of England section of the cemetery has now been cleared of gravestones. The present-day fire station uses part of the wall as its boundary. It is odd to think that this ordinary looking wall now greatly neglected and ignored was once the cause of so much furore and strong religious emotions in our normally fairly staid and prim ancestors.

Bideford Gazette 25.8.1983

71. WHEN HACKLES WERE RAISED BY A SECT

Devon has always had a reputation for religious tolerance. Nonconformity came early to the county and many sects flourished, leaving their mark on the landscape in the shape of the many roadside chapels we see today. One group, however, seem to have raised the hackles of virtually everybody in nineteenth century Devon – the Mormons. Begun in the 1830's in the USA by Joseph Smith their exclusivity and implied superiority in their alternative name – Latter Day Saints – created much bad feeling against them.

The group's practice of polygamy undoubtedly also outraged Victorian sensibilities.

During indexing of past files of the *North Devon Journal* several references to a previously unrecorded group in North Devon have been found. The first comes in August 1850 when the paper's correspondent in South Molton reported, "A body of this peculiar sect have lately been formed in this town." Their leader was a Mr Hanham who created a stir with his first sermon, a direct attack against a sermon given earlier in the day by the local Methodist minister. He followed this with another attacking all the other clergymen in the town. The reporter had obviously listened to these but dismissed them saying, "neither the reasoning of the lecture nor his style was satisfactory."

Evidently his view was not shared by all in South Molton as four years later there is an article violently condemning the Mormons who had grown enough to have a 'church' in a room in East Street. The article talks of the "humiliation", "dishonour", and "scandal" of having such a "religious group" in this town. This attack followed two public lectures by "a person styling himself Dr Patrick" which the correspondent had attended. He noted there had only been a "small audience" and said "Many of them getting tired of the dry discourse, left before it was concluded."

Seven months later, however, the reporter returned to the attack with a vitriolic piece headed "The Mormonites Tea Party". A party had been held in the meeting room where a meal had been eaten, followed by a foot-stamping sing-song. According to the article "the orgies were worthy of Hotentots or New Zealand cannibals and their filthy and obscene conversation must not be represented on paper." The cause of this extreme language was the singing of such songs as "Over the hills and far away" and "You must not buy tripe on a Friday"; music hall songs, yes – but obscene probably no. the report carried on in the same vein with "How is it that public morality which is outraged thereby, does not indignantly suppress these disgusting scenes of hypocrisy and blasphemy?" It concluded with a demand that the sect be stamped out in the same way they had been "rooted out from Barnstaple".

A further report six months later is the last note I have at present to the South Molton Mormons. It deals with the expulsion of John Vickery of East Street from the group. Apparently Vickery had been "admonished for sin" in that he had missed some meetings and been seen entering a pub.

Two other references have been noted to the sect in North Devon. The first is from May 1857 when a Mormon (probably from South Molton) preached in Taw Vale Parade, Barnstaple, but received a poor reception. The last reference I have located is from January 1858 when two young Mormons began to preach on Ilfracombe's Quay. One was the son of a local man who had been converted to the faith and journeyed to Salt Lake City several years previously. Before the pair had said much, however, a Captain Williams whose boat was moored alongside the Quay interrupted them with some caustic remarks. Perhaps his most startling one concerned two local girls called Tuckfield whom, he alleged, had gone to Salt Lake City and been murdered!

The two Mormons gave up trying to preach and the *Journal* ended its report by saying they had left Devon on their way to Salt Lake City to join a Mormon Army which had been raised to protect their homeland against the US Government. The sect appears to have vanished from the area for many decades after this last Ilfracombe appearance.

North Devon Journal 15.11.1984

72. BATTLING WITH THE EVILS OF THE DEMON DRINK

Temperance groups are no longer very strong in Britain but in the mid-nineteenth century they were a powerful and popular movement against the "evils of drink". Powerful they may have been, but successful they were not. The battle over drink was fought everywhere – including North Devon.

In December 1877, a meeting of the wonderfully named "Association for Stopping Sale of Intoxicating Liquors on Sunday" was held in the Assembly Rooms at South Molton. National secretary Edward Whitwell was the speaker, accompanied on the platform by four local clergymen, one of whom, the Rev Uriah Butters, acted as chairman. After prayers Mr Whitwell spoke for an hour "amidst considerable noise and interruption from the lower end of the room by a few of the licensed victuallers and their friends." Whitwell struggled bravely on, doing his best to ignore the hecklers.

A Rev Dodge took the floor and thought it a pity that "the great evils of the demon intemperance" could not be discussed "with dignity, calmness and charity." But he rather spoiled his appeal by going on to denounce "the evils of intemperance" which "had become so extensive and frightful" that he for one wanted "to remove the temptation out of the way of the working classes." The vicar thought it a "safe and reasonable proposal to close all access to the public house on Sundays." All this, needless to say, was accompanied by further heckling from the publicans in the hall. Nothing daunted the Rev Dodge proposed a motion to the meeting against Sunday opening as it produced "a large amount of drunkenness, irreligion, pauperism and crime among the people."

Before a vote could be taken, however, Mr W Cole of the Unicorn Hotel jumped on to the platform and attacked the resolution as it would deprive the population of civil liberty and "rob the poor man of his beer." He added that "the rich in their clubs would be able to get their liquors and the poor man would not." As a further argument he noted that if the principle of not selling drink on a Sunday was accepted, then "they also must stop the traffic in milk."

The vote was then taken by a show of hands and the temperance supporters won though Cole "rose to question the decision of the chairman." Amidst tremendous uproar the votes were counted and the result was 95 to 90 in favour of the anti-drink group. This didn't satisfy the publicans and "the meeting broke up in great disorder." Stirring times indeed that give the lie to our image of po-faced Victorians!

North Devon Journal 2.11.1989

73. TROPHIES OF A FAITH HEALER

The Salvation Army today is generally regarded as a good organisation doing a difficult job – yet on its first introduction into North Devon just over a century ago it was reviled, attacked and the object of much journalistic sarcasm. One episode, admittedly somewhat bizarre, stands out.

In March 1887 Major Pearson of the 'Army' headquarters staff visited Barnstaple. He came at the invitation of the local 'Army' group leader, Captain Topping, who was a great believer in Biblical authority for faith-healing – of which Major Pearson was apparently a well-known practitioner. The major's first public meeting opened with his stating his beliefs "with a good deal of force and some amount of unpolished eloquence." The reporter who attended the meeting admitted that Pearson had "a somewhat patriarchal appearance, to which his high forehead, full, florid countenance, and long flowing beard...lend no little attractiveness."

Some 300 people attended this meeting held in the "Army Barracks" which had been converted from a theatre. They were regaled with stories of "wonderful cures" but were told that these only occurred with "fervent prayer and unlimited faith." Pearson then "invited those who were endowed with sufficient faith" to come down to him – and twelve people came forward. They knelt in a line in front of him and he anointed each with "sweet oil" praying all the time as he did so. Within hours several of the people reported improvements in their illnesses. One was a boy named Charles Mullins, of Higher Maudlin Street, whose arm had been badly broken and gone very stiff – yet he could now flex it easily.

News of these results spread rapidly and a second meeting that evening saw "some eight hundred persons occupying every available inch of space in the body of the 'barracks'." After a short address Pearson once again called for people to come to the front and this time fifteen did, one a Mrs Cann of 'Sunny-bank' experienced an instantaneous cure of her inflamed eyes. Another was Mr Pearce, a cripple from Marwood, who "had come into the town for the purpose of having a large boot made, and entered the meeting with the aid of crutches." He in fact left these behind for Pearson to add to his collection of "faith healing trophies." Other less dramatic cases were also reported, each one being hailed as another success for the Salvation Army.

The next morning people came on foot in large numbers and coaches containing "female invalids" arrived outside the house where Pearson was staying. He saw all of them and anointed each. A Mrs Lapthorne of the Poltimore Arms public house in Barnstaple showed definite signs of improvement in her paralysis.

Another girl afflicted with St Vitus's dance walked away "with marked firmness of footing."

The reporter didn't know quite what to make of all this. He notes that the local Salvationists "anticipate much benefit to the movement from the visit of Major Pearson," but adds that "much scepticism is openly expressed as to the genuineness of the cases." He went on to quote, rather oddly, a case when Winston Churchill's mother, though paralysed, apparently leapt out of bed and ran downstairs when she felt the shock of an earthquake. What this was meant to prove I don't know.

The report ends, "But, whatever be the opinion as to its genuiness or otherwise, the brief faith healing mission of Major Pearson, the Salvation Army Apostle is at any rate, certain to attain the dignity of 'a nine day's wonder'." One is curious as to when the Salvation Army gave up faith-healing as one of its weapons against Satan?

North Devon Journal 1.5.1986

74. FOLLOW THE BAND WITH PARSON

Go to church or chapel today and it is almost certain that the hymns will be accompanied by an organ. Large or small, warbling or booming – the organ is the instrument of religion, without a doubt. In the past, however, as with so many things, the situation was different with only the largest congregations being able to afford the hand-built organs then available.

Music did exist, though, even in the smallest churches. This was provided by the church bands. These were small groups of men who played a variety of instruments. The usual complement was a violin, a clarinet and a bass viol or cello as we would call it. In some bands there might also be a bassoon or a flute. These bands would sit in a gallery and scrape and blow their way through the sacred tunes. At Christmas they would tour the parish as 'waits' collecting money towards the upkeep of the church. With the introduction of the portable and inexpensive harmonium, however, these bands rapidly died out becoming just dim memories in most areas by 1900.

Records of these parish musicians are fairly rare. Indeed, most people only know of their existence through reading Thomas Hardy's novels, especially *Under the Greenwood Tree*. A few notes about some North Devon examples were published by old men in the early twentieth century and these make interesting reading.

At Hartland the band consisted of William Cann, the parish clerk, on cello, James Rowe, a "substantial yeoman" on violin accompanied by Sam Walter on another violin with William Short on flute. These men were "learned" or taught by one "Painter" Heard. They were disbanded about 1848 when the old West Gallery was removed.

Petrockstow apparently claimed to have the best band and choir in North Devon in the mid-nineteenth century, under the forceful leadership of the Rev John Knight. He and John Darke played the cello while a Mr Honey of Holsworthy played flute and William Trace the violin. The person who remembered this band also recalled that when "a new fangled harmonium was installed in the church, he (John Darke) sat hidden in the shadows...and wept audibly throughout the service."

Claims to have had the last surviving band were made for several parishes with Countisbury putting in a strong bid by pointing out that even as late as 1886 they were still paying for repairs to their band's cello. A later example, however, eclipsed them. In August 1895 the *Musical Herald*, a national magazine for musicians, carried a picture of Mr Anthony Tucker of Yarnscombe. He had played the violoncello in his parish church up until the 1840s when, because of changes in church practice, his church band was discontinued. Tucker was 72 years old when he was once again invited back to play in the church.

The vicar of Yarnscombe at this date was the Rev J B Singleton and he wrote a letter to the *Musical Herald* saying that he deplored the disappearance of such bands, citing one odd reason that "being a member of the church band a man has something to do for, instead of against, the old church." The vicar had arrived in Yarnscombe about 1884 and "saw the old fiddle hanging up in (Tucker's) shoemaker's shop, and in course of time I asked him to bring it to church and help to supplement the little harmonium." Not quite a true church band but nevertheless a fascinating survival.

Some church-goers today condemn the introduction of guitars and other instruments to modern services – but it is clear that organ music by itself was never the sole music of religion.

North Devon Journal 11.12.1986

75. BIZARRE EVENTS IN QUIET PLACES

Combe Martin is a sleepy sort of place, but in 1928 it was the centre of a bizarre series of events focusing on the rector the Rev R Seymour. These events began when a Mrs de Beaumont-Checkland and her grown-up daughter came to live in the village. Of French extraction they were very excitable and soon gained a reputation for annoying people.

In February 1928 they overstepped the mark which led to a court appearance for "riotous and violent behaviour" in Combe Martin Church. At the court hearing the Rev Seymour told his long story of harassment. It all began when the daughter came to him and "professed to be in communication with the rector's late wife" – presumably via spiritual seances. She went on to claim that this spirit had told her that she must marry the rector!

Things came to a head after an evensong service, when the daughter stayed behind and began shouting and gesticulating. The rector asked her to leave, but she refused and bolted the church door from the inside. The police were sent for and a Pc Bolt arrived. Unfortunately the mother also appeared and began abusing the rector for exciting her daughter and accused the clergyman of a "serious and painful charge".

During the court appearance the rector produced several of the letters he had received from Miss Beaumont-Checkland containing much "nasty matter". Various other witnesses testified to the irksome behaviour of the mother and daughter. When called to give an answer, only Mrs Beaumont-Checkland was in court. The mother didn't try to defend herself merely saying that her daughter suffered from "hysteria" adding, somewhat oddly, "We are French, thank God, not English."

The magistrates imposed a fine of £5 and awarded costs against Mrs Beaumont-Checkland. They also ordered that her daughter be bound over for a year to keep the peace and forbade her from entering Combe Martin or communicating with the rector again.

Colourful times in old North Devon, yet things just as odd go on today.

North Devon Journal 23.8.1990

MILITARY

76. SUPPORTING A SURVIVOR OF THE CIVIL WAR

War destroys most things – the only things it creates are misery and illness. It is now 350 years since the English Civil War tore this country apart. In January 1649 King Charles I lost his head to the executioner's axe and the Commonwealth under Oliver Cromwell was ushered into British History. It was to be eleven years before Charles II was called back by a nation tired of puritanism and hard religion.

Eleven years was a long time even for the most ardent Royalists to sustain hope that their sufferings would be repaid. For those who kept the faith with their exiled king, however, the day of reckoning did come. The nobles who had fled with Prince Charles were rewarded with lands and honours – and even the common soldiers of his father's army were not overlooked by the new king.

In February 1663 one Symon Jefferye, a Bideford sailor, penned his "humble petition" to "The Right Worshipful the Justices of the Peace within the County of Devon". This petition recited how Symon had fought in "the late unhappy wars" where he had "for divers years faythfully served his Majesties own royall ffather of ever blessed memory". Presumably he had been in the very small part of the Royal Navy which had remained loyal to the king. During his service Symon had "by wounds and long imprisonments etc." become "decreeped in all his body" so as to be "not able to helpe himselfe but is now in a very low and sadd condition." He was one of the war's casualties – at a time when little provision or thought was given to such cases.

Previously, in May 1662, he had appealed to the newly restored king and had been given a pension of £2 per annum – not a great deal it must be admitted but enough to live on. Unfortunately "since which time he is growne into a more deploreable state than formerly". Whatever his wounds were they had rendered him totally helpless.

A note added to Symon's letter says, "The contents of this petition is really true" being signed by Abraham Heiman (probably we would write it Heyman), then Mayor of Bideford. In addition the vicar and six other leading townsmen also signed. It was these men who added a note to the effect that because of Symon's infirmities "he may very well and justly deserve an addition into it (his pension) as you in your discussions may think fit." A further testimonial signed by fifteen other townspeople also accompanied this petition. In this second document it was related how Symon has served seven years under the command of Major Richard Pomeroy and Captain John Zealand. It added that Symon was "an object of all people's pitty and compassion."

Clearly these letters did the trick for there is an order attached to them signed by Richard Coffin and Robert Cary that Symon was to get £3 per annum pension paid at quarterly intervals – an increase of £1 a year. One wonders how long poor Symon lived to enjoy his new wealth!

North Devon Journal 12.3.1987

77. GRUESOME CLUES TO FATE OF PRISONERS

Skeletons, prisoners-of-war and murder are a heady mix, but they come together in one odd story in Bideford's history. The tale is complex and begins back in 1758 when Britain, as was often the case in that century, was at war with France. Bideford had sent her men and ships to help fight and, in return as it were, had got more than 1,000 prisoners-of-war billeted in the area.

These were apparently housed in two places – an area called Pillmouth just in Landcross and at Drum Field (where the fire station now stands). They were guarded by soldiers from the Somerset Militia rather than the regular army. Pillmouth and possibly Drum Field were used again in the later Napoleonic Wars.

In 1758 the first issue of *The Plymouth Magazine* carried a small paragraph which read, "Last Sunday morning (October 15) the prisoners in the French prison at Bideford (in number 1050), attempted to make their escape; but were discover'd, and fired on, by the soldiers on duty, one was killed on the spot, and several others were much wounded. They have attempted to escape twice before, but were timely discover'd." Which prison this was isn't stated but, as a result of this attempted break-out, the Admiralty (who were in charge of them) decided to remove the prisoners to Bideford town prison. Now the town jail at that time was nowhere near large enough to hold a thousand men, so I assume that only the officers or trouble-makers were moved to this more secure place.

Inkerman Rogers, in his *History of Bideford*, quotes a letter from Bideford dated 26 August 1759 which mentions that the families of these officers were living in the town and paying high rents for the privilege – obviously the eighteenth century was a civilised time in regard to prisoners' dependants. The conditions for the officers themselves, however, could not have been very pleasant as in 1761 the Admiralty noted that the prison was lacking in air.

We now jump to 1820 when a Mr Puddicombe, a farmer of Eastleigh Higher Barton in Westleigh parish, was riding into Bideford. He never arrived and his body was never found. All sorts of wild rumours were flying around and for years afterwards every skeleton that was unearthed in odd places was claimed to be his.

In 1832, for example, Mr Robert Prior discovered, near Pyne's Lane in Bideford "the whole of the upper parts of a human skeleton in the field where the other portions of the same bones were found the other day, with some nails also." These were claimed as the remains of Mr Puddicombe but again, in May 1867, some more human relics, the leg and thigh of an adult male, were found "in a field at Pines' Lane near the Hartland turnpike-gate, Bideford," (the toll-house is still there and is now called Twinaways). The report of this discovery adds about this site, "It was used as a burial ground for the victims of cholera and French prisoners." Clearly the area was handy to the Drum Field prison.

In July 1877 workmen were digging some wall foundations for the Bideford Gas company at its premises in East-the-Water and two feet down came across two adult male skeletons. Someone had taken them by the next morning but this didn't stop speculation that they were the bones of French prisoners and that this was the site of another wartime jail – though there was no evidence for this. Interestingly Inkerman Rogers claimed, in 1938, to have seen those bones, so whoever took them must have kept them carefully for some years.

Again in August 1904 when the foundations were dug for the new library and Town Hall extension at the end of the Bridge, the excavation hadn't gone very far when 16 skeletons "laid side by side" were discovered and claimed as the remains of prisoners-of-war who had died in the old town jail which stood on this site. The bones were later interred in St Mary's churchyard.

There is one more strand to the story. When interviewing an old Bidefordian a year or two ago, he told me how, in the 1930s when the houses in Clovelly Road were being built, the builders unearthed a whole series of skeletons, devoid of clothes or coffins, lying head to foot and running the length of the road. These would appear to have been more of the "French prisoners" buried unceremoniously in unhallowed ground. Although the skeletons were disposed of the skulls were thrown into a well which was and still is on the site.

We will never know for certain whether these various finds of bones were the remains of Frenchmen who had died far from home. All we can say is that it is possible. They remain as mute reminders of an earlier epoch of our history.

Bideford Gazette 28.2.1985

78. DAYS OF BIDEFORD RIFLE VOLUNTEERS

I once wrote a short article on the founding of the Bideford Rifle Corps in 1860. This was a Volunteer Corps – a group of men who paid for their own equipment and arms who were pledged to defend their own home area in time of war. In the article I described their uniform but bemoaned the fact that no photograph of this uniform existed. Serendipity being what it is, one has now surfaced dating from about 1870 according to an inscription on the back.

The man wearing it is one William Rogers, father of the famous Bideford historian Inkerman Rogers. William had been born in Heanton Punchardon in 1823 and was a groom until he enlisted into the Army at Bath in 1841. The Regiment he entered was the 21st Royal Scots and he stayed with them for the next 21 years and 129 days, as his discharge document records. Whilst there he rose from private to the exalted rank of colour-sergeant. In 1852 he was detached to train raw recruits of the West Yorkshire Militia – for which he received the grateful thanks of the local magistrates who were then responsible for such matters.

A year later Britain declared war on Russia and William's regiment was shipped to the hell of Crimea. Here William won two medals – the Turkish War medal and the British Crimean medal with three bars. These joined his good conduct medal and a silver decoration "for distinguished conduct in the field." Clearly he had been a brave and exemplary soldier.

His discharge papers in 1863 record him as being just under 5 feet 8 inches in height, fresh complexioned with grey eyes and sandy hair. His intended place of retirement was Barnstaple. William, however, had no intention of retiring. As soon as he arrived in North Devon he appears to have joined the newly-formed Rifle Corps.

Clearly his experience was a valuable asset to these part-time soldiers. Not only was William "detached from the headquarters of the Corps as sergeant instructor to the company quartered at Bideford" but he was also responsible for the Torrington company. A letter of 1879 has the major of the Bideford company noting, "I should add that the Torrington corps was raised and formed entirely under the superintendence of Sergeant Rogers – he managed the whole business, including the drilling of the men, in a thoroughly satisfactory manner." Praise indeed.

In 1875 the Bideford Corps, by then known as the 21st Devon Rifle Volunteers was amalgamated with other local groups to become the 4th Battalion the Devon Rifle Volunteers. William who had been colour-sergeant to the 21st became sergeant-major of the new battalion.

He retired fully on February 6 1883, after 42 years of service. He lived to enjoy 14 years of true retirement, dying in 1897 aged 74 – a real 'old soldier' who finally faded away.

North Devon Journal 16.1.1986

79. NAVY MEN WHO RAISED CASH TO PAY EXPENSES

Britain, as a maritime nation, has always taken coastal defence seriously from the beacons of Armada days to the 'dragon's teeth' of the Second World War the military have been conscious of our vulnerability to attack from he sea. The key to North Devon is of course the wide mouth of the Taw and Torridge which provides easy access to the whole area. It is no surprise therefore to know that Appledore was selected as the site for fortification to defend this entry.

In the Civil War an earthwork fort was erected (and fought over) on Staddon Hill. In the Napoleonic period a battery of six 18-pounder guns was established here – they later being moved to Ilfracombe and then on to Plymouth.

In the mid-nineteenth century the perceived enemy was again France and steps were taken to raise Volunteer regiments to defend their home area and release the regular army for service elsewhere. One part of this force was the Royal Naval Volunteers formed in 1859. An advertisement in the *North Devon Journal* in November of that year was to raise recruits for this new force. Pay at £24 per year for 28 days drill was very attractive to the seasonally employed fisherman of North Devon – none more so than at Appledore where at one time over 200 men belonged to this force.

For many years, however, these Appledore men had no real headquarters or guns – just a "few pop-guns at the Custom House Fort" as one writer put it. In late 1894 this changed with the building of a proper battery for the reserve near the lifeboat house in the village. In March 1895 tenders were invited for the mounting of the guns which consisted of one 64-pounder, a six-inch gun and two-inch "Nordenfeldts" – a type of early machine gun.

On Monday June 3 of the same year drilling of the Volunteers began at their Battery – which still had no guns. Mr Martin, the chief-officer, put the men through their paces and then marched them through the streets of Appledore headed by the local band. The streets were crowded and the people cheered but this wasn't thought grand enough, so two weeks later a proper opening ceremony was held.

It was grandiosely described as "the day of a century at Appledore" and we read "Generations come and generations go, and there is little change at the quaint old town." A contemporary newspaper report pointed out, "It had been hoped that an official opening would be made, but possibly the Admiralty officials saw the quiet joke that would be perpetrated in opening a battery without guns, and so a visiting officer just looked in and examined the building."

The day began with a procession, again headed by the Appledore band followed by 100 RNR men, with rifles, cutlasses and flags flying under the command of Mr Martin. Nearly 2000 schoolchildren and spectators followed. The men stopped on the

Quay to sing 'God Save the Queen' which they repeated at Richmond House and sung once more on reaching their new Battery. Tea was provided for the Volunteers and 850 children in the Church Field.

After this the men marched back to the Battery where they were dismissed and joined in a sports competition. Entry fees for this event raised £22 which "with the charge for admission to the sports will cover all expenses." Volunteer units were designed to be as self-financing as possible! Two months later a presentation marble clock was handed over to a Mr C H Schillers who was apparently the main driving force behind the building of the Battery.

The guns did eventually arrive and were put into place I have been told that although never fired in anger they did claim one victim when one blew up during a ceremonial salvo. The Battery was commandeered during the First World War and again during the Second having fallen into disuse during peace time. The Battery still stands today – though it has been converted into two large bungalows – a somewhat odd end to a military career!

North Devon Journal 23.12.1986

80. NORTH DEVON TERRITORIALS LED BRITAIN

The British Army is one of the last great bastions of tradition. When change does come it is rarely welcomed. But exceptions do exist and a fascinating example of this can be seen from an event in North Devon in 1908.

Fifty years previously, at a time of heightened tension in Europe, the volunteer movement had begun where men banded together in battalions pledged to defend their home town or area. They paid for their own uniforms and underwent regular training – both Barnstaple and Bideford had their own Corps – and to the men who served in these formations they became very dear and a source of good companionship.

By the twentieth-century, however, changes were afoot. In order to streamline the volunteers and make them more useful, the Minister of War decided to reorganise them under a new name – the Territorial Army. In many parts of the country there was opposition to this move – but not in North Devon.

The change was scheduled for April 11 1908 and the local volunteers decided to do something very unexpected. On the evening of the last day of March of that year they held a "smoking concert" in their Castle Street Drill Hall in Barnstaple. Most of the volunteers were present enjoying "tobacco and liquid refreshments kindly provided by the officers" whilst viewing the many musical "turns." The evening began at 8 p.m. and lasted until nearly midnight when 100 of the volunteers lined up and filled in enlistment forms to join the Territorial Army.

They were sworn in before a local magistrate who was also present. Following this their buglers assembled in the Square by the present museum and sounded 'The Last Post'. As the clocks struck midnight they changed to 'The Reveille'. The rest of the men formed up outside the Drill Hall and marching behind their band which was playing 'Hail, Smiling Morn' marched through the Square, up High Street and down Cross Street to their headquarters. This was to the great surprise – and probable annoyance – of the local populace who had already gone to bed.

The parade was a complete surprise as the secret had been kept so well. It finished with the singing of the National Anthem and 'Auld Lang Syne' and cheers for their officers outside the Drill Hall. At the same time a telegram was sent to the War Office which read, "Devon leads the way again. The first parade of the Territorial Army is being held in Barnstaple, Wednesday, 12 a.m. – Brown, Captain."

The Ministry replied thanking them as the first 'Terrier' unit in Britain – a novel record for North Devon and a good example of initiative from these part-time soldiers – though what the rudely woken townspeople thought isn't recorded.

North Devon Journal 9.7.1987

81. VICAR KEPT THE HOME FIRES BURNING

In October 1917 the Revered G Payne Cook, vicar of Northam, sent out a letter from his vicarage asking for contributions to a fund to send a "Christmas parcel" of food and other items to all Northam men serving in the forces abroad. He reckoned that about 150 would be needed at a cost of 25p each. The response was such that every local man got his parcel – and many of the men sent

Barnstaple – *Cross Street in 1901 when the beautiful Elizabethan building said to have been built by Pentecost Dodderidge was being demolished to clear the site for the new Post Office (now the offices of Slee & Blackwell).*

Torrington – *Frank Dyson's atmospheric chemist's shop c.1930.*

Instow – *The famous thatched pavillion at the cricket ground c.1955 plus a shot of its interior at the same date.*

Appledore – An aerial view from the late 1950s showing a quayside empty of parked cars.

Barnstaple – A peaceful scene at Rolle Quay around the 1920s with a rail waggon and traction engine in the background.

Barnstaple – The Strand looking towards the building now housing 'Zenaxis' and the North Devon Advertiser c.1920.

Bideford – The Bridge in 1926 when it was being widened.

Torrington – *The Electricity showroom with posters advertising the latest advantages of cooking with electric ovens c.1950*

Torrington – *The well-loved 'Green Lantern' cafe in the Square with an interesting pavement display next door.*

Taddiport – The now closed milk factory at full steam next door to the medieval bridge in the 1960s.

Torrington – *The stand-down of the Torrington Home Guard in 1945.*

Torrington – *The Pannier Market in better days – though the original glass roof had been taken down by this date – mid 1950s.*

Barnstaple – *Packed quayside where the bus station now stands.*
The now demolished curved iron bridge is in the forefront
of the photograph c.1910.

Westward Ho! – *One of the earliest photographs of the village taken by*
W C Murphy of Bideford around 1870.

Ilfracombe – *The famous Chapel seen here from an unusual angle c.1948.*

Bishops Nympton – *A newly thatched cottage in the village exhibiting the Freemason's symbol on its roof May 1948.*

Barnstaple – The fair in typical Devon weather in the 1930s when it was held where the Civic Centre now stands.

Bideford – Workers in 1911 at Hansen's shipyard at Bank End on the site now occupied by Riverbank House. Note the curtains on the windowless lorry.

Bideford – Green's china shop which stood on the corner of Allhalland and High Street. Lloyds bank is there today.

Barnstaple – *The Pannier Market crowded with both panniers and people c.1900. Note the gaslights.*

Barnstaple – *The Square with some top-hatted and bewhiskered Victorians c.1890 before the fountain was erected.*

Bideford – *The old toll house at the top of Clovelly Road which is now a shop called 'Twinaways'.*

Devon County Show 1874

Barnstaple *– A triumphal arch at the corner of Joy and Boutport Street in 1874 when the Devon County Show was held in town.*

Barnstaple *– Boutport Street Adams Brothers selling boots, shoes, ice cream, tea, tobacco and newspapers. The shop now sells fruit and vegetables.*

Lynmouth – The English Alps' show to good advantage in this engraving from the mid 19th century.

Barnstaple – A print showing the Strand and Queen Ann's Walk in the early years of the ninteenth century.

Bideford – Early print of the Old Quay.

Bideford – Early print of the High Street.

Ilfracombe – A close-up view of the Chapel c.1860. The vertical scale is somewhat exaggerated.

Westward Ho! – Bathing huts on wheels and a curiously flat pebble ridge at this resort in the 1860s.

Appledore and Instow – The railway station with primitive signal device c.1860. Note 'Chanter's Tower' at the extreme left.

Ilfracombe – *The 'genteel' villas of mid-nineteenth century Ilfracombe.*

Barnstaple – Part of the opening ceremonies for the Lynton and Barnstaple Railway 1898.

Hartland – *The main street at rush hour! The view is from a postcard dated December 1905 which tells the recipient that the writer's teeth were better.*

Northam – *A procession of the mounted band of the North Devon Yeomanry just before the First World War.*

Lynmouth – Showing the famous Beacon Tower c. 1860.

Clovelly – A very atmospheric view of the tiny village harbour with two fishing boats present c. 1860.

Barnstaple – The men of the town fire brigade march along Taw Vale c.1930.

Appledore – *One of the village's narrow cobbled lanes replete with two old seamen and a tiny corner shop c. 1910.*

Bideford – *The Quay in 1944-5 with a military march headed by the Town Marshal.*

Westward Ho! – *In 1930 showing the construction of the sea defences. Note the octagonal building in the centre of the photograph which was moved there from Bideford Quay.*

Ilfracombe – *The Royal Britannia Hotel by the harbour at the turn of the century – note the three faces at the middle window.*

Barnstaple – *Part of the opening ceremonies for the Lynton and Barnstaple Railway 1898.*

grateful letters to the vicar – who then kept them. Today they are in the Devon Record Office and, although all are censored, we can still get some taste of what "the war to end all wars" was like for the common man caught up in it.

Thus Private A Braunton writing from "a dugout in the trenches" noted, "It was three years ago I joined the Army, now it seems nearly a lifetime" and added "I must bring this letter to a close, old Fritzys is sending over some big shells just outside." He also described how he and his mates had just eaten the tin of salmon in the parcel – "it was a nice change from our usual biscuits and jam."

Thomas Branch, serving on HMS Achilles, wrote "the cocoa you sent me was very good and when we had to turn out of our hammocks at 12 o'clock and keep a watch until 4 o'clock in the morning in the cold and wet we always had a basin of cocoa."

Not everyone was so happy – poor Sapper W Hayle complained that his parcel took three months to reach him "so of course the cake was gone bad." And another complaint came from Sapper A Maggs of the Mesopotamian Expeditionary Force. He got the vicar's parcel but never received others from his family – a loss he put down to theft as he was "afraid that those who are left to deal with the Parcels have a hand in helping themselves."

Other comments are equally sad. Sapper J Gale wrote unhappily, "I shall be spending Xmas in the (front) line." And Private Stacey of the Ordnance Corps reckoned, "You cannot tell how pleased we feel when we receive a parcel from home, we know we are not forgotten." Perhaps the most poignant letter came from S Harris who wrote, one feels more in hope than expectation, "The boys out here are very optimistic as to the War finishing at an early date."

The war in fact went on for another year and the Rev Cook was sending out Christmas parcels again in 1918 – although by then the armies had laid down their weapons and called a halt to the slaughter.

North Devon Journal 1.9.1988

82. THE LAST VICTIM OF THE WAR

The slaughter that was the First World War ended in November 1918, yet three months later 'war' came again to Bideford. In

February 1919 the Bideford Schools Management Committee met "to decide the question of the reinstatement of Mr Guard, a conscientious objector."

Harry Guard was about 45 and had been a well-liked teacher at Old Town Boys' School (on the site of the present fire station) before the war. In 1917 men of his age group had been called up but Harry had announced that his conscience would not allow him to kill. If a man said he was a 'conchy' then he had to attend a tribunal to put his case. This Harry did and his grounds for exemption were accepted and instead of being conscripted he went to work on a local farm. He was the only man in Bideford who registered as a conscientious objector.

When the men were demobilised many went back to their old jobs and Guard applied for his – which led to the meeting in February 1919. Public opinion was strongly set against a 'conchy' getting his job back again on the same terms as men who had served in the Forces. After long discussions the committee decided to reinstate Guard but the longest-serving member, Mr T Pollard, jumped up and resigned on the spot saying, somewhat oddly, "How...on May 24 were they going to celebrate Empire Day with a man like that leading the boys of school?"

The committee did not reach this decision lightly. The chairman "reported the receipt of a protest from the Bideford branch of the National Federation of Discharged and Demobilised Soldiers and Sailors...also a resolution from the Barnstaple branch of the Comrades of the Great War," the secretary of which wrote, "It is evident and imperative that the rising generation must be taught patriotism before all other subjects. It is on one hand, a disgrace to place teaching in the hands of a person who refuses to fight for his country and protect his women and children, and on the other hand it is a gross injustice to the parents and children who are compelled to attend this school."

Guard began work on Monday February 10, but "on the assembly for afternoon school Mr Guard was given a hostile reception by large numbers of boys and some of their mothers. About 60 lads declared a protest strike and spent the afternoon parading the streets in procession and singing patriotic and other songs." I have talked to an old man who was one of these boys and he sung me one of these 'songs' – a crude but effective pastiche of a then popular tune directed against all 'conchies'. Worse followed when at 4 o'clock the absentee boys returned, with children from other schools, and "mobbed Mr Guard, who went home accompanied by the Rev H Trotman and two policemen, the boys following and booing. Some potatoes and other missiles were thrown."

This state of anarchy continued for several days with the people of Bideford taking no steps to restore peace. Indeed we read that "beyond exhorting the boys to be orderly the public did not interfere with them." The size of the mobs can be judged from the fact that the schools attendance officer reported 123 boys absent.

Mr Guard was not without his supporters. A Henry Woodcock who had actually been at the tribunal which judged Guard's case as a conscientious objector reckoned him a very brave man in that he stuck by his principles and did not "bolt into a reserved occupation" as many other Bidefordians did.

At the next school managers' meeting Guard's headmaster noted that "the opposition had died down, and...his class had got up to 37, more volunteering to go into his class." The old man I referred to earlier told me that this was partly due to the headmaster threatening to flog every boy who did not come back! At the same meeting, however, a pile of letters was produced condemning Guard. The Mayor of Bideford commented that Guard "must be living a wretched life" and "it would be better for him to seek a situation somewhere else."

The Mayor's suggestion seemed to put the seal on the poor teacher's fate. His resignation was gladly accepted and so fell the last victim of the war – hounded to disgrace because of his personal convictions.

North Devon Journal 11.9.1986

83. WAITING FOR THE BOMBS TO DROP

With all the talk of nuclear bunkers and civil defence it is perhaps interesting (and less frightening) to look back to the Second World War and see what Bideford citizens were doing to protect themselves from expected German air-raids. We can do this by examining a small booklet entitled *Air Raid Precautions* dated June 1941 and printed by the *Gazette*.

It begins by listing the town council who made up the civil defence committee under the Mayor, G H Braddick. Also listed are the various "emergency officials" including the rescue party officer F Gray, the evacuation clerk A Blackwell and the chief billeting officer W Langford.

The duties of the air raid wardens are then detailed and included "To give warning of gas – by the sounding of rattles – and to notify the public – with hand bells – when the danger is past." Their most vital job was "To co-operate with the police in enforcing lighting regulations" – the source of many complaints from the public. The wardens were organised on a group basis and a typical one was that run by H Vickers of Chudleigh Terrace which ran from Barnstaple Street to Vinegar Hill and up to Chudleigh and Fort Terraces. The group warden of group 'O' was Miss Hutchinson of Orchard Hill – still happily with us today – who covered the Orchard and Raleigh Hill areas.

The "first aid post" for the town was the White House in Meddon Street – now the hospital, and this had two first-aid parties with ambulances based there. A similar group also existed in East-the-Water. The White House also contained a "gas cleaning station" though details for 'do-it-yourself' decontamination techniques are also given. This section of the booklet ends with the exhortation "Carry Your Gas Masks Always" – a suggestion generally ignored by most people once it became clear that the Germans were not going to use gas bombs.

A sombre note was struck in the section headed "Civilian War Deaths" where we read, "Particulars will be posted up at the Police Station and the Town Hall as soon as possible after their occurrence." The emergency mortuary was in the Old Town Cemetery Chapel kept by Mr J Ackland.

Details of the two fire engines and seven trailer pumps "with efficient crews" are then given with a page of "Hints for fire-fighters." Eleven "public shelters" are listed and there were in addition premises in town with suitable basements – a notice displayed in their window identified which shops these were.

There follows four pages of "What to do in a raid" and another eight pages on "After an Air Raid" including details of accommodation for the homeless (at the Convent and the Strand Cinema among other places) and temporary feeding places. Listed in this group was the "British Restaurant" in the Brigade Hall in Allhalland Street. Repairs to bombed houses would be carried out by the borough surveyor and "no charges for repairs will be collected from the owner of the property until after the war." So even in 1941 we were looking to the end of the conflict!

It is gratifying to add that during the war only three bombs were dropped on Bideford and they caused very little damage even though one was a 1000lb parachute bomb. It is clear from this booklet, however, that if the town had been more heavily attacked the people of Bideford would have been prepared for it.

Bideford Gazette 4.1.1985

TRANSPORT

84. STORMY NIGHT OR JUDGEMENT OF THE LORD

North Devon has had its share of shipping tragedies – though one of special note occurred in 1828. At 4 p.m. on Sunday October 28 twelve fishing boats left Clovelly pier in good weather with a calm sea. The boats were small, containing only 26 men between them – all local and all very experienced. The men put down their nets "with a promising prospect of an abundant catch" and all went well until midnight when a sudden wind of hurricane force sprung up and completely overwhelmed the little fleet.

A contemporary report of the storm talks of its "irresistible violence" and it must have been terrible as, with all their experience, only one boat managed to outride the huge seas and mountainous waves. The fleet must have been near to the shore as it was noted that "the shrieks of distress from the poor fellows were heard on shore" – but the weather prevented any rescuc attempts.

On the following morning the one surviving boat struggled back to Clovelly bringing little comfort to the waiting crowds lining the beach and pier. Of the other eleven boats nine sank completely whilst another two nearly made land but were dashed to pieces on the rocks. When the count was taken it was found that 21 men had been drowned that night.

Although the greatest impact was on Clovelly, other villages had their mourning widows and orphaned children. Three men came from Bucks Mills including John Braund of the famous family there. Two others, both married with children came from Ilfracombe. James Kelly and Richard Lock were from Appledore and had nine children between them. Three Hartland men also drowned along with one from Bideford, one from Bude and another "whose name was unknown" from Cornwall.

Many of their bodies were washed up over the next few weeks being claimed by their families where still identifiable. The Bideford man, Henry Pooley, was thought to have actually made it ashore at Northam "but by the violence of the surge was afterwards destroyed by being dashed against the rocks, as his corpse was disfigured with wounds and contusions."

The inquests returned verdicts of accidental death, it being noted that "the tide at Clovelly on the night was higher than any that had occurred within the memory of the oldest inhabitants." Contemporary reports of the disaster end rather sententiously with the suggestion that "the Christian moralist" might "discover in the awful visitation a mark of Divine displeasure at the flagrant breach of his sacred command – remember the Sabbath day." Not much comfort to the bereaved perhaps – but then the nineteenth-century believed in an inflexibly stern vision of religion.

North Devon Journal 26.2.1987

85. HARE-BRAINED BALLOONISTS GO BACKWARDS

Planes have been a common sight over North Devon for at least 75 years but the history of aerial endeavour in this area goes back before that ... in the form of ballooning. In March 1882 Captain Molesworth, of Northdown, Bideford, chaired a meeting of the grandly-named Balloon Society of Great Britain when it was decided to attempt an aerial crossing of the Bristol Channel from Westward Ho! Mr Joseph Simmons was the daring "aeronaut" and he announced boldly that "nothing whatever should stand in the way of his crossing, providing that the weather would permit him to do so."

The only difficulty he could see was an easterly wind "which would take the balloon out into the Atlantic". Even this danger was to be met as Mr Cornish "an inventor" had offered to fit his new life-saving apparatus to the basket of the balloon. The proposed date for the attempt was April 12 and the costs were to be met by local subscriptions.

Only a week after the meeting Mr Simmons attempted to cross the English Channel but came down in the sea and had to be rescued by a passing mail ship – not an auspicious omen to say the least. His balloon was rescued and repaired and a week later turned up at Westward Ho! A Captain Jerman prepared a favourable weather forecast and everything looked set. Unfortunately the residents of Westward Ho! showed little interest and Mr Simmons moved his balloon to Ilfracombe – attracted by more generous supporters.

It was thus at Ilfracombe and not Westward Ho! that on April 10, Mr Simmons set out. The day broke "magnificently fine, with a clear bright sky, and the wind almost a dead calm." At 7 a.m. the balloon "was brought into the field at the rear of the Independent Chapel, which had been engaged by the Committee." A special five-inch gas pipe which had been laid for the purpose was connected to the balloon "but notwithstanding the size of the pipe" it still took four hours to inflate. In fact, "no less than 37,000 cubic feet of gas" were needed.

A small pilot balloon showed the wind to be blowing from the south west. The main balloon, still tethered by ropes, was sent up to 300 feet carrying Mr Simmons, R and W Huxtable and a Miss Street – a brave Victorian lady! On the third 'captive ascent' too much rope was paid out too quickly and "the men in charge narrowly escaped losing the rope altogether." One of the helpers Mr Vickery received a rope burn and Coastguard Rowley was carried 15 feet into the air and was badly bruised when he fell heavily to the ground.

After this slight mishap Simmons was joined by two men from London and the real attempt began. The balloon rapidly rose to a mile accompanied by the cheers of the vast crowd that had gathered. Unfortunately the balloon began moving eastwards and then turned to the west and drifted towards Barnstaple. Some hours later it gently descended to land at Hacketts Farm, Swimbridge – 16 miles away in the wrong direction! A rather ludicrous end to a brave enterprise.

The newspaper editorials were very severe over the whole thing, one writing, "It is difficult to write with patience of such hare-brained follies as occupied attention in North Devon on Monday. Ballooning under any conditions is sufficiently hazardous, but it argues suicidal mania or idiotic recklessness to select for the scene of an ascent the margin of the sea." The general feeling seems to have been that the whole was a "ludicrous and contemptible farce."

As if to rub salt into the balloonist's wounded pride it was announced two weeks later that a loss of £40 had been made on the affair. A sad start to North Devon's aerial history.

North Devon Journal 29.8.1985

86. WRECK THAT LEAD TO LICENSING

We are approaching the centenary of one of North Devon's worst disasters. On Friday, August 26 1887 The Monarch, a 10 ton yacht, set sail from Ilfracombe harbour on a pleasure trip. On board were 24 passengers, mainly tourists, and two local boatmen – Captain William Rumson and Charles Buckingham, an ex-naval man.

The sea was smooth and the party cheerful but as the boat sailed past the Tunnels Bathing Beach a "puff of wind" hit it and blew a boat-hook overboard. Captain Rumson decided to retrieve this and immediately began tacking back. It was then that another "puff of wind" hit and "the boat heeled over and shipped water at the stern." At the same time the passengers were all tumbled together and their weight concentrated at one end sent the boat diving rapidly to its doom.

What followed was a scene of horror where "the screams and shrieks of the unfortunate people were heartrending." Many could not swim and the suddenness of the event saw them entangled in rigging or encumbered with heavy coats. One young man, Harold Baker, went down with the boat yet managed to surface briefly before being dragged down again by desperate hands. It took frantic efforts to free himself and cling to floating wreckage.

The disaster had, however, been witnessed from the beach and local boats pushed off with haste. Many bodies, living and the dead, were brought ashore at the pier being "taken up the steps on stretchers or on the shoulders of stalwart men." The rescuers were soon forced back by high waves that followed the first squalls. Medical men on holiday in Ilfracombe helped in resuscitation attempts. In one case "a medical coil (for electrical stimulation) was used for over an hour, and ether was injected" but in vain.

Amidst all this confusion it took some time before any casualty figures could be finalised – by the end of the day, however, it was known that 14 had drowned, including three women. At the inquest soon afterwards the coroner talked of "an occurrence which had cast a gloom over the whole of the town, and had plunged several families into a state of great distress." He then went on to take identification of the five bodies so far recovered and hear evidence from Captain Rumson who had survived. The jury gave as their verdict "accidental death."

A reward of £3 for each of the nine missing bodies was offered and many local fishermen "have been out with lines grappling for bodies, and a long line with hooks on has been laid, in the hope of hitching the clothes of any bodies that may be washed along the bottom by the tides." At the same time a subscription was opened for the widow and nine children of Charles Buckingham, the second boatman, who went down with the yacht.

Within a week two more bodies had been recovered and another inquest followed – a pattern repeated once more when another two bodies came ashore. One of these latter corpses was of Buckingham being identified by "a blue jersey with the word Monarch in large letters on the breast." By this time the subscription to his family had reached £382 – a tremendous sum in those days.

Such a disaster called for serious investigation and within two weeks a Board of Trade inquiry was opened at Bristol. It heard much evidence but put most weight on that from John Pollard an Ilfracombe shipwright. Some time earlier he had lengthened the Monarch by 8' amidships to increase its length to 36'. The ballast loading, however, was left unchanged. The newly enlarged boat was checked by Ilfracombe police who freely admitted they had no expert knowledge. Perhaps more attention should have been paid to local coastguard, Lieut. Dyke Acland, who had announced that he would no longer sail in the Monarch after its change as he regarded it as unsafe.

The inquiry inspector absolved Rumson from blame but did suggest he should have had his main sail fastened when he tried to tack. In addition he called strongly for the Ilfracombe Local Board – the council – to introduce proper licensing and be much more stringent over inspecting pleasure boats. As a contemporary remarked, however, it was a great pity that it took 14 deaths to bring about such an obvious change.

North Devon Journal 19.6.1986

87. WHEN MINSTRELS PLAYED AT WESTWARD HO! RAILWAY STATION

Many people in Bideford still fondly remember and mourn the passing of the Bideford, Westward Ho! and Appledore Railway.

Several pamphlets and numerous articles have been written about the little railway with its custom made engines and carriages. Recently I came across a copy of an obscure article on the line which appeared in the *Monthly Gazette* of the British Electrical Traction Co. Ltd. in August 1902. This was one of a long-running series on 'B.E.T. Lines' in Britain and its contemporary details add some points of interest to the story of this local railway.

It begins with a short history of the company which was established in 1896 to build the line. As the writer notes, "A glance at the map will show that the route followed is somewhat circuitous, but this is necessary owing to the difficulties which would have been experienced in constructing a line direct to Westward Ho!" The only alternative to this route would have been "a tunnel almost the whole distance" which was clearly an uneconomic proposition.

The route is then described in some detail. Beginning on the Quay the line was "a tramway along the centre of Broad Quay" for some 300 yards. The route then went around the Pill on "bull headed rails" whatever they were. The Pill was then just waste ground through which a stream had run – this had been filled in by the company.

The yard (still standing in Kingsley Road,) is then dealt with, the locomotive shed being capable of holding four engines. An inspection pit was provided here for the fitters to repair the three locomotives actually housed in the building. The engines were, of course, steam driven and a clever system of ventilation had been constructed to carry the steam and smoke away from inside the shed. The writer says, "It is provided with wooden troughs suspended from the roof over the centre lines of the rails for the purpose of preventing the fumes eating away the iron; these troughs slope upwards and communicate with wooden chimneys." Each of the engines had its wheels "cased in thin iron plates for the better protection of wayfarers and vehicles" on the Quay.

Next to the engine shed stood the "car shed" which housed four carriages. These carriages were described as "handsome structures of teak," with seating for 10 first-class and 40 third class passengers.

After this description of the yard the writer moved on to the rural part of the route along the Causeway and Kenwith Valley. The stream here had given some trouble early on in the life of the line but agreement with the landowner over straightening the stream's course had solved this. The two stations of Kenwith and Abbotsham Road are briefly described, the latter being "a pretty station in the midst of trees." Near this halt the company had made "a path for the benefit of volunteers who wish to make use of the range that is situated near the line." These volunteers were the local militia based in Bideford.

After this the line ran along the top of Cornborough Cliffs "giving the passengers an opportunity of enjoying what is undoubtedly one of the most beautiful views in North Devon." The writer then breaks into highly coloured prose to describe the view much of which is still here today.

At Westward Ho! the company had a "fully fledged station with waiting room, bookstall and refreshment room, the latter being exceeding popular." To increase passenger traffic the company were subsidising 'black and white' minstrels who gave two shows a day during the week and one on Sundays near the station.

The terminus at Northam is then described, a note being added that many passengers were golfers, going to the links on the Burrows. Some discussion then follows as to the advisability of continuing the line to Appledore. One reason advanced as to why this should happen is that it would help break down Appledore's isolation. To support this point the writer quotes an anecdote as follows, "A visitor on his first visit to Bideford was looking up at the Bridge Hall, and asked some men who were lounging on the quay what building it was. The men gazed at him and at the hall in silence, and at last one of them said in reply. 'Us don't know; us be Appledore men'."

A story to be taken with a pinch of salt, no doubt, but interesting in any case! On this humorous note the anonymous writer ends, little realising that within a few years the railway would have disappeared as a part of the 'war effort' never, sadly, to return.

Bideford Gazette 11.5.1984

88. TAKING TO THE AIR FOR ONE SHORT MINUTE

Today the North Devon Show is one of the major events in the calendar of North Devon attractions. In the past, however, many smaller shows were held and they often vied with each other to obtain the best 'draws'. In 1911 the South Molton Show committee under the Hon G W Bampfylde must have been congratulating themselves on obtaining a visit from an intrepid aviator. Air flight was still at that date in its infancy and a scheduled fly-past was a certain crowd-puller. The pilot who had agreed to show off his flying machine to North Devonians was a Capt Clayton of the Midlands Aviation Syndicate.

His aircraft was a single wing Bleriot which arrived by road along with its own canvas hangar. This was erected about a quarter of a mile from the showground which was at Great Hele Barton. For a shilling (5p) the curious were allowed to inspect the machine. The local reporter went and admitted that "a technical description of it is beyond his powers" but that everyone who saw it thought it "impossible that the machine could bear its own weight of 560 lbs" plus the weight of the pilot. The nine-foot propeller seemed to be "the only really substantial part of the machine."

Poor Capt Clayton nearly didn't make it to the show at all as the plane's engine had caught fire the previous week and a new one had to be hurriedly ordered. Clayton admitted "it would be impossible to test it fully before attempting a flight." The brave captain, however, did not want to let the public down especially as a record crowd of 4,298 had turned up – so he announced he would try a flight at 6 p.m. He was hopeful "of being able to fly to the show ground, a distance of a quarter of a mile, to encircle the ground, and return to the field where he started – if the engine worked satisfactorily."

At 6 p.m. a tremendous crowd gathered and waited "with exemplary patience for an hour." At 7 p.m. the aeroplane was towed out of its hangar and the engine started. It didn't run smoothly – the noise it made being described "as of a fractious motor cycle" whilst the propeller revolved "jerkily". Nothing daunted, Capt Clayton climbed in and set off. Unfortunately it took three attempts before he got it airborne and then it "soared to a height of perhaps fifty feet" – but only for a minute. The propeller apparently refused to revolve at a fast enough rate and Clayton thought it wiser to descend. He had covered only 400 yards.

He managed to land safely but his troubles weren't over. Although he turned the engine off it continued to fire and kept the aircraft running along the ground. Clayton jumped out and his plane ran on to crash into a hedge and crumple up "like tissue paper" in the graphic phrase of the local newspaper reporter. The damage was repaired by local coachbuilders Moor and Son, of South Molton, and the bill came to £20, which seems cheap. When asked why he had taken off when he knew his aircraft might not make it Clayton replied in true British style "he did not wish to disappoint the public and would sooner lose £100 than get a bad name for refusing to fly."

North Devon Journal 13.8.1987

LAW AND ORDER

89. WHY BAILIFF WAS HAULED UP IN COURT

There has been no military invasion of these islands since 1066 and this long period of security has resulted in a massive accumulation of records from the past. One of the earliest surviving records for this area consists of a series of court rolls or legal proceedings for the Manor of Alwington, near Bideford. These date from the middle of the fifteenth century and record events at the 'court leets' of the Lord of the Manor. These court leets had control over such matters as 'petty common law misdemeanours and public nuisances' as well as governing agreements between the lord and his tenants.

Before looking at these early records it is interesting to remember that Bideford still retains its manor court which meets once a year in the town hall. Such a survival is rare today and links us directly to our ancient forebears though the range of topics covered today are different to those of the past.

At Alwington the Lords of the Manor came from the Coffin family and their manor did not just consist of the parish of Alwington but probably extended into adjoining parishes as well. The day-to-day work of running the manor would have been carried out by a bailiff. It would almost certainly have been this official who called the court to order on October 4th 1456 (the first date for which records survive).

The bailiff was actually the subject of the first case to be heard. He was summoned to explain why "he did not distrain John Denys of Orlegh to do homage and fealty"? This odd-sounding passage may be explained as follows. John Denys as tenant of "Orlegh" owed a 'rent' to the Lord of the Manor but this had yet to be paid. The bailiff had been ordered to seize goods to the value of this 'rent' but had not done so – thus explaining why he was being presented at court rather than the 'rent' dodger. Although I call it a 'rent' it wasn't exactly this. Under the old manorial system, with its feudal basis, rich tenants owed a term of military service to their lords though by the fifteenth century this had been changed to a straight money payment.

The bailiff was ordered to carry out his duty and the court then passed on to other matters including the presentation of one Baldwin Viell for non-payment of his 'rent' for houses at "Wode" and "Forde." Anyone who knows Alwington will recognise the place-names in their present forms of Woodtown and Ford – clearly these hamlets date back at least 500 years.

At the same court John and Johanne Whiteman gave up their tenancy of "Ivehous" and were replaced by David Prust and his wife. There is still an Ivy House in the parish and such a link across 500 years I personally find fascinating.

The next court in 1457 saw John Dolyner, Richard Buys and John Rixlake being presented for not giving up to the Lord of the Manor a "toppe" of a ship and half of a small boat "shipwrecked at Cokynton." Such wreckage was the property of the Lord and had to be surrendered to him where and when it came ashore. Cockington cliffs are still a prominent landmark along this coast and still provide rich hunting grounds for beachcombers. The next case dealt with was one of debt between Richard Morcombe and Richard Alyn. The bailiff seized four animals worth 10/- from Alyn to settle the money owed.

In December 1458 it was reported to the court that Richard Cavell who had been a tenant of a cottage at "Fayre-crosse" (the modern Fairy Cross) had died and that the "heriot" to the Lord of the Manor was one cow. A "heriot" was a sum due to the Lord whenever any of his tenants died – an odd reversal of our present-day 'key-money'! In May 1462 another "heriot" was noted when the death of Robert Coffyn of "Alwyngton" (presumably related to the Lord of the Manor) meant that a horse had become the Lord's due. His widow Edith took over the tenancy but still had to hand over the horse. At the 1458 court Meliora Durehill gave up her cottage at "Fayre-crosse" and Anthony Sompter took it over though a note by his name in 1459 reveals that he had been taken away to the "kings prison." As an indication of how regulated were the lives of feudal tenants one can quote the 1471 court records where Nicholas Wode was ordered to make an oven in the chimney of the hall at his house in "Bikepitte" – probably the modern Baggepit.

Of such small details is history made, however, and we in the twentieth century can only be grateful for the patience and care with which our ancestors noted such minutiae – without it local history would be far poorer. The Alwington records continue until at least 1619 and can be found today housed in the Devon Record Office. Reading the originals is difficult but the job has been made much easier by a modern typed transcript in English which is also available.

Bideford Gazette 14.12.1984

90. TRANSPORTED FOR THE THEFT OF A FEW TOOLS

North Devon was, for many years, a major source of emigrants to the colonies. No one knows for certain how many thousands left to seek their fortunes elsewhere, but numbers were very large. Not all emigrants, however, went willingly. For 200 years – from the 17th to 19th century – criminals were sent from Britain to our colonies in North America and Australia.

One such unwilling colonist was Matthew Crang, apparently born in 1697 at Chittlehampton though he married at Cornworthy in South Devon in 1726. At the time he was an agricultural labourer and his bride was Alice Wadland.

His downfall came in August 1736 when he was arrested for stealing a few tools from James Soper of Cornworthy. On the document describing his case the tools are valued at 3s (15p) and include. "One scythe with sneed, hand-pins and crookes" (a snead or sneed was the handle for the scythe). Matthew was sent to the bridewell or gaol in Exeter to await his trial. Unfortunately no records of the trial exist but we do have the verdict – "Try'd found Guilty of Petty Larceny To be transported for Seven Years". Such a vicious sentence for such a small crime seems terrible to us but it was nothing unusual in those days.

The "transport order" tells us that Matthew was to be sent to "one of his Majesty's Colonies or Plantations in America." Six magistrates were appointed to draw up a contract with a private ship-owner to carry the convict to his new home – privatisation of government responsibilities is nothing new! The man who was awarded the contract was John Buck of Bideford, described in the records as "merchant". From other sources it is clear that this Bideford 'merchant' often undertook the job of 'floating gaoler'.

At this time of course Bideford still had strong trading links with North America. Buck agreed to transport Matthew and six other unfortunate men to Maryland within three months of signing the contract. He also agreed to produce a "certificate of their landing under the hand and seal of the governor or principal officer of the port" where he landed them. In another clause he agreed to pay £30 a head to the court if any of the convicts escaped!

A slightly later document records that Matthew and his fellow convicts were taken to Bideford and delivered to John Buck and "were shiped off to sea" – but it adds that this was "illegal irregular and contrary to law". Apparently the proper formalities had not been gone through and John Buck's father George was fined £10.10s, though as he was one of the leading townsmen at this time it probably didn't bother him too much.

Unfortunately this technical error did not lead to Matthew being brought back and so he disappears into history. His wife and five children left behind in Cornworthy did appear, however, in the records of the Overseer of the Poor for the parish. The removal of the breadwinner meant they had to seek poor relief and various payments are recorded for clothing and other expenses. In August 1775 there is an entry referring to money being paid for a shroud and the digging of a grave for poor Alice. As it was rare for a convict to return, even after serving his sentence, we can only assume that Alice remained a 'widow' for 37 years after her husband was forcibly taken from her – all for a sum of less than 3s – harsh justice indeed.

North Devon Journal 28.12.1984

91. CRIME-CRACKERS WHO PRECEDED THE POLICE FORCE

One of the fastest growing anti-crime schemes today is the Neighbourhood Watch. However, as with most things it is not a new idea. Our ancestors had their version of the scheme but it perhaps went further than ours does today. One example was the grandly named Barnstaple Association for the Protection of Property. Such organisations were particularly common in the late eighteenth and early nineteenth centuries and consisted of groups of shopkeepers, farmers and other tradesmen who banded together to offer rewards in cases where their members had been the victims of crime.

Very few records of their activities survive but in 1827 we get a brief glimpse of the Barnstaple Association, when three young men, Thomas Ward, George Greeny and James Harvey, were arrested for "numerous thefts in and around the town". They had been reported by a woman named Miller who lived in Litchdon Street and cooked for them. Her reward was paid by the Association.

The following month the Association members placed an advertisement in the *Journal* which began, "This Association was formed in the Year 1812 and at present consists of about 60 members, with a fund of upwards of ONE HUNDRED POUNDS." The advertisement continued by listing the various rewards available on conviction of offenders, e.g. £5 for burglars, "Footpad" robbers (today's muggers) and arsonists, £2 for thieves, £1 for hedge destroyers and the same amount for those "Wilfully breaking glass lamps or windows, or destroying knockers, bell pulls, or pulling up any scrapers, or doing wilful damage to any dwelling house." Membership of the Association was open to anyone within 20 miles of Barnstaple on payment of £1 plus 12½p a year.

It apparently continued for many years afterwards but with the formation of the first professional police force in the 1830's the original reason for its foundation disappeared and it seems to have ended as a local company insuring members' plate glass windows.

Perhaps our modern Neighbourhood Watch schemes might offer rewards? The results could prove interesting – but one thing is certain – it would be nothing new!

North Devon Journal 17.11.1988

92. BIDEFORD RIOT IN 1816

In an earlier article I wrote about the local military volunteers known as the North Devon Yeomanry Cavalry. This regiment was raised during the Napoleonic Wars but saw no action then, being confined to local guard duties. Their first taste of action came, sadly enough, after the war ended and it was directed against their fellow country-men.

After the Battle of Waterloo in 1815 the Government, ever keen to save money, disbanded large numbers of soldiers and at the same time cancelled many orders for military equipment from British manufacturers. This had the not unexpected effect of increasing unemployment and depressing business. Among the poor, hunger quickly became common and in Bideford in 1816 the lack of both work and food erupted in a violent riot. Its initial cause was when a local shipowner loaded a cargo of potatoes at the Quay – presumably with the intention of taking them to a place such as Bristol or Plymouth where he would make more profit than in Bideford. The townsmen clearly could not tolerate this. Gathering in large numbers they unloaded the potatoes by force and made off with them.

The event was noted briefly in the *Exeter Flying Post* of May 23 1816 which said, "A serious riot took place in Bideford on Wednesday last occasioned by an interference on the part of the populace to prevent the shipment of potatoes, and which was not quelled until Saturday. Four of the rioters were brought up here on Sunday morning, escorted by a party of the North Devon Yeomanry Cavalry and lodged in the Devon County Gaol for trial at our next Assizes."

At this date a professional police force for Bideford was still some 22 years in the future – the ineffectual parish constables were the only 'police' available to the town Mayor. Faced with such a riot the Council could only call in the local military to quell the disturbance. With four of the rioters in Exeter gaol one would have thought that the authorities could have relaxed, but evidently they viewed the event as something very serious.

The Home Secretary at this date was Lord Sidmouth – a Devon peer whose personal records are now in the Devon Record Office. Among these is a letter to Lord Rolle dated six days after the riot started. This reads, "My dear Lord, The late Proceedings at Bideford, of which I received an Account from your Lordship by this Day's Post, are of a Description so flagrant that I have thought it necessary to adopt the most prompt and decisive Means for the Discovery of the Offenders. With this in View I have directed the first Clerk in the Bow Street Office, a most intelligent and experienced man, to proceed immediately to the Spot and to take the most effectual Steps, in Conjunction with the Civil Authorities there, to bring to Justice the Persons principally concerned in these criminal and dangerous Proceedings. The name of the Person to whom I have alluded is Stafford, and I well know his peculiar

Fitness for the Service on which he is ordered having employed Him frequently and with great Advantage, on similar Occasions."

Thus Bideford played host, probably unknowingly, to the chief of the Bow Street Runners. This famous body of men – the first professional policemen in Britain's history – had been formed in 1792 by Henry Fielding (author of *Tom Jones*) to patrol the streets of London. Early in their history, however, their expertise as detectives was utilised by the authorities of provincial towns. Mr Stafford apparently achieved some success as by the time of the trial of the rioters in August 1816 five men were in gaol – one extra to those originally gaoled. Their names were, William Moyrick, James Stapledon, George Veal, Thomas Croscombe and Thomas Trace.

By August 15 the trials were over and the sentences announced. Trace was imprisoned for two years, Croscombe for 18 months, Moyrick and Stapledon for a year and Veal for six months. The sentences appear light considering the amount of energy expended by the Yeomanry and the Bow Street Runner but one must remember that any sentence of imprisonment in a gaol of this period was often tantamount to a death sentence, so common was disease in the insanitary cells and among the vermin-infested prisoners.

Bideford Gazette 25.5.1982

93. POISON PENS THAT REACHED WHITEHALL

I have written elsewhere about the Bideford "food riots" of 1816 when townspeople took to the streets to protest over the export of potatoes at a time when local supplies were running low. Recently, however, I have come across reports from 1801, 1802 and 1812 which point to similar trouble.

In January 1801 the *London Gazette,* which was published by the Government, carried a notice signed by Home Secretary Lord Portland offering a reward of 20 guineas and a free pardon to anyone informing him who was responsible for "several anonymous and inflammatory papers threatening the lives and property of the inhabitants of Bideford". These papers had "lately been dispersed and dropped in various parts of that town". What the "papers" referred to is not stated, but in December 1802 the

London Gazette again carried news of threatening letters from Bideford.

This time it reprinted the text of one of these messages which had been addressed to Israel Doidge, a prominent merchant. The writer alleged that 200 people had agreed to force Doidge to stop exporting wheat from the Bideford area and instead "sell it out to the inhabitance or whomsoever shall apply for it". If he refused then "you may depend Death will be your portion, your house on fire, your property destroyed, your Family in flames, to dust and ashes this is your portion". The writer added, "You'll not deceive us by Night or Day as we keep a true watch on the Quay every Hour of the Night as well as the day." The letter ended with a general condemnation of such "villains" as Doidge who made money at the expense of his starving fellow townsmen. As a parting comment the writer reckoned that "the Devil will grind your head in powder as the mill grinds corn".

In this instance the Home Secretary promised a free pardon and 25 guineas reward for information. Anonymous letters were again used in the 1812 case, although this time they were directed at a Mr Skurray of Alverdiscott. He had incurred the wrath of the letter writer for informing on a poor man selling wheat in the town slightly deficient in weight. Skurray was warned to be cautious as the writer intended to murder him if possible, "If you chance to escape the hand that guides this pen," he wrote, "a lighted match will do equal execution. your family I know not, but the whole shall be enveloped in flames, Your Carkase, if any part shall be found, will be given to the dogs."

Another letter dated from Bideford talked of bets being made in the local market that Skurray would have left the area in six months or indeed that he would be dead within three. Again the Home Secretary offered a pardon to any informer and Skurray himself offered a 50 guinea reward.

In no case have I traced any arrest or trial of the letter writers. Such letters were a common way of expressing dissatisfaction, but it is rare they have survived in such detail – though their survival is a sad reminder of the harsher days in which our ancestors lived.

The extracts are taken from *Devon Extracts from the London Gazette 1665-1850* available from the North Devon Athenaeum.

North Devon Journal 28.9.1989

94. A MURDER MOST FOUL

No single crime exerts such a fascination as murder. This, the ultimate sin, has been uncommon in North Devon, but in 1821 a case hit the national headlines. It occurred two years prior to the foundation of the *Journal* and we have to go to the *Sherborne Mercury* to find our story.

In December 1821 twenty-year old Philip Chappell, an apprentice with Mr Baget, a Torrington glove maker, murdered his sweetheart and fellow-servant, Mary Stevens. The trial came on at Exeter in March 1822 and many local people gave evidence. The first of these was William Handford, a Torrington labourer, who found the girl's body one Monday morning in the mill leat at the bottom of Castle Hill. He called Thomas Vicary a surgeon who, after pronouncing her dead, found three wounds "inflicted with some weighty substance," and noted that she was "far advanced in pregnancy".

A whole succession of witnesses then appeared to depose that Chappell and Stevens had been "keeping company" and that the apprentice had been expected to make an honest woman of poor Mary. Chappell, however, appears to have had different ideas. When one Elizabeth Chambers asked him several weeks before the murder, "I suppose you intend to marry her", he brusquely replied. "I know nothing at all about marrying."

Mary Thompson of Castle Street was Mary's landlady and she recalled how her lodger had been meeting Chappell every Sunday night. William Passmore, a constable, gave evidence as to searching Chappell's house, where he found a newly washed pair of leather breeches whilst his fellow constable, William Thomas, found a pair of men's stockings, also newly washed. At this point, Chappell's parents identified the clothes as their son's and admitted that they hadn't washed them and didn't know why their son had done so.

When asked to explain all this damning evidence, Chappell replied, "My Lord, I am as innocent as anybody in the court. I loved her too well to murder her." The judge then went through the evidence again and the jury "without much hesitation" returned a guilty verdict. The judge then pronounced the death sentence and Chappell was carried away weeping bitterly with a "trembling, unsteady step."

Exactly a week later, the prisoner was brought to the scaffold outside Exeter prison in the presence of a huge crowd. During the preceding week he had admitted his guilt and confessed that he had kicked Mary down and drowned her.

North Devon Journal 2.3.1989

95. GRAVE ROBBERS WHO STRUCK NORTH DEVON

The silence of the grave is a truism – yet the grave has not always been so quiet. In the early years of the nineteenth century the infant science of medicine had a seemingly unquenchable demand for human bodies to dissect. Legally only hanged criminals could be anatomised (the polite term for dissection) so grave robbing was the only alternative. It was mostly confined to cities where the medical schools were situated, but graverobbers nevertheless made their appearance in North Devon on several occasions.

The first was in April 1829 at a committee meeting of the governors of the North Devon Infirmary in Barnstaple. During the meeting a Welshman turned up and announced himself to be a "body snatcher, and that the object of his visit was to make a tender to the medical gentlemen of his professional services". He was thrown out.

A month later, however, the *Journal* carried a long warning to its readers that "sordid and relentless Resurrectionists" were operating in North Devon – an area that had "been free from all anxieties relative to the safety of the mortal remains of our departed friends".

This warning seems to have put a stop to grave robbing though in July 1829 the *Journal* did print a long letter signed 'Medicus' of Bideford which set out the necessity for dissection if medicine was to improve.

All was quiet for two years until February 1831 when the *Journal* carried a report of an actual grave robbery at Barnstaple. The corpse was that of a man called Bishop who came from Torrington. He had fallen ill and entered the North Devon Infirmary where he died. His body was interred in St Peter's churchyard and the funeral was conducted by the Rev Luxmoore.

Mrs Bishop, however, soon afterwards received an anonymous letter telling her that "the remains of her husband were still in the

Infirmary". She hurried round to the Torrington Overseer of the Poor who accompanied her to Barnstaple and took out an exhumation order. The coffin was disinterred and "on being opened was found to be full of earth". The widow then rushed to the Infirmary where "after some little delay the body was surrendered to them, having been disembowelled and exhibiting signs of the commencement of dissection". Mrs Bishop put the "mangled remains" in a coffin and took them with her to Torrington for proper burial.

The Governors of the Infirmary discussed the case at their next meeting but in a curiously limp statement merely expressed "the most marked reprehension of the conduct exhibited on this occasion".

Interestingly the doctor(s) involved could not be arrested or sued as a dead human body was not legally recognised as having any value – and therefore stealing it did not mean a crime had been committed.

In 1829 though, the Burke and Hare case (where people were murdered to supply anatomists) had come to light and it, along with a similar case in London, had led to a national panic and the passing of the Anatomy Act in 1832. This laid down that all unclaimed bodies of workhouse inmates could be dissected – thus giving rise to the horror still expressed today by some elderly people of ending one's days in the workhouse or a 'pauper's grave'. These three references are the only ones I have found to the very Georgian crime of grave-robbing in this area.

Many people today of course will their bodies to medical science and many others carry a donor's card stipulating what parts of their bodies are to be used after their death. How human feelings change!

North Devon Journal 21.9.1989

96. WHEN THE POOREST RIOTED

1830 was a bad year for the poor – harvests failed, work disappeared and wages fell – adding further problems to the many hardships suffered by those on the poverty line. In Britain the poor reacted in time honoured fashion – they rioted. In North Devon the most serious trouble occurred at Swimbridge in December as the result of the greediness of local landowner, John Nott. Five of the rioters were arrested and their trial was deemed important enough to be held at Exeter a month later – and fascinating reading it makes.

The case for the prosecution opened with the testimony of Nott's servant Robert Bowden. He told how "a crowd of persons came to his master's house" on December 9 and demanded money and a reduction in rent and tithes. Nott had purchased the right to collect the local tithes – traditional rents paid to local clergymen – and as such the poor thought he should apparently share the money with them. Bowden thought their demands preposterous and told them to go, but one Richard Barrow said, "Damme your master shall have a warm shirt" which was taken to be a threat of arson.

A fellow servant, John Bear, said that he had heard another member of the mob, James Thorn, say of Mr Nott "You should have a bloody shirt." Bear estimated the mob at 50 strong and noted they were armed with sticks. The two servants only managed to disperse the crowd when they gave out free cider.

Thorn and Barrow were not so easily bought off, however, and they spread the rumour that the local landowners would meet with the labourers to settle their wage and rent demands on December 11 at Kerscott Hill, Swimbridge. On that day they apparently went round demanding that their fellow labourers follow them to Kerscott. To one young labourer Barrow said that "if the gentlemen did not raise their wages they would dip a handkerchief in blood and tie it on the top of the pole and carry it about" – as a sign of their violent rebellion.

On the 11th, Lord Ebrington a local magistrate who had heard rumours about the Kerscott meeting, rode there to see what was happening. He arrived to find a huge mob growing rapidly and "vainly tried to persuade them of their folly and danger of the course they were pursuing." All in vain, and the mob made a rush for Mr Nott's house 300 yards away. Lord Ebrington made a desperate attempt to turn them back saying that "what they were doing was a hanging matter" but even this could not stop them. On reaching the house they shouted and cat-called and Thorn tried to inflame them more by shouting that "we will take the gentlemen and lay their heads on a block that is the best way to serve them."

This dire threat, however, appeared to have the opposite effect in that it scared many of the men and they began to slink away although onlookers heard them muttering that "they would meet again on Tuesday, a thousand strong, when they would have their grievance settled." Various other witnesses were called and implicated three other local labourers – George Goff, Thomas Rowcliff and Philip Shaddick.

The prisoners were called to make their defence. Thorn alleged he had been told to go to the Kerscott meeting by one "Farmer Powell" – a suggestion that the labourers were 'encouraged' in their actions by local small farmers who would have felt the burden of tithe payments far more than landless labourers.

Richard Barrow "said he had a wife and five children in a state of starvation" whilst Shaddick had a wife, eight children and earnt "but 8s. (40p) a week". Both Rowcliffe and Goff alleged that only the threat of force had persuaded them to go to the meeting. In the event Thorn was gaoled for 18 months with hard labour, Barrow and Shaddick got a year each, Rowcliff nine months and Goff six months.

Within two years a great tide of reform swept Britain with the vote being given for the first time to the great mass of adult men. One can date the beginning of the end of such rioting from these sweeping political changes.

North Devon Journal 13.3.1986

97. HOW A TOWN'S POLICE FORCE WAS FOUNDED

May 1986 will mark the 150th anniversary of the police force in Barnstaple. In 1835 Parliament passed the Municipal Corporations Act which reformed many old, self-appointed and corrupt local councils and replaced them with the democratically elected town councils we see today. New powers and duties were given to these bodies – including the right to raise a professional police force paid for out of the rates money. Up until this time parish constables were elected annually from the ratepayers of the town – an election nobody wanted to win as the job was arduous, sometimes dangerous and always unpaid.

The new Barnstaple Town Council met in January 1836, and set up a Watch Committee whose first decision on the 26th of that month was to appoint three salaried night watchmen. They were to be supplied with "Great Coats, Staves, Rattles and Lanthorns."

These rattles were the forerunners of police whistles, though these men were not really policemen in the true sense. The advertisement that went out asking for men had one oddity in that the applicants were asked to tender for their own wages. Some 49 candidates offered themselves, their tenders ranging from 8/6 (42½p) to 15/- (75p) per week. The committee, however, could (or would) only offer 8/- per week in summer and 12/- per week in winter.

For some reason they disregarded a Mr Thomas Baker who had offered to do the job free and appointed William Gabriel, a local bailiff and town beadle, William Cousins, a plumber, and Thomas Norman. The committee also decided to turn one of the shops under the Guildhall into a 'watch-house' or police-station with two cells, a fire and a gas-light. The rooms are still there today, although they are now offices. At the same meeting they also decided to appoint a 'day constable' – the equivalent of our present policemen.

The first note of disagreement came when one of the councillors, Mr Arter, reckoned that the force was too small, saying "it was absurd to expect that the same men could do the duty every night. At Torrington, with scarcely a quarter of our population, they had appointed twelve policemen; and if the council of Barnstaple intended to have anything like an efficient force, they could not engage less than 15." He, however, was shouted down as the other members weren't too happy with the expense associated with hiring policemen. Indeed, Councillor Mortimer stood up and confided that "many of the most intelligent men in the borough had spoken to him upon this subject, and so far from thinking the measure necessary, they agreed with him that it would tend rather to disturb the peace than to keep it." An interesting idea if nothing else!

Councillor Bencraft answered the critics of the watchmen and planned policeman by saying that such a force would cure the "singing, fiddling, tippling and brawling" that went on in the town's public houses. His argument was ignored, however, and the council voted 11 to 7 against appointing a day policeman. The night watch was apparently continued, though the records are rather confusing.

The result was predictable. Crimes at night declined, while daytime ones increased. At the April meeting of the council, the

Mayor reported that between £60 and £70 had been stolen from local people in the Friday market by a gang of pickpockets, there being no constables on duty.

The Watch Committee hastily reassembled and on the 20th of May 1836 appointed John Evans, a bookseller who lived in the Cattle Market, to be the first Superintendent of Police in Barnstaple at 12/- per week with William Gabriel as his solitary police officer. They took up their duties three days later and these, for Evans, included the following, "He will be particularly required to be constantly on the alert in perambulating the streets during the day, to attend to the Police Office until two o'clock every morning, to direct the proceedings of the Night Police when appointed and to be very active on Market days in regulating the markets and the disposition of Carts."

Superintendent Evans only served 7 months before resigning, but at least the Barnstaple police force had been founded. Its later history was very turbulent for some years, but that is another story for another time.

North Devon Gazette 15.3.1985

98. DEPORTATION FOR BOY THIEF

I have often referred, ironically, to the 'good old days'...which were anything but. Public hangings, unsolved murders, child slavery and harsh living conditions do not paint a pretty picture of the past. But I recently came across a case which is appalling even by our ancestors' standards.

On Friday December 23 1836 a farmer's wife set up her stall in Barnstaple market. She sold a fair bit of produce and had some £6.42 in her handbag. In a moment of forgetfulness she put her bag down, and it disappeared. She raised the alarm and town constables made enquiries which led to 13-year-old Robert Ellis and his brother-in-law Robert Passmore, also 13.

They had been walking through town and had met nine-year old George Thorne. Coming to the market, then held in the streets around the churchyard, the older boys were "window shopping" when George said there was money in a basket. The youngster picked up the basket and ran, closely followed by the two Roberts, through Church Lane, across the churchyard and up Bear Street to open fields and there divided up the money. Hearing that the constables were searching they panicked and threw the money away. On questioning, however, the boys admitted their part in the theft.

Within three weeks they came before a judge. The jury had no hesitation in finding a verdict of 'guilty' against George for the theft. The judge then began to pass sentence with "the greatest tenderness and humanity" – a quite unbelievable phrase in the light of his actual decision. He was worried that if George was allowed on the streets with his companions he would "be led on to further crimes, till he came to an ignominious end." So to save him from himself the judge sentenced the nine-year-old to be transported to Australia for seven years adding that the Secretary of State might just change the sentence to one to be spent "in an asylum in England."

North Devon Journal 6.12.1990

99. GREAT ALARM THAT BROUGHT A DETECTIVE

In an earlier article I wrote about the creation of the three-man Barnstaple police force in 1836. In July 1839 the Watch Committee who oversaw the police passed a resolution which spoke of "frequent and daring burglaries lately in this borough, unparalleled in the recollection of the oldest inhabitant" and went on ominously to note "the insufficiency of the present police force to detect and bring to justice the burglars," from "want of experience".

Mayor William Avery was empowered to write to the Home Secretary and ask for an "efficient police officer" to be sent from London 'incognito' to detect the criminals. A day after this decision the local bank was burgled. This was noted in the Mayor's letter to the Home Secretary he adding that Barumites "are living in a state of great alarm, uncertain whose house may next be attacked."

A reply came three days later saying the Home Office would send an officer – his identity only being known to the Mayor and Town Clerk. His name was Charles Otway. He was Barnstaple's first detective and he immediately set to work by examining the bank and another house that had been burgled. He reported, "I am decidedly of the opinion that these burglaries were not committed by any experienced and regularly trained thieves, but by some idle and dissolute characters living in the town." He reckoned the same men were responsible in each case adding a recommendation "that a watchful and suspicious eye be kept by the police on the actions of several men whose names I have given to the magistrates of the borough."

Having completed the job he commented on the local police. One, named Chanter, would "become a useful officer" given the right leadership. The other two, Davey and Purchase "I conceive to be of little or no use as police officers". To replace them with better men the Watch Committee would have to offer better wages – higher than "the trifling salaries which I understand they receive." Two other things had caught the Londoner's attention – the poor quality of lighting in the town, which helped thieves, and "the great number of prostitutes which infest the streets of Barnstaple – a greater number in proportion than is to be met with in London." These women were "invariably connected with men of the worst characters, with whom they plan and carry into execution various thefts."

This report was printed in the local paper and was speedily followed by a petition for a better police force. Under this pressure the council were forced to act and rapidly appointed a Mr Steel as their new superintendent of police at £100 per year with two constables – Chanter and Fairchild – at 75p a week each, although extra lighting of the town was deemed too expensive.

North Devon Journal 26.3.1987

100. TRIAL IN 1844 STARTED ALLOTMENTS PLAN

Allotments are so much a part of the British landscape that few ever ask themselves what their history is, but in some cases they can have a long and fascinating background. In Bideford, for example, the idea of allotments can be directly traced back to a criminal trial in 1844. In January of that year one John Babb, a 27 year old labourer, was committed to Bideford prison to await trial on charges of theft. His case came up a week later when he was tried for receiving 3lbs of bacon, the property of Philip Colwell of Meddon Street, a farmer, knowing it to have been stolen.

The first witness called was Mary Anne Halls who was a parish apprentice to Mr Colwell. Such a person was usually an orphan or illegitimate child, whose apprenticeship indentures were paid for by the parish authorities. She worked at Mr Colwell's farm at Tennacott and admitted stealing the bacon to give to Babb but only after he had incited her to do it. Although she was the actual thief presumably her youth led the court to see Babb as the major criminal in the case.

She was followed into the witness box by Elizabeth, the wife of Philip. She told how she had discovered that the bacon was missing and called the policeman (there was only one at the this time). he came and quickly got the truth from Mary Ann whereupon he arrested Babb.

The luckless prisoner then appeared and, after some discussion of his poverty as an alleviating factor, was gaoled for six months. It was the account of his poverty, however, that led to a long and unusual editorial in the local newspaper. This dwelt on the fact that Babb's wages were six shillings a week – that's 30p today – on which he had to support a wife and three children. Out of this came one shilling for rent which left a shilling a week each for his family – or ½d each for each meal allowing three meals a day. This of course, left no money for fuel or clothing. As the editor put it, in the expansive rolling prose of the mid-Victorians, "What spirit can a man have to go to his daily toil, himself so scantily fed as to be scarcely able to stand at his work from early day to dewy eve, and his feelings (for the labourer has the feelings and sympathies of humanity!) exasperated by the constant recollection of the home of want and woe which his toil cannot ameliorate, and the wife of his bosom and the children of his youth whom the stern law of necessity dooms to be the sharers of his half-starved lot!" The editorial went on to suggest that the provision of allotments might help the labouring man to eke out such pitiful wages as were being paid in Bideford.

In succeeding issues many letters were printed arguing about the case. These ranged in tone from a Beaford farmer who alleged "the remedy must be in the man himself" and that Babb should not have married or had children if he couldn't support them. Others were more charitable and argued that 6 shillings a week was scandalously low and that the average wage in North Devon was 9 shillings a week, often being supplemented with free cider or ale.

These letters were answered by two from actual labourers who poured scorn on the idea that 9 shillings was the general wage claiming that in many places "the very best men" only got 7 shillings a week. One letter in support of Babb thought that his case would help improve the labourer's lot if action followed. It ended up with a choice example of Victorian paternalism when the writer added, "Let him (the labourer) have but a sufficiency of employment and with his present wages his children can be clad and fed, and he can live a happy and an honest man in that state of life in which it is the will of God to place him."

The upshot of all this fuss and publicity was a public meeting called in the Bridge Hall in Bideford (on the site of the present Torridge District Council offices) to set up the 'Bideford and Northam Allotment Society.' The meeting was convened by the Mayor, Mr Buck, who was voted the first chairman of the new society. His first action was to call for subscriptions to allow the purchase of land suitable for allotments. Some £60 was immediately pledged and the society soon purchased enough land to develop the first allotments seen in Bideford.

Poor John Babb served his term of imprisonment – one can only hope that he was given one of the new allotments on his release. Unknowingly perhaps, he was the true instigator of the system we see today, no longer organised on a private basis but still fulfilling the original hopes of the founders by providing the working man with an area of land he could work for himself to help feed his family.

Bideford Gazette 20.1.1984

101. ORGIES SPILLING INTO THE STREET

Mention of the Victorians to most people will conjure up pictures of solidity, economic expansion, sternness etc. etc. Above all else, however, there is the idea of extraordinarily severe moral attitudes summed up by the old tale that even piano legs were covered to preserve modesty. Such a picture is, of course, only partly true. Then, as now, there was a criminal underworld behind the law-abiding face of normal society. In many ways the Victorian underworld with its total hopelessness, misery and extreme violence was worse than we know today.

These nineteenth-century criminals were not just confined to the great cities – both Barnstaple and Bideford had their hard core of criminal elements. Very full records have been left behind, especially in the pages of contemporary newspapers which seemed to follow the same policy as many today believing that 'crime sold papers.'

The most extraordinary aspect of North Devon at this time, at least to my mind, was the number of prostitutes and brothels that existed. Every town except Ilfracombe appears to have had its quota, the largest number being in Barnstaple, and reference to the cases that came before the local magistrates over the years 1850-54 provide a fairly typical example.

In February 1850 the local paper reported, "Many of the respectable inhabitants of this town (Barnstaple) more especially those near and at the Boutport Street end of Back Lane, have for some time past been subjected to considerable annoyance by the manner in which the house number 5 in that lane has been conducted. Under the auspices of one Elizabeth Williams (herself not altogether a stranger to the police) it has of late been the nightly resort of the most dissolute and abandoned of both sexes, whose midnight orgies (not confined exclusively to the interior of the house, but extended to the streets, and thus annoying strangers passing as well as neighbouring residents) have become such an intolerable nuisance, that the adoption of legal measures was considered not only advisable but absolutely necessary."

The report is typical in that it concentrates not on the moral aspect but merely on the "nuisance" created to "respectable" neighbours. Back Lane was the original name of Queen Street and this brothel was near where the Post Office now stands. Elizabeth Williams was tried and found guilty on the evidence of the police, various neighbours and "a party who confessed himself to have been a visitor for a disgraceful purpose."

The judge's comments are of interest in that he admitted he was "disposed to be very tolerant of such establishments so long as they were conducted with unobtrusive decency, regarding them as things that must exist, yet could not suffer them to degenerate into common nuisances." Again notice the lack of moral condemnation, the main point being the nuisance created. Elizabeth, who was aged 24, received four months imprisonment with hard labour. She was released in August 1850 with a warning not to molest anyone – especially Pc Chanter who had arrested her.

In the same month that Elizabeth gained her freedom a girl called Lugg was charged with creating a disturbance late at night in Rendell's Court which was off Green Lane. The police were called by the proprietor of the house where she was found. This was a woman called Slader who, with her accomplice John Brailey, described as "an elderly man of uncouth appearance," were themselves charged as being brothel keepers. Slader's call to the police for help had obviously backfired on her because, after arresting Lugg, the police had proceeded to search the house and found several well-known prostitutes and their no-doubt embarrassed customers in bed. Brailey was fined 10 shillings with costs and Lugg was discharged with a caution, both sentences contrasting strangely with Elizabeth Williams' gaol term.

In May the following year Elizabeth Hazel of Myrtle Place was charged with "keeping a disorderly house." Again her appearance in court was due to the noise created by the "young women whom she was in the habit of harbouring." Among these girls was Elizabeth Williams! Indeed in every report one reads concerning Barnstaple brothels at this time one comes across the same names re-appearing. This particular case was dismissed on a complicated legal technicality.

Two months later "two notorious prostitutes," Ann Milton and Thirza Turner, "who have infested this town for some time past," were arrested and gaoled for keeping a brothel "of the most disgraceful and disgusting description" in Queen Street. The case was brought as a result, once again, of complaints made by respectable persons living in the neighbourhood.

In April 1854 the police were called to a house in Bell-meadow (where the car park next to Brannam's now is) to sort out a fight between a man and a woman. The woman, described as a "buxom lass of some 18 or 20 years", was asked "How do you get your living?" to which she could make no reply. The newspaper reporter evidently knew about the building in this case as he wrote, "It appeared to be the practice at this house to entrap these stupid fools on Saturday nights, when they received their wages, and get them drunk; some one of the women then taking her victim off to bed, another partner in the dark trade robs him of his money, and in the course of the night he gets bundled out penniless, mad with drink and rage."

The woman was dismissed on paying costs after the magistrates requested strenuous efforts by the police to close the place down. Their plea was answered a week later when the owner, one John Hill, was presented at court. He claimed that the house, which he admitted owning, was split into two and he had no idea what went on in the other half! He was fined 15 shillings but claimed to have no money. The magistrates decided to issue a distraint order on Hill to meet the fine but the police said that all the furniture had been removed earlier to prevent this happening. On hearing this the Bench ordered that Hill be gaoled, whereupon the money for the fine was rapidly produced and grudgingly paid over.

From just these few cases a few conclusions might be drawn. In strait-laced, stern Victorian England brothels were apparently seen as a 'necessary evil' and as such were tolerated by police and public alike. It was only when they became the focus of rowdy behaviour that public opinion and police action forced their closure. It is intriguing to speculate how many such places were carried on with "unobtrusive decency" that we do not know about. Certainly Victorian Barnstaple was a very 'colourful' place!

North Devon Gazette 13.1.1984

102. PRISON AT BARUM IN 1851 WAS A MIXED AFFAIR

Today Barnstaple may not be free of crime but it is certainly free of a prison. In the last century there were three successive Barnstaple prisons over a relatively short period.

The first of these, or the Old Prison as it was known, was a very insanitary place and was replaced in 1828-29 with a new building situated in the Square approximately on the site of the relief road. In 1851 the Government Inspector of Prisons visited Barnstaple and produced a report on the Borough Gaol and adjacent "lock-up." His report makes fascinating reading especially bearing in mind today's centrally-heated prisons with their ample diets and other comforts.

The Gaol "consists of 7 cells on the ground floor for males, and the like number on the floor above for females." Clearly Barnstaple was not a tremendously criminal place though it is interesting that males and females had equal numbers of cells – not a situation found today. He went on to say that "the windows of the cells are not glazed, the cold being excluded only by shutters, which renders the cells too dark for ordinary purposes." The coldness could hardly have been helped by the stone flooring. No fires were provided but in very cold weather the prisoners were allowed to cluster in a "dayroom" on the ground floor where there was a fireplace.

There was only one exercise yard though this was "very insecure" the Inspector noting that "a prisoner might easily climb up any one of the walls and the window sills from stepping stones." Any escaping convict, however, would first have to negotiate some poultry which were kept in the yard by the gaoler! The Inspector passes over this without comment – a similar reaction to his finding that "some of the cells at the time of my inspection were filled with wool and other articles, the property of the keeper." He was more annoyed that in the chapel, "a small room" over the lock-up house, there was no screen preventing male and female prisoners from talking with each other.

Turning to the furniture in the cells he noted that beds consisted of "a straw mattress, the stuffing of which is changed every 6 weeks" – presumably when it was totally verminous, the prisons (and prisoners) of Victorian Britain being notorious for their dirty condition. Bedding was four rugs but no blankets or sheets. Prisoners wore their own clothes, even if they arrived in rags.

Diet was based on a weekly menu. Each inmate got 144 ozs of bread, 1 lb of bacon, 4 lbs of potatoes, a pint of soup, ½lb of rice, 3½ pints of milk and, somewhat oddly, 2 ozs of treacle. Notice there was no fruit. This fare was luxurious when compared to that given to any imprisoned vagrants. All they received was 168 ozs of bread and all the water they wanted. After such a diet they would presumably hasten away – this being the whole aim of the sparse regime of course.

As to keeping the prisoners occupied, "the only labour performed in the prison is the picking of oakum (i.e. unpicking old tarred rope into separate strands), of which 2½ lbs are required to be picked daily by each prisoner; as however, no penalty attaches to the non-performance of the stipulated task, it is very doubtful whether that amount of work is ever performed."

Judging by his salary the gaoler was probably not to blame for this lax state of affairs. He earnt £40 a year out of which £5 went, as a pension, to the widow of his predecessor. His own wife acted as matron and was supposed to get £5 but apparently at this date the Council were refusing to pay her. The report noted that she had delivered three babies in the prison in the past year – this in addition to her normal duties.

The "lock-up" or temporary prison, next to the main prison was, optimistically, called the House of Correction. It simply consisted of two cells, 12 feet by 6 and 10 feet high. The only furniture was a "barrack-bed" with straw and rugs whilst the windows were unshuttered and unglazed making the rooms "very damp and cold."

The report paints a picture of a rather casual state of affairs and this continued for some years until the prison was moved. In 1874 a new prison was built in Castle Street adjoining the Cattle Market as the earlier prison had been condemned as unfit. This new prison contained 32 cells – a sad comment on declining honesty in the town. Unfortunately only four years later a new Parliamentary Act meant that all Barnstaple prisoners had to be taken to Exeter and the County authorities took over Barnstaple's new prison. To add insult to injury the town, in order to regain ownership of the building, was forced to buy it back for £1123. This last prison only disappeared in 1978 when it was demolished by the local council.

North Devon Gazette 4.11.1983

103. WHEN APPLEDORE SACKED THEIR POLICEMAN

As we approach the 130th anniversary of the county police force it is fascinating to look back at the beginnings of the professional, full-time force...and the local opposition generated by its introduction. One of the clearest examples of this resistance comes from Appledore. Before the county force was established the village followed the time-honoured practice of annually selecting a parishioner to be the honorary constable for the ensuing year. The post involved a great deal of work and was sometimes dangerous. To be chosen was not a cause for rejoicing.

In April 1852, however, the parishioners tried an experiment and appointed a full-time paid policeman. This was a Mr Baker "formerly of the detective force at Cardiff." The local papers reported, "The establishment of such an officer here seems to give general satisfaction."

This "satisfaction" seems to have soon changed for in February 1854 we read, "A good deal of unpleasant feeling has been manifested by some of our parishioners of late with respect to our policeman, in consequence of which a parish meeting was convened last week, to consider whether he should still be retained, or whether it is desirable to elect a paid constable in his stead, which latter proposal was unanimously decided upon."

We are not told how Pc Baker offended the locals but clearly he had and they decided to revert to electing a local man. The reason was probably economic – a locally-elected, poorly-paid man was far cheaper than a paid professional.

After four months without a policeman the Appledore correspondent of the *North Devon Journal* reported that the village had remained quiet and maintained itself in good order.

Poor Pc Baker had been suspended and in order to live had evidently become a shop-keeper. A court case in July 1854 however, showed the ex-policeman in trouble. Mr Rock, a miller of Marwood, had sold Baker a large amount of flour which the latter immediately sold very cheaply. Baker then made preparations to leave Appledore and return to Wales – without paying the miller's bill. The judge who heard the case ordered that Baker pay the debt and be imprisoned 40 days for fraud. Baker was in fact arrested on the very morning he was due to depart.

Thus ended the policeman's unhappy stay – but the penny-pinching people of Appledore had their just rewards when in the same month, the *Journal* correspondent reported on the breakdown of law and order in the now unpoliced village.

He wrote, "Since the opposition on the part of the landowners and tenant farmers to the appointment of a policeman in this place, the town has been frequently disturbed after midnight by the brawls of drunken men, and petty robberies are constantly taking place. Other breaches of the public peace in some respects more deplorable are every now and then witnessed."

He goes on to quote an instance where a poor Cornish woman was abused and stoned "by a rabble of several hundred children of both sexes." He adds another case concerning the servant of the local vicar who "on passing through Market-street was seriously injured by some boys intentionally driving a wheel-barrow against her. The night being dark, they escaped with impunity."

A mere 22 months later something was done. In May 1856 the "principal parishioners" put together a petition calling for a paid policeman once again to be stationed in Appledore. Indeed the state of Appledore was so bad that the new Chief Constable of Devon, after his appointment in 1858, gave orders to build a police station with cells in the village and appears to have despatched not one but two men to the village to police it.

North Devon Journal 10.1.1985

104. MURDER: WHEN CROWDS BAYED FOR REVENGE

Murder isn't common in North Devon...so imagine the thrill of fear that went through newspaper readers when they saw the headline "A Murderous Affair" in their *North Devon Journal* in May 1854. The victim, young glovemaker Mary Richards, of Langtree, was on her way home from taking completed gloves to her employer, Mrs. Wills, in Torrington when she was attacked at Cross Hill near Taddiport. Her assailant had beaten her unconscious, raped her and left her for dead behind a hedge where she was found next morning, still alive, by passing waggoner William Millman.

Attracted by her groans and seeing what state she was in he hurried for help – but by a terrible twist of fate the first person he met was Mary's mother who had come looking for her. Together they rushed Mary to Torrington Workhouse Infirmary where surgeons treated her terrible head wounds as best they could. As well as being viciously assaulted she had been robbed of 11 pairs of unmade gloves and 4/7½d (23p).

People in Taddiport said they had seen her in company with a whiskered vagrant whose description was circulated. The same day Barnstaple police arrested a suspect after "a desperate resistance" at "a house of ill-fame in Myrtle place." Llewellyn Garrett Talmage Harvey was a chimney sweep. He was clean-shaven but the police superintendent suspected his whiskers had only just been removed. Harvey had been living with his wife and child in Thornhill-head, Buckland Brewer, but was a common sight on the North Devon roads as he plied his trade.

He was taken back to Torrington where Mary identified him from her death bed. By this time a large crowd were baying for revenge but the police managed to get Harvey safely back to Barnstaple gaol.

The police then went to the prisoner's house and found a recently cleaned hammer which they considered to be the murder weapon. Pc Cole, of Torrington, matched Harvey's boot soles with footprints at the scene. A barber came forward to identify Harvey as a man he had shaved on the day of the murder.

Harvey was committed for trial on a charge of attempted murder but on that afternoon Mary died and the charge became murder. After an inquest she was buried a few days later at the Baptist Chapel cemetery, Langtree, her funeral attracting a large, silent crowd. Harvey came to trial at Exeter Assizes a month later and after evidence from numerous witnesses the Judge donned the black cap and sentenced him to death. He tried to interrupt but was dragged off to the cells apparently in a state of shock.

On August 4 he was publicly executed outside the walls of Exeter prison before a crowd estimated at 10,000. He is reported to have said "he would show the people he could die firm" and he kept his courage to the end – his last words on the scaffold being "Lord have mercy on my soul."

Just before this he had written his confession which was rapidly printed (along with many other catchpenny items) and sold widely. Edward Capern, the local 'postman poet' wrote on the case and a fund was opened to send Harvey's widow and child to Canada where they might start a new life.

For years afterwards Cross Hill became a place to be pointed out with dread.

North Devon Journal 7.2.1985

105. FAIR 'TARGET' PROVED TO BE REAL SHOCKER

The Victorians were nothing if not strait-laced. We have all heard how they went so far as to cover up piano legs and referred to cockerels as 'he-hens.' One only wonders, therefore, what the good people of Barnstaple made of a court case in September 1855.

James Smith of Green Lane in the town, described as "an itinerant vendor of nuts" and keeper of the Beehive public house, was charged with exhibiting a disgusting figure in The Square on Fair Day. The figure was produced in court being described as in the shape of a human body with two horns on its head whilst "over the lower part of the abdomen was a tin covering." Smith had made the figure himself and set it up as a target at the shooting gallery he ran at the fair.

He exhibited it for two days without any hindrance from the police until they were informed of its true nature whereupon they instantly seized it. The reason for this was that when anyone shot and hit the head a spring was activated which "suddenly removed the tin covering and exposed the lower parts of the body in a manner most outrageously indecent." A contemporary newspaper report added, "We cannot defile our pages by giving a closer description." The police took the view that it "must have had a tendency to familiarise youthful minds with all that is disgusting and obscene."

When asked why he had made it, Smith said it was "to zill a vew nuts" – a bag of nuts being the prize. The Mayor, who was the magistrate in the case, thundered that "No language...could express the disgust felt by the bench; if they allowed such conduct to pass unpunished they would be reprobated by every moral and decent person." He also attacked Smith personally for "doing his best to deprave the whole community...to pollute youthful minds – to do the work of Satan by tempting them from the ways of virtue." After this he sentenced Smith to a month's gaol.

Interestingly, the police superintendent noticed that "in the course of his experience he had seen many such figures, but this was the worst he had ever seen." Just how many such shows were there? Perhaps we would seriously question our ideas of so-called Victorian values!

North Devon Journal 7.4.1988

106. DISGRACED IN 19TH CENTURY BARNSTAPLE
In researching the past, one often comes across odd characters. These people seem to keep cropping up and one cannot but help becoming interested in them – in my case one of these was a

certain Elizabeth Williams. I first came across her in a newspaper report from February 1850 when she and Mary Jane Perryman were charged by William Lemon with the theft of his silver watch. William had been to Landkey and was returning to his home at Marwood, when he dropped in at a Barnstaple pub and later went to "a house of ill-fame, kept by Elizabeth Williams." Here in the course of events about which we read "much...is unfit for publication," he lost his watch. Charges weren't followed up as he got his watch back – no doubt he didn't want the publicity.

Brothels weren't uncommon in nineteenth century Barnstaple – bearing in mind that the town was a thriving seaport and that 'disgraced' servant girls had few honest options to support themselves in hypocritical Victorian Britain. Elizabeth's house was 5 Back Lane (now Queen Street) which was near the Boutport Street junction.

The theft brought the wrath of the local police down on her. Only a week after her court appearance, she was arrested as her house "has of late been the nightly resort of the most dissolute and abandoned of both sexes, whose midnight orgies not confined exclusively to the interior of the house, but extended to the streets, and thus annoying strangers passing as well as neighbouring residents have become such an intolerable nuisance that the adoption of legal measures was considered not only advisable but absolutely necessary."

Poor Elizabeth couldn't raise any bail and she was thrown into prison where she remained for two months until her case came to court. At her trial evidence was given against her "by a party who confessed himself to have been a visitor for a disgraceful purpose" to her house. Naturally she was found guilty and sentenced to four further months in gaol with hard labour. Her landlord, Harry Martin, was upset as she "was a weekly tenant and paid her rent very regularly."

Elizabeth was released in August with a caution not to break the law again. However, only eight months later she was arrested once again – this time as an accessory after the fact in a theft case along with another Barnstaple prostitute, Mary Ann Dendle. The case had begun when one Charles Ridd had come to Barnstaple in February 1851 to do some business. His business done, he had a few drinks and eventually ended up in Back Lane in Elizabeth's house. Here he was 'rolled' or robbed of £30 by two men, Thomas Stoyle and James Whitefield.

Charles immediately reported his loss to the police and at 5 a.m. returned to the scene of the crime. Here he met Elizabeth "leaning against the wall under an archway" and she asked "Are you the man that has been robbed?" – it seems that she wasn't the guilty party this time. She even asked, "If we try to get the money back, you will not do anything to the fellows?" She was as good as her word, and tracked down the two thieves who were in a carriage on their way to Bideford, but they refused to return their loot. The police then appeared and arrested the men plus Elizabeth and her friend, Mary Ann Dendle.

At the trial the men were transported to Australia – one for fourteen, the other for seven years. Mary Ann got a year's gaol and Elizabeth eight months – both with hard labour. Elizabeth had shown her mettle at the beginning of the proceedings by challenging three of the jurors and having them replaced. During the trial she "conducted herself with great violence, casting looks and words of the utmost indignation at the court and jury."

In the Census of 1851 Elizabeth appears in the Barnstaple Borough Gaol (then in the Square – approximately where the Relief Road enters) as "Elizabeth Williams – prisoner – unmarried – aged 27 – occupation: prostitute – birthplace: Combe Martin." Her friend, Mary Ann Dendle was only 20 and came from Braunton.

After this date I have not come across Elizabeth again – presumably Barnstaple became 'too hot for comfort' for the young woman and she left. Objective Victorian writers on the subject of prostitution were forced to admit that such women often ended up marrying well and settling down to a happy married life – I have a sneaking hope that Elizabeth managed this.

North Devon Journal 31.12.1986

107. ONE IN EIGHT BARNSTAPLE WOMEN PROSTITUTES IN 1856!

I wrote an earlier article about the brothels of Victorian Barnstaple and the colourful stories attached to some of them.

Further work in the nineteenth-century newspaper files has furnished me with many more colourful details.

One intriguing item came in 1856 when three "fallen women" came before Barnstaple Magistrates Court on theft charges. The journalist covering the case called the women, "Three out of the three hundred of that degraded class of females said to be found within the precincts of this borough."

Now in the 1851 census the female population of Barnstaple was found to be 4,831 – probably half of this number would have been too young or too old to be members of the "degraded class." This leaves us with the amazing statistic that 300 out of 2,400 (or 1 in 8) women in Victorian Barnstaple were prostitutes! So much for Victorian sobriety and staidness.

Although the editors and the public often attacked these women for their bad influence not everyone was so hard-hearted. In the mid-1860s the vicar of Barnstaple, the Rev Wallas and a helper, Captain Walters, founded the 'Barnstaple Female Rescue Association' which was designed to help local prostitutes who wished to leave the profession. The society was small with a very low income, while the work must have been trying as 'rescue' was often followed by 'relapse.' The main job of the society was to persuade the women to enter the 'Devon and Exeter Penitentiary' or the 'Exeter Home for Reclaiming Fallen Women.' The first of these, with its prison-like name, exactly summed up the idea of the society – to reform, one had to be sorry.

Women from Barnstaple were "kept in these institutions, trained in industrious habits, and provided, after suitable probation, with respectable situations as domestic servants." If they stayed in their 'situation' for a year they were given "a reward of a guinea." In 1872, for example, three women received this reward and exhibited "every sign of being really reclaimed" and were "leading useful and respectable lives."

In the association's annual reports letters were often quoted from these women about their successful escape from the streets. Thus in 1872 one girl wrote, "I hope the Lord will lead me in the right road as long as I live. I thank God I have seen my folly." Another girl returned to Barnstaple to visit the chairman of the association and we read that "It was not easy to recognise in this modest-looking neatly-clad, well-spoken visitor, the lost, poverty-stricken, unhappy girl whom they had sent to Exeter five years before."

At first sight the association and its aims were indeed praiseworthy but one is left asking questions. Why was the 'relapse' rate so high? The very strict regime at the two refuges was probably to blame – a distinct change from the free and easy life of the streets. Again why did so many girls enter into a life generally presented by Victorian writers as having only one inevitable end – degradation, disease and death?

In the Victorian world, dominated by men, and without any real form of unemployment benefit, prostitution was often the only avenue open to many poor girls, and one wonders whether the 'Female Rescue Association' might have been more successful if it had tackled the cause rather than the symptoms of the problem.

North Devon Gazette 4.1.1985

108. LAWS THAT FIRST BEGAN THE FEMINIST CAUSE
Currently there is much debate about AIDS and whether compulsory testing of suspected carriers should be carried out. The debate has, however, been held before. In 1864, 1866 and 1869 three Acts were passed by the British Parliament. The Contagious Diseases Acts allowed policemen to stop any woman they suspected of being a prostitute or "immoral" and have her examined to see if she were suffering from venereal disease. If she was diseased then she could be interned in a secure hospital for up to nine months until cured (or dead).

The Acts applied to eighteen "subject areas" of the country – all of them in southern Britain around military or naval depots and they were an attempt to control the spread of venereal disease amongst the Victorian armed forces whose manpower was seriously affected by these types of illness.

The Acts were, however, in typical nineteenth-century fashion, extremely demeaning to women; any woman could be stopped and the law only applied to women – men were not stopped or checked and certainly were not forcibly detained. If a woman refused to be examined she was taken to court and had to prove herself "virtuous" – she was guilty, until proven innocent. If found guilty of "non-compliance" she could be jailed until she changed her mind.

It is not surprising perhaps that women got together to fight these Acts supported by a few, more enlightened men. Indeed many feminists date the beginning of their movement from this date.

In June 1873 James Coutts, a member of the National Association for the Repeal of the Contagious Diseases Acts, spoke to a public meeting in Barnstaple. Only about 50 people attended – all men. The newspaper report of the occasion was heavily censored to avoid stress to delicate Victorian readers – but we can still get the flavour of it.

Coutts said he opposed the Acts because there was no provision "for the moral benefits of those who were subjected to it." He put the blame for the spread of the disease squarely on the armed forces whose men "lived a life of idleness, and therefore were tempted or driven to licentiousness."

He went on to denounce the inequality of forcing inspection on women but not on men and followed this up with a denunciation of State regulation of prostitution as he saw it. The only way to solve the problem was education and jobs for single women where they could actually earn enough to support themselves. Barnstaple was praised for its practical education programme via the local Female Rescue Association which had reduced the town's population of "women of the abandoned class" from 50 to 29.

He finished his long speech with a ringing passage, "By their sense of justice to all men, by their sense of domestic home love, by their sense of constitutional rights of personal freedom, he would ask them to press for a repeal of those immoral and unconstitutional Acts." This proposal was put to the meeting after some hesitation over who would actually propose it – no-one wanted their name attached too publicly! Once it was put, however, it was passed unanimously.

Even though most meetings held against the Acts went this way it was to be another 13 years before the Acts were repealed, having, it was thought, achieved very little. Coutts was almost certainly right – education was the only way to change human nature not legislation – a course as true today as it was then – even though the initials of the disease may have changed.

North Devon Journal 3.12.1987

109. LUNDY ISLANDERS IN RIOT

Many times during Lundy's varied history the island has acted as a refuge, for Royalists during the Civil War, for ships in distress, and latterly for those seeking peace and quiet. In 1866, however, the island played host to a very different sort of refugee – those escaping justice. In that year a case of debt came before the county court at Bideford but could not be settled as the defendant had fled to Lundy.

The journalist reporting the case noted that Lundy had become a shelter "to what was termed 'blacklegs' who resisted the authority of policemen and county court bailiffs." Apparently, once they arrived on the island these 'blacklegs' "smiled contemptuously on any pecuniary claims their creditors on the mainland might make on them." Police and bailiffs had gone to the island but had been "defied and resisted" to such an extent that the law officers retreated. The local judge, a Mr Petersdorff, stated that Lundy had no legal right of exemption from English law and anyone who refused to recognise this would be arrested.

Taking heart from this expression of support the local court bailiff, Mr W Ley, set out for the island "and promptly served three summonses." No doubt he congratulated himself on this but as he returned to the ferry boat the *Ranger* "he was assaulted on all sides by about 100 of the islanders, who commenced hooting, halloaing, beating kettles etc." until as the local paper put it, "they worked themselves into a state of fury."

It was then that they started hurling "gravel, turf, stones and every conceivable missile" at him – poor Ley retreated to the house of the island's owner Mr Heaven. Here he stayed until the mob had gone and only then did he emerge and, with an escort from the *Ranger* made his way down to the landing beach.

The crowd had, however, only hidden and they rushed out "hooting" and "yelling" and once more began stoning the hapless court official. The captain of the *Ranger* was hit in the face and the mob "then began to shout 'Pitch the .... over the cliffs! Pitch the .... over the cliffs!'"

The sailors and Mr Ley beat a hasty exit to the beach and only just made their boat in time as "A rush was made by the infuriated islanders, to upset the boat, and one huge ruffian seized the bailiff, who was sitting in the stern of the boat by the skirts of his coat and attempted to drag him into the water." In imminent danger of drowning Mr Ley only saved himself by clubbing his attacker with a stick. Even after launching the boat the islanders continued to throw "A perfect storm of missiles" at them.

Poor Ley got back to Bideford and reported to his superiors who were unsure what action to take. What made it worse was that "some of the chief men of authority on the island were smilingly looking on" while the attacks took place. Oddly enough nothing public seems to have been done though it appears that Mr Heaven received a very sharp warning and he defused the situation by persuading the 'debtors' to find sanctuary elsewhere. Whatever actually happened the occasion can only be regarded as another oddity in the history of this very odd little island.

Bideford Gazette 25.1.1985

110. HONEYMOONERS WHO SET A MAN FREE

"I am the only surviving member of the old Barnstaple Borough Police Force," ran the opening sentences of an article printed in the *Journal* in June 1935 recording the reminiscences of Richard Holland then living at 2 Salem Street, Barnstaple.

Mr Holland was born at Combrew Farm, Fremington, and had many stories to tell of his boyhood days in the village. He most clearly recalled the various celebrations in the village – especially "Revel Sunday and Monday" every July which "were kept up with great rejoicings." A stand was erected outside the New Inn from which "Waldron's band contributed a programme of music" whilst at the same time "revel sweet stalls lined the road."

Apparently the 'revel' had been even livelier in the past. Holland had been brought up on tales from his grandfather, William Sloley, about the old-style wrestling competitions in the early 1800's. The competitors followed a very 'free-style' type of fighting, the winners being presented with silver spoons. These "trophies were proudly worn by the winners in their hats on going in to church the following Sunday."

Other annual events in Fremington were ploughing matches attended by men from all the local areas. Large scale "rabbit hunts" and sheep-shearing competitions were also popular. The successful completion of the harvest was marked by a day of feasting when all the labourers were treated to breakfast, lunch, dinner, tea and supper! They almost certainly ate better on that day than on any other.

One other "annual festivity" took place in Fremington when "Mr Blackmore, the station master, used to give a supper at the Fox and Hounds Hotel to the employees at the station quay." The station was then a busy place "what with the discharging of vessels, and the operation of several lime-kilns, upon which much labour was engaged in conveying lime to farms."

Although cheered by these festive occasions Holland's life was hard and he was ambitious. In 1879 he enlisted into the North Devon Hussars and then in 1882 joined the Barnstaple Borough Police Force. At that time it consisted of a superintendent, a sergeant and 10 constables, the latter earning 18s. 7d. (93p) a week. Richard served 21 years and was presented with a purse of gold and an "inscribed album" on his retirement.

A few memories of his police service stood out such as accompanying the Mayor and Corporation "in a barge down the river on the occasion of the beating of the Borough bounds." On one occasion he was sent to Bideford to take possession of a Russian boat and its crew which had been in an accident with a local craft. A fight broke out between the two crews and "knives were freely used" though Holland managed to separate the two groups.

Nothing is new ... and vandals were common even in the 1880's as Holland shows when he talked of Queen Anne's statue "often adorned in the most grotesque attire, and the Albert clock and the fountain in the Square were frequently informally decorated." One night he returned to the police station to find it "surrounded with plants and flowers that some of the young bloods had transported from various gardens in the town.

His oddest occurrence was on Barnstaple station when he was with two handcuffed prisoners bound for Exeter jail. A train from Ilfracombe drew in and a man got out and asked what the prisoners had done. Holland replied that they were being gaoled for non-payment of fines – upon which the man replied, "I am on honeymoon and I would like them released if possible." He backed up his words with a cheque to cover the fines and, as Holland says, "I immediately took off the handcuffs and released the men." A large crowd that had gathered cheered both Holland and the 'Good

Samaritan' but the ex-policeman added, "I was rather worried ... until the cheque handed me had been honoured."

North Devon Journal 3.1.1986

ODDS AND ENDS

111. WHEN PLAGUE SWEPT THROUGH BARNSTAPLE

In earlier articles I wrote about the parish registers of Barnstaple and Bideford and, using early 19th century entries, showed what they could reveal about life – and death – at that time. Earlier entries also have a story to tell – especially the burial entries from the mid-16th century.

From 1539 until 1545 the average number of burials in the town was 40 a year. In 1546, however, there was a marked change. The first ominous note was sounded when, at the beginning of September 1546 there is a note in Latin "Syc hic incept" or "Plague begins here." What the disease was is unknown – it could have been the dreaded bubonic plague that periodically swept Britain or it might have been typhus or the odd-sounding 'sweating sickness'.

It is impossible to tell how it arrived in North Devon though there is an entry for August 23 1546 noting that Peter a "pantynkler of Exeter" had been buried. Perhaps he brought the infection with him or possibly a ship pulled over the bar with the flea-carrying plague rats on board. We can never know but one thing is certain – the disease spread rapidly and was a killer.

From September to October 27 1546 80 burials are recorded – twice the annual average in just two months. Children and adults suffered on the same scale. On October 12, for example, William, son of Dennis Curke, was buried – followed a day later by Joan his mother and Katheren his grandmother. On several occasions five people were buried in one day.

The registers have a gap of 13 days until November 10 – possibly the vicar had too many deaths to record. From then until the end of November another 45 people were buried. In December numbers began to decline – possibly the cold weather was keeping the rats in their nests or people were keeping themselves isolated from neighbours out of fear.

There is another break in the records from December 9 until February 25 1547 which could hide another increase in deaths. Another possibility is that the town's cemetery next to St. Peter's was full and 'plague pits' were opened outside of the town. Not being consecrated ground the vicar may not have bothered recording the burials there. It is interesting that when recording again commenced the entries were in a different hand suggesting that the vicar himself had succumbed to the disease.

The numbers dying may have fallen but over March, April and May 1547 another 40 people were buried – not as high as in the preceding few months but still much above the usual. By the summer of 1547 the disease seems to have disappeared – doubtless to the relief of the survivors in the town. Over the next eight years the burial rate returned to its usual average of 40 per year.

By estimating the number of deaths in the missing months we can reckon that some 200 people died in this particular outbreak – at a time when the town's population was only around 2,000. Thus roughly one in ten had been killed. The reasons were simple – lack of hygiene, overcrowding of old houses and the primitive state of medical knowledge. Once the plague arrived these early Barumites could only pray that they would be spared and the disease would soon abate. It was another 33 years before the town once again experienced the plague though not on such a scale as this terrible outbreak.

North Devon Journal 22.8.1985

112. PAID 2P FOR A CRIER'S CALL

The office of Mayor is now sadly diminished. Local government re-organisation has taken its toll and from a position of great power in the community the Mayor now fulfils just a symbolic role for the most part. It is interesting to look back to earlier times to see the all-powerful Mayor dispensing justice and favours and actually running his own town (women Mayors being a modern innovation!). Each year in Barnstaple at the end of his term the Mayor made up his accounts and these have come down to us today. A typical one was drawn up by John Baker, Mayor in 1715-16. The town's income came from the market tolls and rents on land and buildings and these accounts yield little of human interest. However, the expenditure is a different matter.

They began in October 1715 when Mr Baker came to office and let the tolls to the highest bidder. This job was evidently a thirsty one as eight gallons of wine, two bottles of sherry and one of "Canary" plus 22 "Bottles of Ale" were needed to complete it – at a cost of £3.89. Five days later 45p went on "powder spent in fireing the chambers on the day of election of members of Parliament" – an apparent reference to heating rather than shooting.

Somewhat oddly Mayor Baker had to settle up a bill incurred two years before when £3 went on wine "being a day of publick rejoycing for the victory in Spain" with another £2.84 being "spent at the Swan in the evening". This was during yet another of Britain's interminable eighteenth-century wars.

Rather more prosaic entries then follow – 16½p for five "quire of paper" for keeping the accounts with John Conibear being paid for "binding ruleing and alphabet" the said paper. In January a new set of bread weights was purchased for the town from London whilst "soft wax" for sealing documents was bought locally. One common entry was 2p for a "hue and cry" – a payment to the Town Crier for "crying" or announcing a theft or other crime and asking townspeople to both supply evidence and be on their guard.

Two payments went to cover the costs of the beadles' suits – "Paid George Exter for makeing the beadles cloaths" 75p and "paid Mr Mounier for the beadles hatts" 87p. The beadles were the Mayor's officers and their hats must have been very ornate to have cost more than the suits – the hat maker Mounier was one of the Huguenots who fled to Barnstaple from France and made such an impact on the town.

Other officials were also paid by the Mayor from the town incomes. Thus George and Jon Coulscott were paid 12½p "for beating the drums to give notice of bringing in th'arms into the hall." Presumably this refers to an official survey of the weapons held by the local militia men – though I am open to suggestions. There was even 12½p for "Widow Carwick for sweeping the High Cross and Shambles" or outside the present church gates and along Butcher's Row.

And so the entries continue over five pages. The receipts totalled just over £448 with expenditure coming to a little more than £412. It is very difficult to compare prices between then and now but one might multiply the totals by one hundred times to get a modern equivalent – clearly being Mayor at this date was big business!

North Devon Journal 4.9.1986

113. WHEN RIVERS AND LIMEKILNS WERE DEATH

Records of inquests are rare survivals from the past, probably because coroners were always private individuals and not State employees and their records were their own property. Luckily, however, a few have survived for Barnstaple, and they make fascinating reading. They date from the 1730's and 1740's and most follow a set pattern. There is usually an order to the Sergeant-at-Mace of the town (the Mayor's mace bearer – an office that still survives) to summon 24 "good and lawful men" to "sit on the body" of the corpse. Nobody actually used the body as a seat but the 24 jurymen did have to view the deceased – not a very enjoyable business in most instances!

In the first surviving case, from August 1735, coroner Thomas Harris was holding an inquest into the drowning of John Sandis. Two witnesses, Lewis Norris and John Blaney, both of Barnstaple had been standing on the Long Bridge and had seen Sandis strip off and swim in the river near the Litchdon lime kilns which used to jut out from what is now Taw Vale. The witnesses "saw a large fish leap near him" and Sandis began swimming after it but soon disappeared from sight. The jury returned a verdict of accidental death and all 24 signed or made their mark as well as impressing a wax seal on the paper noting their decision. The coroner and three aldermen also signed and sealed this paper making it an imposing document.

Some inquests reveal fascinating sidelights on the history of the people and town. In March 1740 Joan Milton was the subject of a fatal accident. She, with three fellow workers, Anne and Priscilla Drew and Ellizabeth Velley, were handling a load of salt on a vessel moored at Barnstaple Quay when Joan, who had "a sieve full of salt on her head" overbalanced and "reeled backwards" overboard. She was quickly rescued but was "taken up speechless and dyed in a very short time after". Women dockers were a common sight around North Devon with so many of the menfolk away at sea. Indeed the women of Appledore were renowned for strength developed through unloading limestone from South Wales. The river was a dangerous place if we are to judge from the number of fatalities in or on it.

Another main cause of death was the limekilns which provided a dry, warm haven for the local poor and other vagrants. Unfortunately fumes produced in these kilns could, and did, poison those who sought refuge in them at the wrong time. In November 1737 John Wilkey and Thomas Honeywell found the body of George Webber in a kiln owned by a Mr Tucker. He had been overcome by fumes.

But one case shows us a worse death. In 1742 Thomas Drewet was found dead. It was noted during the inquest that "for some time past he hath been lunatick and out of his senses." The poor man cut his throat with a razor. Such suicides were denied burial in consecrated ground their bodies usually being buried at a cross-roads with a stake through the heart to prevent their ghosts walking – a practice that survived until the mid-nineteenth century.

North Devon Journal 20.12.1984

114. CLUE TO ORIGINS OF KINGSLEY'S *WESTWARD HO!*

It is well-known that Bideford was the home of Charles Kingsley whilst he wrote his classic *Westward Ho!* He came to the town in 1854 and rented Northdown House, which today forms part of the Stella Maris School. The house still boasts a beautiful curving staircase which Kingsley would have known for apparently he wrote the book in a back room on the first floor overlooking the garden.

Westward Ho! itself is one of that large band of 'unread classics' – those books that people have heard of but few have actually read. For the most part it seems too heavy-handed and slow moving for our modern tastes. Its long moralising passages do nothing but interrupt the flow of the story.

All writers on Kingsley have noted how he used local North Devon settings and local people as a basis for characters and scenes in the novel. His descriptions of Bideford and the local area are fairly accurate and give a great deal of verisimilitude to the story. In a letter to his brother, written just prior to beginning the book, he says he wishes to live in Bideford "To be on the spot to enable me to get some local colour." Behind the excitement of the central tale there runs a strong anti-Catholic strain. This is not surprising when one considers Kingsley's marked 'low-church' views and the fact that when the story was written Britain was going through a marked period of 'No Popery' and anti-Catholicism.

The novel is said to have been based on local events but what they were has never been discovered or made clear. During recent research, however, I feel I may have stumbled across one strand of the original story that fired Kingsley's imagination.

The roots of the tale go back to 1685 when one Elizabeth Chester of Arlington in North Devon was eleven years old. Brought up as a member of the Church of England, she embarked in this year for Jamaica with her uncle. Her father was a widower who apparently was quite content to see her go. On the passage, however, they were attacked by Turkish pirates near the Spanish coast. There was "a sharp engagement, in which many of the English were kill'd and amongst the rest her uncle." The ship managed to escape and travelled on to Madeira where Elizabeth, totally destitute, became a servant to an English family until 1696.

In that year she married Manoel Cardosa de Vasconcellos, a local doctor, the ceremony being performed by an English naval chaplain. She was careful to note that during her marriage she never gave up her Protestant faith though married to a Catholic. In 1704 whilst her husband was on a voyage to Brazil she "fell dangerously ill, and being light headed, the parish priest came into her house and gave her the sacrament" – that is, the last rites according to the Catholic church. She herself remembered nothing of this afterwards.

When she recovered she was told "that she had turn'd her religion, and must conform to the Romish church". She refused and was consigned to the Bishop's gaol where she stayed seven months after which she was sent to the Inquisition at Lisbon. Here she was treated as an heretic, being imprisoned for a further nine months, whipped, branded and having her foot burnt in "a red hot slipper". Under this treatment she broke down and signed a recantation of her faith. Being then released she fled to some English merchants in the city who took her in and sent her home to Devon.

The story is related in a monthly publication called *The Gentleman's Magazine* for 1745. I am not sure how true it is – no Chester family, for example, appears in the parish registers of Arlington. Also it must be said that Bonnie Prince Charlie came to Britain in this year and raised an army of Highlanders which gave rise to many anti-Catholic articles in the English press.

Leaving aside the finer points of authenticity, one can now suggest links with Kingsley's story. Those who have read *Westward Ho!* will remember that it hinges partly on the sufferings of a woman at the hands of the Inquisition. The woman was Rose Salterne, the original "Rose of Torridge". In Kingsley's story she was burnt at the stake along with the brother of the hero Amyas.

Is it too fantastic to suggest that we have here one of the original sources of Kingsley's story? Such a tale as that of Elizabeth Chester would have been told and retold many times in North Devon and Kingsley, with his love of folklore, must have heard it during his many holidays spent in this area when a child. Its powerful imagery of good and evil with the binding theme of revenge would have appealed greatly to the author's sensibilities. As far as I'm aware no other source has been suggested. A story using local scenery and local people that is itself based on local events would appear to make sense – I will say no more than that. It is a suggestion with a fair possibility of being true.

Bideford Gazette 8.7.1983

115. A MYSTERY OF MISSING BOOKS

In 1765 a John Watkins was baptised at St Mary's church in Bideford. He grew up in the town leaving it to be educated for the nonconformist ministry. In 1785, however, he joined the Church of England and began a school somewhere in Devon. Three years later he published some sermons preached in Bideford and in 1792 he published *An Essay towards the History of Bideford* – the first book about the town.

According to the preface this book "originated in the intention of giving some small assistance to the present ingenious historian of Devonshire" which apparently refers to Richard Polwhele who published his county history in 1793. Up until very recently I and everyone else assumed that Watkins was the first local historian of

Bideford. A chance find at the Devon Record Office has, however, altered my view.

In a small anonymous notebook presented to Mr Glynn, Mayor of Bideford in 1857-58, occurs the follows, "There are two histories of Bideford, the first is now rarely to be met with, indeed only two copies have ever come within my recollection. It is supposed to be the production of Mr Donn, a schoolmaster here." The second is Watkins' which the writer notes "is generally acknowledged to be very incomplete."

The Donn referred to is Benjamin Donn (1729-98) famous as the author of the first detailed map of Devon in 1765. His father was a churchwarden at Bideford and his son was brought up in the town. We do know that Benjamin was the author of a short essay on the history of Bideford which appeared in the *Gentleman's Magazine* for 1751.

If, as the writer asserts, Donn also produced a history in book form then no-one seems to have a copy now. The writer refers to one "which was in the possession of Mr George Buck of Daddon ... and is now at Moreton" (in Bideford). No copy is listed in any bibliography I have consulted and I would give my eye-teeth to see one.

There is also a further mystery; in the Record Office there is a letter dated June 1852 written by John Wilson, a Bideford bookseller, to a noted antiquarian James Davidson. In it he enclosed a manuscript advertisement written by Watkins which reads in part, "Preparing and nearly ready for publication, The History, Antiquities and topography of the Town and Neighbourhood of Bideford in the county of Devon." This apparently covered every village between the Torridge and Hartland as well as Lundy, the whole being illustrated with "a map, plan, and several views." The mystery, however, is whether the author ever produced any of this projected work and, if he did, where is his manuscript today?

North Devon Journal 13.4.1989

116. A STORM OVER NORTH DEVON'S FIRST HISTORY

The first person to publish a history of North Devon was one Thomas Cornish in September 1828. He had been preceded by historians of the whole county, but to him goes the honour of first tackling just this area in any depth. The book had a wonderful title, *Sketch of the Rise and Progress of the Principal Towns of the North of Devon together with the scenery and local advantages.* It cost 10p and was printed in Bristol. Copies are very scarce today.

Unfortunately, attacks on the book began only a few weeks after publication when a Mr Brooks of Pilton wrote a scathing poem which appeared in the *Journal.* This prompted Cornish to a reply printed in an Exeter paper and this in its turn gave rise to a magisterial response from the editor of the *Journal* himself, J Avery. I have read many such literary attacks but this one stands head and shoulders above any other for its marvellous use of language. Avery took a whole column to himself and began satirically by saying that the piece in the Exeter paper couldn't possibly have been written by Cornish as it was so bad; it was "no doubt scribbled by some aspiring witling, who is anxious to see his trash fill up a whole column of some minor periodical, and who has presumed to hide a farrago of nonsense and asperity, under the transparent veil of your illustrious name".

Avery reckoned Cornish was "entirely void of learning, genius, or any other qualification" to write a history of North Devon. Strong stuff, but it got stronger. Cornish had apparently cast aspersions on some of Avery's friends. For this he lacked "reason or common sense" and his work was "disgraceful in its matter, its ideas and its language". Indeed Cornish as an author was a "scurrilous ignorant donkey".

At this point Avery drew breath and admitted that his only reason for attacking Cornish was "to display to that very small part of the world which takes interest in your productions, particularly to those whom your scrawlings have in some degree injured, the stupidity, negligence and asinine tastelessness of that host of plagiarism you have presented to the public as the genuine effusions of your shallow brain".

Avery was clearly enjoying himself as he went on to sketch Cornish's career. He was born in Barnstaple and at school there he was distinguished by "the prominence of his parts, which were often publicly exhibited as an example to his schoolfellows" (i.e. caning). He was apprenticed to a local printer but "kicked out" before finishing his term. Avery himself then took him on in his printing works but after two years Cornish left under a cloud and became an advertising agent for a London soap firm. When Avery began the *Journal* in 1824, Cornish sent him "large and expensive" weekly parcels of his writing which Avery refused to print as they were so bad.

After such an attack lesser men might have given up but Cornish was made of sterner stuff. He went on to turn the tables on his attacker and publish his own newspaper. Although "well got up" it wasn't a success and Cornish sold out after a year. Another indictment of his lack of literary skill perhaps? Whatever the case, clearly Avery had the last laugh and Cornish soon after disappeared from the literary history of North Devon.

North Devon Journal 3.8.1981

117. WHERE THERE'S A WILL

We are all nosey, or perhaps I should say curious, about other people's wills. Our local papers print details of how much the recently deceased left, and everyone reads these lists with interest. This interest is, of course, doubled in the case of local or family historians who can get valuable details of the past from old wills. Unfortunately here in Devon, all our wills dating from before 1857 were destroyed by fire during a bombing raid on Exeter during the war.

This calamitous loss can partly be made good by reference to a collection of Devon wills made for tax purposes by the Inland Revenue and dating from 1812 to 1857. I have slowly been reading through the 130 or so made by Bideford residents and they contain some fascinating material. They all give name and occupation of those who made them and so we find a linen draper, an innkeeper, a hatmaker, a timber merchant, a victualler, a printer and a joiner among others. Women are usually just described as either a widow or a spinster.

All follow a general pattern, with legacies being left to close relations coming first followed by those to more distant relations and friends. Thus Thomas Brook, a draper, left £200 to Elizabeth Hodge of Bideford in 1832 – a truly tremendous sum in those days. I have yet to find someone being left the proverbial 'shilling' but the oddly-named Class Brook left her three children just 1 guinea each (£1.05).

John Bishop, who died in 1845, left his money to his son John as well as a deathbed declaration that this child was "by Mary Bishop otherwise Mary Minards formerly of Polperro in the County of Cornwall who lived and resided faithfully with me for many years prior to her decease." Presumably they never married and poor John senior wanted the world to know that he accepted paternity of her son.

Most legacies are in the form of money, but other more personal belongings are willed away. Charles Colwill, described as "yeoman" of Bideford left his "best bed with the Bedstead, Bedding, and Bed furniture" plus 12 china cups and saucers to his wife Grace in 1826. James Clifton, gentleman, left the family bible and prayer book plus three volumes of sermons and two volumes of "lectures" to his son Thomas as well as 11 silver tea spoons and other silver. This James seems to have gone round his house just before his death in 1835 earmarking every item for someone as his will goes into great detail as to who gets what – even to the extent of listing "flat kettles" and "the metal pan for boiling pickles." Susanna Bartlett, who died in 1813, left careful instructions as to who received her jewellery. Her diamond ring, for example, went to one daughter, while "a small pair of diamond earrings" went to another and "my gold watch" went to a third.

The most important legacies often came last when the person making their will named those to inherit their property. Some, such as John Cotton in 1813, simply left their house to their spouse. Others, however, had much more property to leave. Richard Balch, a sawyer, left his house, three other houses in Torrington Lane and a pub called the Currier's Arms at East-the-Water to be equally divided between his three sons, Richard, Samuel and Stephen. One wonders how they divided five buildings between three men!

One of the most complex wills I have come across is that of Richard Taylor, who described himself as a joiner and who died in 1842. At his death he owned all of New Row (which he probably built) plus houses and shops in Allhalland Street, Tower Street, Buttgarden, Mill Street, Lower Gunstone and Coldharbour. These were left to his six children. One of his daughters had married Edward White, a local builder, who went on to become Mayor twice and the biggest builder in Bideford, being responsible for, among other places, Lavington Chapel, the Town Hall and the present Midland Bank building on the Quay. Another daughter married a local printer and Richard's complete web of family and business connections intertwined with most of the main families in the town.

These are but a selection of the wills I have so far looked at – many questions have been answered but, as ever in local history, many new ones have been posed. Perhaps I will return to this subject at a later date when I have completed my researches.

Bideford Gazette 2.1.1986

118. 166 NOT OUT FOR CRICKET CLUB OF NORTH DEVON

Kipling may have described cricketers as the "flannelled fools at the wicket" but cricket still has high esteem among the British. Here in North Devon we apparently have one claim to cricketing history in that the North Devon club has the longest unbroken existence of any – with the exception of the MCC itself. This claim was put forward in a *Journal* article marking the club's centenary in 1923.

The club dates from 1823 when it was set up by a "few devoted enthusiasts" and was based in Barnstaple. Its first pitch was at Pottington and here it stayed until 1837. In those days it must be said that the game seems to have been secondary to the social activities of the club. Unfortunately few records of those early days have survived. The first mention I have found comes from the *Journal* in May 1827 when a small note on the Barnstaple Cricket Club says that their clubhouse could hold 100 people.

The first actual match report appears in July 1827 when North Devon played the Gentlemen of Teignbridge, a match which the visitors won. At this period Teignbridge appears to have been the only other cricket team in Devon – which must have made the job of the fixtures secretary fairly straightforward! The social aspects are well shown in a match report from July 1828 when we read that at the club dinner some 150 people attended, being "the greater proportion of the rank, beauty and fashion of the neighbourhood."

It was in 1837 that Colonel Cleveland of Tapeley Park, Instow invited the club to move to the site it still occupies on Instow sea front. The centenary report describes the "quaint old thatched roofed pavilion" which had survived various fires over the years including two in the early 1890's.

As the years advanced so the game became more serious, though it still seems very casual to us. In the 1860's for example the club members would meet every Thursday during the Summer, split into 2 sides (sometimes with only 6 a side) and play from mid-day until 3 p.m. when dinner was taken. This consisted of fresh caught Torridge salmon, cold beef and cheese followed by "hot grog and baccy". The match was resumed later and sometimes "considerably later" – surely an understatement. At this date the local train from Barnstaple to Bideford drew up at the "very gates of the ground" to allow the visiting team and their supporters to alight, which seems a very civilised way of behaving.

The 1923 article also mentions some of the club's historical exhibits, then in the pavilion. These included the dinner gong like a "huge brass tray" which still exists, various cricketing prints and even "a stuffed bird that was killed some years ago by a ball bowled by Mr J Tweedie of Braunton which struck it as it flew across the pitch." The unfortunate bird was mounted with the ball that killed it. The centenary year was marked not just by the article but also by a special match played by teams dressed in "garb similar to the olden days," with top hats in evidence.

Will a similar match be played in 1998 to mark 175 years of North Devon's cricketing history?

North Devon Journal 31.8.1989

119. A DEAD MAN'S HAND PROVIDES A CURE FOR ALL

I have written before about the folklore of this area – yet it can still come as something of a surprise to discover just what bizarre things our ancestors believed in. There seems to be a general rule here – the less they knew about something the odder their stories and beliefs about it. A good example of this is medicine – we still don't actually know a great deal about our own bodies – but our ancestors knew even less as a case from Combe Martin shows.

In July 1824 a man was found in a hay loft there "apparently dead". The discoverers of this gruesome find made "a minute examination of his person to discover if any external marks might be found whereby to ascertain the cause of his death" but could find none. That he was actually dead was demonstrated by the powerful stench his body gave off. Then, as now, a suspicious death meant that the coroner had to be called in and a horseman was dispatched to Barnstaple to fetch him.

In the meantime, however, a local woman "long afflicted with a sore leg" made her way to the hay loft where the body still lay. Here she proceeded to "strike" the dead man's hand over the sore leg in the expectation of a cure. This "striking" was a well-known and widely believed remedy at that time – though it seems totally weird to us today. Unfortunately for the woman as she was doing this the 'dead' man suddenly revived "and to the consternation of the poor woman, and to the surprise of the rest who stood around him, he bawled out with a stentorian voice 'let me alone'." He had in fact been dead – dead drunk – so the woman didn't get her cure. Indeed she probably needed medical treatment for shock after seeing the man's revival.

There are many references to this supposed cure in the literature of folklore though I can only find two for Devon. One was at Plymouth in 1879 and the other occurred in November 1890 at Hartland. In this latter case an unnamed villager used the hand of a drowned sailor who had been shipwrecked when the s.s. Uffington struck the rocks at Hartland.

I don't know how successful this operation was in these cases – presumably, in this more scientific age, the chances of anyone carrying out a test are rather remote!

North Devon Journal 27.10.1988

120. SPORTSMAN WHO WALKED AWAY FROM HIS DEBTS

We take sport for granted today. Yet in the past there was very little in Britain – horse-racing, wrestling, boxing, hunting and fishing were about the only sports our eighteenth and nineteenth century ancestors indulged in. There was one other, however, pedestrianism or long distance walking. This might seem odd given the state of the roads then, but the sport was highly regarded.

One champion was a Mr Sutton who came from Kent and made his living by accepting bets as to his prowess; in 1825 he came to North Devon. He began taking bets as to whether he could walk from Barnstaple to South Molton and back again three times a day for three successive days – a distance then of 72 miles. He began well by completing the first day easily but on the second day, when he arrived for the second time at Barnstaple, he decided to show-off and leapt over the rails which surrounded the Square – and managing to sprain his leg. Thus lamed he began walking back to South Molton but rapidly exhausted himself and "was compelled to relinquish his undertaking at Swimbridge."

Nothing daunted he waited two weeks and set off to try again. Although the weather was "unfavourable" he managed to complete the wager this time and then announced that he would walk from Barnstaple to London and back again within five successive days for a purse of ten sovereigns! Nobody took him up on this amazing offer and the next episode of his stay in North Devon was rather sad.

A week after completing his walk to South Molton he carried out "a much commoner feat by walking off with the money he had procured to the discomfiture of the landlady of the house, where he lodged."

North Devon Journal 30.12.1988

121. 'MISSING' YEARS OF HISTORY

In writing these articles over the past few years I have read my way through the complete run of the *Journal* from its inception in July 1824 up until 1914 – that is except for the 18 months between June 1825 and December 1826. The reason for this is simple – the original issues for that period have completely disappeared. However, Barnstaple library has recently purchased a microfilm run of *The Sherborne Mercury* which covers the missing months and I have now read through them extracting North Devon news – and what news.

Barnstaple was experiencing something of an economic boom. In July 1825 it was announced that a new customs house was to be built in the town while two months later Symonds & Co., the owners of the lace factory at Rawleigh, leased some land in Newport Road from the corporation in order to build a new "lace manufactory" – thus laying the foundations for one of Victorian Barnstaple's most important industries.

At the same time as this was happening a new quay was begun at Pilton in order to help the collier (coal carrying) ships to berth more easily. That this was needed was shown by a note in February 1826 when a journalist counted 31 ships lined up along Barnstaple Quay – "further proof of the rising commercial prosperity of that town" as his report puts it.

Even better proof had come two months previously when the *Mercury* announced the sale of two acres near Barnstaple "at the outstanding price of £2,000." This was soon developed with various streets of lace-worker's houses being laid out on it (Union Street etc.). The foundation stone was laid by an 18-month-old child. To round off this hectic period the new Guildhall in High Street "built in the Grecian style" was officially opened in November 1826.

South Molton's main development was the rebuilding of its old church. Tenders were invited in July 1825 and the foundation stone laid 10 months later. The enlargement was "to provide accommodation for the increasing population of that town." The new church could also have provided a home for a bust of the human form, "of exquisite symmetry, with the arms broke off just below the elbow" discovered in a new limestone quarry opened up in the parish. No more details are given which is a pity considering how bizarre this discovery sounds.

In July 1825 Bideford's market building was roofed over for the first time, which it was thought, "will afford great accommodation to the public." In the same month it was announced that a lifeboat was to be stationed at Bideford – presumably this was actually at Appledore – within the Port of Bideford area. Also the old bridge across the Pill which joined Bideford to Northam was condemned and the council decided to build a new road inland – the road is now the Northam Road which apparently stands on a much earlier 'causeway'. In August 1825 one Samuel Facey announced that he would build a lace factory in the town and in January 1826 the Bideford Bridge Trust placed lights on the bridge for the first time as "a result of numerous accidents."

The oddest story from Bideford was the one where an apprentice of Mr Crocker, a local shipbuilder, had an argument with his master. Nothing unusual in that – except that it took place some 30 foot up a mast and when Crocker lost his temper and threatened to throw the apprentice off the lad immediately "clasped him round the waist, and exclaimed 'Will you? then we will go together' and jumped off. Luckily the tide was out and the deep mud cushioned their fall!

Torrington during this period saw the opening of the Rolle Canal which allowed freight barges to reach the town from the Torridge estuary. The canal was accompanied by a new road (the present Bideford-Torrington link) described as "one of the most picturesque in the West of England." Lord Rolle, who financed the canal, also ordered two lime kilns to be built alongside his waterway in July 1826. The canal and road were designed to open up local opportunities – but in September 1825 Torringtonians could have extended their horizons considerably. A "gentleman" with a huge cattle ranch in Uruguay came to the town seeking glove makers who were willing to emigrate to South America to establish a glove industry there! Whether any went or not we are not told.

Two other main news stories occurred at this period – one at Clovelly and one at Appledore. At Appledore unemployment among the local seamen was great. They had worked on the sailing boats taking coal from South Wales to Ireland but "By the establishment of steam vessels this trade has been annihilated, and these poor mariners are left in a destitute state."

At Clovelly heavy seas had destroyed much of the "Pier" around 1823 and the local herring fishery was in such decline that it looked as though it might disappear entirely after the 1825 season. In February 1826, however, Sir John Williams the local squire decided to rebuild the pier – "to the great joy of the inhabitants of that place."

Much else was, of course, covered over this 18 month period in the *Sherborne Mercury* but these few items I have dealt with give the flavour of a very active time in North Devon's history.

North Devon Journal 23.1.1992 & 30.1.1992

122. MIRACLE CURES AT 90 PENCE A BOTTLE

In reading through the files of the *Journal* I have come across many peculiar stories, compared to which the advertisement columns have been staid and dry. In 1830, however, there appeared an extremely odd advert. One John Pearse of Pilton who termed himself an "oculist" offered for sale some "invaluable prescriptions". Pearse had invented some "medicine" and "salve" but owing to increasing age had decided to offer his secret recipes for these medicines to the highest bidder.

If a bidder failed to meet his expectations, Pearse announced that he would pass the recipes on to anyone supplying him with a rent-free house and garden (of at least a quarter-acre) "surrounded by a wall eight feet in height" whilst "the garden should be filled with such herbs as will delight every beholder." Failing this, Pearse offered to become personal physician "to any lady or gentleman for a salary of £150 per year" – but in this case the recipes would remain his secret. Pearse's medicine was sold under the name of "Comfort of Life Drops for Blindness, Deafness etc." at 30p for a half-ounce bottle, at a time when labourers' wages were about 50p a week.

He claimed they "rescued from the hands of sickness, those who seemed on the very verge of the grave." More specifically it "takes films off the eyes", "recovers the hearing of those who retain a rumbling, singing noise in the head", "cures cancers", "cures the rheumatic gout", "destroys worms" and "cures declining or consumptive persons." His "salve" was equally effective curing at least 20 different illnesses including snakebite, scalds, cancer, bloody flux, salt phlegm face (whatever that was) and piles. The price of this magic substance was 90p a box.

To bolster his claims Pearse printed a series of letters from grateful users of his preparations who had been cured of their ailments. Jane Stacey of Torrington wrote that she had been paralysed for three years, "Twelve months I was carried up and down stairs and all this time I would not turn in my bed without assistance." She had consulted many doctors and tried many different treatments, including the "steam bath", but got no relief.

After seeing one of Pearse's leaflets she bought some salve as well as some pills and the results were wonderful. She lost all pain and "can walk, I suppose, twenty miles a day." Pearse added that many other similar testimonials could be seen at his office.

Whether the Pilton "oculist" ever sold his secret recipes I don't know, but his advert continued to appear for quite a few weeks which suggests there weren't any takers. One would love to know what the medicines were actually made of. After all, the claims made for them would suggest they were virtually miracle cures!

North Devon Journal 26.10.1989

123. DISPUTE BETWEEN LAWYERS DRIVES THEM TO THE DUEL

The duel, as a means of settling an argument, has long gone out of fashion. The last one I have found in North Devon occurred in January 1832 when, rather bizarrely, two Barnstaple solicitors took part in an "affair of honour" as it was termed. Charles Roberts and Mr Clay were lawyers who had clashed during a court case where Roberts was prosecuting and Clay had appeared to give evidence on behalf of the defendant. The defence won but Roberts demanded a re-trial on the basis that Clay had lied when giving his evidence. Indeed Roberts produced nine sworn statements from other witnesses alleging that Clay had lied in the witness box, but the judge refused a re-trial.

On the morning following the case Clay called on Roberts and said, "You yesterday accused me of perjury." Roberts rather lamely denied this but Clay held up and shook his cane at Mr Roberts and told him to consider he had applied it to his shoulders. Shortly afterwards Roberts sent a challenge to Clay for a duel with pistols over this implied insult. The two solicitors agreed to meet at 4 p.m. that afternoon at Pottington Marsh.

Roberts, his second, a Mr Nicholetts and Doctor Budd turned up and were met by Clay, his brother-in-law Mr Marshall, plus a surgeon Mr Curry. The two duellists stood twelve paces apart, raised their pistols and fired together.

Clay's shot missed entirely but the ball from Roberts' pistol hit his opponent just above his left knee. The two doctors present "instantly ran to his assistance" and he was carried home in a carriage where, as a contemporary journalist put it, "we are glad to hear there is at present every prospect of his speedy recovery."

Roberts presumably felt his honour had been satisfied but the *Journal* editor wrote a stern denunciation of the case. He thought duelling "a practice so barbarous and inhuman, and...utterly at variance with every dictate of sense or justice." The editor reckoned it shameful that honour "should be so perverted that acts so monstrous should be gilded by an appellation so imposing." Indeed he thought duellists were no better than assassins and finished his tirade by "sincerely regretting that in the present instance, gentlemen who stood so high in public estimation should have been betrayed into such an exhibition of intemperance."

With that magisterial statement closed the history of duelling in North Devon.

North Devon Journal 29.12.1989

124. BRING OUT THOSE EARLY FAMILY ALBUMS

A survey has put the family album as the first thing most people would save if disaster struck their house. Photographs are the strongest link we have with our past whether they show people or places.

The photographic process was invented in the early nineteenth century – the first actual photograph, known as a daguerreotype, was taken in 1837 but not publicised until 1839. These first efforts were on copper plate and needed very long exposure times. In 1840 the process was refined and speeded up – allowing the first portraits to be taken.

It is remarkable, therefore, to find an advertisement in the *North Devon Journal* of June 9th 1842 headed "NOW OPEN IN BARNSTAPLE...photographic portraits taken by the reflection of light". The proprietor of what is called "the reflecting apparatus" promised to produce "faithful miniature likenesses of the human countenance and person...in the short space of a few seconds." Thus the first photographs taken in Barnstaple were 'snapped' only three years after the process was announced to the world.

The advertisement announced with a flourish that "The extraordinary process is now open to the public in the upper floor of the premises adjoining the Old Bank, and opposite the Guildhall." The 'Old Bank' was run by Messrs Drake, Gribble and Marshall and the adjacent building was the Three Tuns. Evidently the photographer was lodging there and set up his studio at the inn.

Business cannot have been overwhelming in terms of numbers as we read, "The price of each portrait is one guinea (£1.05) exclusive of the frame." This was at a time when the average wage for an agricultural labourer was barely 8s (40p) a week – so clearly only the very well-to-do could have afforded this new novelty. Anyone who did go for a sitting would have been well advised to choose a sunny day as in the various supporting quotations given in the advertisement it is pointed out that the process took five seconds if the day was bright, but two minutes if it was cloudy. Sitting perfectly still for two minutes takes some doing!

The photographer, whose name is never given, stayed in Barnstaple for six months and only left in December 1842 to go on to Bideford taking his "extraordinary invention" with him. At Bideford he introduced another refinement − colour tinted photographs. He plied his business here for another three months and then left the area altogether.

In his nine months here he must have taken a fair number of photographs and it would be fascinating to see if any have survived to today. The photograph will probably be small − about four inches by three inches − and set in a velvet lined box or frame. One can only be certain of course if a date is given as well because this style of photograph lasted a long time. Can any readers lay claim to having one of these photographs − the first ever taken in North Devon?

North Devon Journal 21.3.1985

125. DIED IN THE TENT WHERE SHE WAS BORN AND LIVED

Gypsies don't get a good press today. Why this might be so isn't hard to work out − unsightly scrap yards by the side of busy roads don't endear the Romanies to the average inhabitant of Britain − even though many people profess to like 'real' gypsies. 'Real' gypsies, of course, live in caravans pulled by horses, tell fortunes and generally look quaint.

Even our ancestors had a fairly romanticised picture of gypsy life as shown by a story from January 1852. An article in the *Journal* from this date is headed 'Habit stronger than life' and concerns one Matilda Boswell who claimed, and was believed, to be a daughter of the 'King of the Gypsies.' Her family had travelled round the West Country for many years, but in January 1852 she was living in a tent at Lilford in Abbotsham. Whilst here she had fallen ill and consulted a local doctor − Mr W H Acland of

Bideford. He had prescribed some medicine for her and tried to persuade her to leave her tent and go into lodgings in Bideford – which he very generously offered to pay for.

"Her reply," we read, "was at once prompt and characteristic of this wandering tribe of Egyptian Ishmaelites." She actually said, "Do you think I could leave the tent, where my fathers and mothers were born and died?" She answered her own question, "No, my good gentlemen, God bless you for your kind offer, nevertheless I cannot live in your dangerous houses. I was born in the tent, and in the tent I am determined to die."

True to her word, she did die in her tent only a few days later, aged 51. A contemporary newspaper report says how "this romantic creature breathed her last amidst the bitterest lamentations of the whole party" of her fellow gypsies. This report also adds that notwithstanding the gales then raging, "she rested on her dying pillow as warm, soft and safe as the minion of luxury on a downy pillow." To emphasise the romanticism of the event the journalist added a verse to the effect that she died in her tent where she,

"Had cheerily passed her Summer days
In sunny nooks and sultry ways."

Traditionally, gypsies were cremated in their caravans, but clearly Matilda didn't have a caravan. Indeed, few local gypsies seem to have owned such vehicles. A few years ago I interviewed an old gentleman whose grandfather had been a local sailmaker who also turned out tents for the local gypsies.

I have searched the burial registers for Abbotsham but no Matilda Boswell appears – where she was interred I don't know – perhaps on the site where she died or perhaps by the roadside – a suitable resting place for such a romantic character.

North Devon Journal 20.10.1988

126. SOUP KITCHEN TO FEED THE HUNGRY POOR

The nineteenth-century was hard for the poor – but in many cases the rich tried to help, one good example being the establishment of the Barnstaple Soup Kitchen. This had its beginning in the harsh winter of 1855-6 which came at a time when there was a recession in the North Devon economy and money was scarce. The Rev Henry Luxmoore of Barnstaple was so moved by what he witnessed in many of his poorer parishioners' houses that he suggested in January 1856 that a soup kitchen be established to provide at least one nourishing meal a day to the starving poor.

His suggestion was quickly taken up and at the inaugural meeting of the soup kitchen committee in early February 1856 many of Barnstaple's leading men promised their help – both with money and organisational skills. William Gould was voted in as secretary with the Mayor of the day, the resoundingly-named Cadwallader Edward Palmer, as chairman along with an eighteen strong committee. Their first job was to raise funds and to do this Barnstaple was divided into seven "districts" and collectors appointed to secure contributions in each. Within a year £193.19s.6d had been accumulated – a huge sum in those days.

Whilst the money was coming in the committee had approached the town council to obtain a room for their 'kitchen.' They tried to get one next to the newly-built market. They were refused but were eventually offered and accepted a room in the corn exchange (now Queen's Hall) with an entrance from Boutport Street.

Once premises had been secured a "boiling plant" was installed at a cost of £87.18s. by a Trowbridge firm. Other work and equipment brought the committee's outlay to a total of £177.11.10d. The coal-fired boiler must have been good as it lasted at least 84 years! In November 1856 adverts went out to secure a cook, and out of sixteen applicants one William Perkin was appointed, His duties consisted of lighting the fires, mixing the soup ingredients and ensuring everything went smoothly. The job was, of course, seasonal, the 'kitchen' only being opened in very cold periods.

The soup itself consisted of pork, oatmeal, peas, flour and onions, and was sold very cheaply. Rich patrons could purchase books of 'soup tickets' and dispense them to deserving cases at their discretion – patronage flourished in Victorian England.

From its inception the soup kitchen was a great success and was well supported by the townspeople – both as subscribers and patrons. A printed poster of 1870 which has survived, shows a huge list of subscriptions – from the Mayor's two guineas to 6d from a Mr Locke. Some £92 was spent that year on providing soup and paying staff wages and fuel costs.

The 'kitchen' continued to be opened in times of need, right the way through the nineteenth century and well into the twentieth. In the 1930s local councillors would don aprons and serve the soup. The end seems finally to have come in 1940 if the minute book of the committee is to be believed. The last entry is dated October 10 1940, and recorded a vote of thanks to the then secretary "for his work and service in feeding and caring for the hundreds of evacuees from London."

North Devon Journal 15.1.1987

127. ELEVEN DIED IN CHOLERA OUTBREAK IN APPLEDORE

Victorian Britain, with its urban slums and poor medical knowledge, was ravaged by a series of vicious diseases – typhoid, smallpox, diphtheria – and perhaps most feared of all, cholera. The worst epidemic of this last killer disease occurred in the years 1831-3 when some 21,000 people died in England and Wales alone. The disease returned in 1849 and 1854 and finally in 1866. During this last outbreak North Devon was affected but only in the village of Appledore.

In South Wales the disease had taken hold in the summer of 1866, but had not spread to this side of the Bristol Channel. At the beginning of August 1866, however, the local papers carried a story about an odd death at Appledore saying, "Some alarm has been created during the last few days by an indiscreet and incorrect announcement that there had been an 'Outbreak of cholera at Appledore'."

Apparently the story began when a customs officer named Oatway was visiting ships in Appledore Pool and on one, which had come from South Wales, took a drink of cold water which gave rise soon after to stomach pains, vomiting and diarrhoea. He died the same evening "after an illness of nine hours." A 19 year old woman called Curtis also had the same symptoms but was recovering. This report was accompanied by a letter from two local magistrates, one the Mayor of Bideford, saying that Oatway had brought about his own death by his "own indiscretion" in drinking "an unusually large quantity of cold water." They also stated that "he had been suffering from diarrhoea for ten days or a fortnight previously."

This attempt to 'play down' the possible outbreak of a dreaded disease rather back-fired when, over the next week, some five people died suddenly in Appledore – four of them in a similar manner to Oatway. The medical men in the village, Dr Pratt and Dr Stuart, now openly stated "there is not the slightest doubt that this was a most virulent case of Asiatic Cholera." Among the five deaths were the young woman Curtis, a Mrs Bynyon of Meeting Street and three children – two from the same family in West Appledore – and a boy called Richards "who was well and at his play on Tuesday evening, and died during the night."

It was the speed of death that frightened the villagers and they hurriedly took all precautions suggested by the local sanitary committee. These consisted of the following, "Tar barrels have been burnt in the streets; disinfectants have been freely used in all parts of the town; our clergyman, the Reverend J J Reynolds has made himself very active in attempting to allay the fears of the people, and in doing all in his power to promote the health of the public. Meetings are being held for prayer in the several chapels, to invoke the mercy of God to stay the pestilence."

Over the next week two more children died, both members of the Richards family. The father Captain Richards was in Ilfracombe and he was quickly summoned home to find his house empty as, "The sanitary authorities ordered the erection of a temporary building in a field on the side of a hill facing the sea, and the remainder of the family – the mother and two children – were speedily removed to their more airy abode." This report from Appledore ended with a phrase that clearly illustrated the lack of medical (and sanitary) knowledge then prevailing, "it is hoped that a change in the weather may prove beneficial to the public health."

The next issue of the paper on the 23rd August saw a massive three column "Inquiry into the sanitary condition" of Appledore by a "Special Correspondent." This makes horrifying reading today as it details, street by street, the awful mixture of overcrowded houses, cess pits next to wells, blocked drains, open privys, dung heaps and filthy water. By now some 18 cases of cholera had been noted in the village – nine of which had proved fatal. The special correspondent called for a complete overhaul of both drainage facilities and water supplies to the village saying that without this work being done the place would remain permanently unhealthy.

Within the following seven days several more cases of illness appeared and an old man named Saltern died of the disease. The end, however, was now in sight. The last person to die in the outbreak appears to have been a Mrs Mary Berry, a sea captain's widow, who lived at the "extreme end of West Appledore." By the 13th of September the local papers could report, "There has not been a single case reported during the past week, and the town may be said to be once more free from the epidemic."

The disease may have left Appledore but its sailors took it with them to other areas. In the same issue as the 'all-clear' was given there was the report of the death from cholera at Swansea of Captain Thomas Brown of the 'Newton'. He left a pregnant wife and four young children in the village. Two weeks later came news of the death, again from cholera, of local man Humphrey England at Marseilles, and he was the very last victim of this particular outbreak.

The epidemic directed attention to the terrible problems of Appledore and the local papers reflected this new focus. From this date forward their columns often carried news of new sanitary works and the removal of "nuisances" from Appledore. As so often in North Devon, however, it had taken a disaster to bring about improvements.

Bideford Gazette 23.11.1984

128. A SCHOOL FROM THE PAGES OF DICKENS

Dickens, in his novel *Nicholas Nickelby,* shocked his Victorian contemporaries with his fictional account of school-life at 'Dotheboys Hall' under the infamous Wackford Squeers. This first appeared in 1838 and readers of the *North Devon Journal* in April 1878 must have been riveted by the headline, "A Devonshire 'Do-the-boys' Hall – Extraordinary Disclosures."

The report concerned a civil action at Holsworthy County Court between James Rawlings, a retired solicitor of Newton Tracey, and Mr and Mrs Charles Veysey, proprietors of the Hampton House Boarding School, Ashwater. Mr Rawlings was seeking £50 damages for the Veysey's negligence in looking after his daughter, Eve.

In 1874 Eve had become an 'articled pupil' at the school. This meant that she taught the juniors for a day-and-a-half a week and only paid £14 per annum to the Veyseys for her own tuition in English, French, music and callisthenics. She arrived to find not only the 20 girls she had expected but 30 boys which she had not expected. Also a surprise were her duties which included helping the single maid-servant make all the beds and also looking after the cleanliness of the girls.

Only four wash-basins were provided for the pupils and she found "a large number of vermin on the pillows and the linen." This wasn't surprising as the sheets were only changed twice in six months. Worse was to come, however, when one of her girl charges "was seized with the itch" – an outbreak which rapidly spread through the school. Apparently no medical help was called, every sufferer (whatever the complaint) being given 'Holloway's Pills' a well known nineteenth century quack medicine. In one case even a child with measles was given these pills. It is a wonder in the light of all this that Eve stayed the two-and-a-half years that she did – on one occasion she arrived home with her head covered in vermin.

Mr Veysey denied everything saying he had "conducted the school for nearly twenty years without a blemish on his character." Under cross-examination he did admit that the 30 boys slept two to a bed in a room only 30 feet long. The judge not surprisingly found Mr Rawlings' case proved and set damages at £20.

The case did not finish there, however, as in May 1878 Eve Rawlings had to appear at the same court to answer a charge of "having committed wilful and corrupt perjury" in her evidence at the April case. Mr Veysey began by producing letters written by Eve to his wife of which one typical one began, "My dear, dear Mrs Veysey – I write to thank you a million times for all your kindness and love to me ever since I have been here," – hardly the letter of an aggrieved person. The schoolmaster then noted that "the inspectior of nuisances had visited the school, but had never complained of uncleanliness." He then produced a string of witnesses including Rose Moore a former pupil who said that "after Miss Rawlings left no one had skin disease." The school laundress Ann Callocott said she washed between 15 and 20 sheets a week and another ex-pupil Elizabeth Harden said the sheets were changed twice weekly (though she added that the cutlery was often dirty!).

Against these witnessses Mr Rawlings produced a series of parents who had withdrawn their children from the school, including a Mr Bartlett whose daughter caught the 'itch' there, came home and was cured but was promptly re-infected when she went back to the school. Another parent had to burn his children's vermin-infested clothes when they came home. One ex-pupil said that her sheets doubled as table-cloths.

The poor judge must have been bemused with such conflicting evidence and he took the easy way out by dismissing the whole case. Very soon, and not unexpectedly after such damaging publicity, Hampton House School closed permanently and its pupils were redistributed to other (possibly cleaner) establishments.

North Devon Journal 4.7.1985

129. REVISITING THE NORTH DEVON GHOSTS OF OLD

We all like a good ghost story – and our ancestors were no different. They, however, had a much more robust and dismissive way of dealing with such phenomena as is shown in the following story reported in local newspapers in March 1881, and headed, rather oddly, "Modern Witchcraft."

The tale comes from Buckland Brewer and evidently had become the talk of the village before reaching the permanency of print. "We don't pretend to vouch for the truth of it, but it comes to us from what seems the most reliable authority," the editor disarmingly wrote, although who this "authority" was isn't stated. The core of the gossip was that "A servant girl living with Mr Lewis Withecombe is (supposed) to be made the target of some foul monster, who amuses himself by throwing stones at her whenever she appears out of doors, and while she is indoors by throwing stones on the roof."

At first sight this seems like a classic poltergeist case – which is really just to give a label to something which is still unexplained. Poltergeist cases are still common today and usually revolve around young girls whose emotional energies somehow cause objects to fly about without human intervention. Poltergeists, however, only seem to happen indoors – and in this case it was outside as well. The 1881 Census for Buckland reveals just one girl servant living with Mr Withecombe at Bera or Bearah Farm – Sarah Ann Budd a sixteen year old from Bridgerule in Cornwall.

Her master resorted to various "tests" but "no solution to the mystery has been arrived at." Indeed "The stones still come, and the girl appears very much distressed thereby," which isn't surprising. The editor added his comment that "We have no doubt it is a hoax" which is a casual way of treating an unusual event well-recorded through history.

Most such cases disappear naturally with time – generally when the young person involved passes through puberty – at which time their emotional energy seems to be dissipated. Be that as it may the final words of the article neatly sum up the probable course of the story, "In the meantime the village gossips are making the most of the circumstances" but how long the villagers kept the story alive I do not know.

North Devon Journal 8.9.1988

130. 'COULSWORTHY WATER' WAS A MAGIC POTION

With all the talk of 'diversification' in agriculture as a means of escaping the problems of over-production it is interesting to examine an early example of this. Around 1902 Norman Forbes came to Coulsworthy Farm near Combe Martin to examine and test the water from a site known locally as St John's Spring. The water flowed out of a solid mass of rock at a minimum rate of about 4 pints a minute and for many years had been noted "for its exceptional purity and marked freshness."

Mr Forbes had it analysed and began encouraging local doctors to use it in various cases of illness as he reckoned it to have medicinal properties. He based this idea on the fact that the spring gave "a specially pure, soft water" and resembled Evian water – still a popular brand of bottled water today.

In a booklet published around 1910 Forbes cites 6 cases from the clinical notes of a Doctor Manning of Combe Martin. These ranged from a retired Indian Army Officer whose digestion had been virtually destroyed to a 25 year old woman who suffered from "indigestion, flatulence, acidity and troublesome neuralgia." In each case, needless to say, a course of Coulsworthy water had restored them to health, vigour and happiness.

These improvements were put down to an "internal cleansing" brought about by the water. Forbes in fact goes on to list 15 conditions where Coulsworthy water could be of use. These included hyperacidity, gout, arthritis, arterio-sclerosis, jaundice, eczema, colitis, appendicitis, sciatica, dysentery, metallic poisoning, bladder stones, diabetes and even "simple obesity" – an impressive list!

The writer suggested that patients could "combine with the systematic drinking of this pure water a 'cure de repos' with a new and salutary regime, spent amid the simpler scenes and more homely character of picturesque villages on the rugged coast of North Devon".

The booklet ends with 2 pages on how to get hold of one's supplies of this wonderful water. You could either order it direct from Coulsworthy or from a wholesaler in London. It cost 30p for a dozen quart bottles with an extra 5p returnable deposit on the bottles. The empties were to be returned to Blackmoor Station on the Lynton and Barnstaple Railway line.

I am unsure as to how long this local industry lasted. A business directory of 1914 doesn't list the company, so presumably it didn't last very long. Interestingly the same directory does list the Lynrock Natural Mineral Water Co. of Lynmouth so the Coulsworthy undertaking clearly wasn't the only business of this type in North Devon.

North Devon Journal 10.3.1988

131. FORTEAN TIMES

Most of us are intrigued by the unusual and the bizarre whether it be UFOs, rains of frogs or the abominable snowman. Newspapers often carry such reports which people read, smile over and forget. In reading through the nineteenth century files of North Devon papers, a few events have been notable enough to deserve resurrecting.

Thus in January 1865 there was a report headed "Strange if True" concerning the quarry opened at Weare Giffard to provide stone for the widening of Bideford Bridge then being carried out. some of the stones were too large to be moved so "the gads were applied to split them" and "in the middle of the largest stone they found a large rat (supposed to be one of the Muscovy breed) of great length from tail to snout, with whiskers 6 inches long". Now frogs and toads encased in stone are not that uncommon though not accepted as genuine by most biologists – but a rat – that really was unusual. The animal was "to be offered to the British Museum as a curiosity." I suspect they threw it in the dustbin.

Such things, however are not confined to the last century. In 1972 a Barnstaple gas-fitter wrote to *Animals* magazine reporting a similar event. He had been breaking up the concrete housing around a gas meter outside a bungalow on the Barnstaple to Ilfracombe road. "My mate was at work with a sledge hammer when he dropped it suddenly and said. "that looks like a frog's leg ... we released 23 perfectly formed but minute frogs which all hopped away to the flower garden."

Another more historic event occurred in 1867 when a "Curious Statement" was made in Ilfracombe. On Saturday November 9 at 5.30 a.m. "Mr Thomas Perriam, of the Coastguard" was out fishing between Brandy Cove and the Outfalls 2 miles west of the town. He looked up and "saw coming swiftly through the air an object resembling a bar of iron thicker than a man's arm, but not quite so long," which entered the water about 12 yards from his boat. It came from the NE (i.e. not from the land) and other fishermen nearby also witnessed this truly 'unidentified flying object.' The story was never followed up and one is left wondering what this strange 'bar' could have been – a meteorite or a long distance cannonball? UFOs of the classic space-ship type were relatively common in North Devon a few years ago – could this have been a prototype?

A third unusual event was recorded some 15 years earlier in April 1852 when an inquest was held at Beaford into the strange death of William Vodden. Poor William was about 60 and had been working at Brinscombe Farm with his wife picking up stones from the fields. At 10 a.m. he went for a break into the "Mowstead" or barn nearby. Two minutes later, William Gilbert, a carpenter also at work on the farm, heard a cry for help. When he arrived at the barn he found that William's "smockfrock was burning" and the flames were all over the poor old man. Two other people came to help, including William's wife, but they couldn't stop the flames and William, of course, died very quickly.

At the inquest, the coroner heard that William "was a great smoker" but that "no pipe was, however, found upon him or near him." The jury returned an odd verdict that "Deceased was found burning, from the effects of which he died, but how the burning took place did not appear to the jury." Such cases are rare and are usually labelled Spontaneous Human Combustion, i.e. where the human body bursts into flame for no apparent reason.

A famous fictional case occurs in Dickens' *Bleak House*, but real cases are recorded and have been photographed. Indeed the last reported one in Britain occurred just before Christmas 1984 at Newton Abbot, though this case is open to doubt.

Bideford Gazette 30.8.1985

132 MYSTERIES IN THE SKY ARE NOTHING NEW

We have all heard of UFO's but do you know the theory that says each generation sees UFO's which reflect their own technology?

Today we see ultra-fast very sophisticated rocket ships whereas in biblical times they saw "flying fiery chariots." In the early years of this century UFO's were seen as "mystery airships." In 1909 for example, there was a whole rash of sightings over Britain beginning in March of that year which, for various reasons were taken as mysterious and inexplicable.

North Devon wasn't left out. In May 1909 a headline in the *Journal* read "Supposed airship seen at Ilfracombe." One William Moon was out walking in Brookfield Place, Ilfracombe, just before midnight, when he saw "a foreign body in the air." He immediately found witnesses and they all described it as being "like a German sausage" carrying "a brilliant light, of a reddish tint, brighter than starlight" as well as "a powerful searchlight."

A second sighting at Ilfracombe came three months later when Pc Clarke and two other policemen saw a "Mysterious Airship." Clarke's testimony begins solidly, "I don't say a thing unless I am sure." He wasn't certain how high up the airship was or even what its shape was but he could describe how, when he was at Widmouth he noticed a "funny star" in the sky – "I looked at it for a minute, and then I saw it moving in my direction." He didn't think it was an airship but thought it was a fire-balloon "as it was dipping up and down like a boat on the waves." "It" was a bright light which came nearer to him and then passed overhead. At this point the policeman says, "I could distinctly hear the 'whirring' of an engine, but the bright light prevented me from seeing anything of the airship itself." Whatever it was disappeared in the direction of Lynton and Pc Clarke continued on his beat.

He met Constables Coppin and Bradbury and told them about his sighting but "they laughed at me" and so he went on until he reached Watermouth Gate. Here he saw the airship again and blew his whistle to summon his fellow officers. They ran to where he stood and all three witnessed the "airship" travelling back towards Ilfracombe "and after that I saw it turn again and head towards Barnstaple." Constable Clarke's testimony ended, "You can laugh as much as you like. I laughed when they said they saw one here before, but I can quite believe it now" – words that are still echoed today by UFO witnesses.

You might wonder what the mystery is about this case bearing in mind that airships already existed at this date. The mystery comes from these odd ones being so fast and having searchlights – no contemporary airship could go as fast or was powerful enough to bear the weight of such lights. Also they were seen over Britain in large numbers at the same time – and yet there were very few "known" ones at that period.

Were these the first modern UFO sightings or not? – we shall never know. Clearly Pc Clarke was certain of what he saw – and as that cannot be easily be explained then we do have a mystery!

North Devon Journal 25.2.1988

133. WIFEBEATERS WHO BECAME THE MAYOR

I have written before about the 'sham-mayors' of Bideford and Derby in Barnstaple but I came across one new to me the other day – the "Mayor" of Buckland Brewer. This wasn't an honour to be sought – as the nomination went to the most notorious wife-beater in the village!

In August 1889 one Herbert Harris told his wife he was off to work and left his house. He didn't get to work, however, but spent the time in the village pub. His wife got to hear of this and went to remonstrate with him and bring him home. As a contemporary report said, "He clearly did not relish being 'looked up' in this fashion, for when he went home later he took what he doubtless regarded as his 'revenge' and beat his wife black and blue."

This was enough to win him the nomination as 'Mayor' and on August Bank Holiday he was presented with a paper bearing the words, "Herbert Harris, Mayor of Buckland Brewer." He was dragged out of his house by five men, tied to a cart and paraded around the village to the ridicule of this neighbours. We are told that he "kicked and struggled with a vigour worthy of a better cause." He was finally tipped out of the cart in front of the public house.

Harris, however, didn't let the matter rest there but had the five summoned for assault. They were Joseph Prouse, William Eastabrook, Fred Jewell, Studley Harris and Montague Squire. At their court appearance they explained that "they were merely following an old custom which had existed at Buckland for many years." They added, rather engagingly, that "no violence was used" and that Harris "was not hurt in the least" – except for his dented ego perhaps.

The magistrates were obviously in sympathy with the five defendants but the chairman "remarked that there were some old customs that could not be kept up now that the law was stronger than it used to be" and that any woman who needed protection could "get it by the aid of the law" rather than from a band of local vigilantes. The outcome indicated these sympathies as the men were merely fined 6d (2½p) each. Doubtless Harris gathered from this what the magistrates thought of him. One wonders when the custom died out? – it might actually be reintroduced – it would certain provide a form of rough local justice.

North Devon Journal 29.10.1987

134. ICE CREAM CLEARED OF TYPHOID DEATHS

In the light of the continuing discussion over local water supplies and sewage disposal it is perhaps instructive to look back some 70 years to a series of events which occurred in Barnstaple in 1911.

In September of that year the medical officer of health for the borough reported that he had seen 28 cases of typhoid, or enteric fever, in the town. The officer admitted that "he could not explain its origin." The mysterious illness claimed another 21 victims by the end of the year, and out of a total of 49 cases, nine died.

Because of the seriousness of the outbreak an outside expert, Dr S W Wheaton, was called in to try and identify the cause. His inspection report was published in 1912 and this small pamphlet makes fascinating reading giving details of housing and social conditions in Barnstaple at that date. Thus of housing in the Green Lane area (now demolished) he says, "they are often so irregularly built as to interfere with the access of light and air, have very small windows, no damp-proof courses, and sometimes neither back doors nor windows in the rear. The woodwork is often much decayed and the mortar between the stones has dropped out so that the rain blows through the walls." In another paragraph he speaks of the dampness owing to the lack of damp-proof courses and dilapidated roofs.

Rents on these properties were about 3/- (15p) a week and many were apparently owned by people too poor to carry out repairs. As if the houses themselves were not bad enough the doctor found that the residents, "usually have large families" and "lodgers are taken when there is already not sufficient accommodation for the tenant's family."

After his brief sketch of the dilapidated state of much of working class Barnstaple the doctor then went on to examine possible causes of the typhoid outbreak. In discussing sewage disposal the inspector talks of leaking sewers often badly damaged, with the raw sewage being discharged straight into the River Taw. The sewage was "carried to and fro" with the tide and gave rise to heavy pollution along the river banks. He considered the shellfish in the river to be polluted by sewage, and notes, "When the factories are working short time, as has been frequently the case of late, the youths go off on days when they are not working and collect shellfish from the estuary." In addition he observed, "The principal bathing place is opposite the principal sewage outfall." So if you ate local shellfish and swam in the river you were asking for trouble!

Leaving the river the report moved on to the housing conditions where the doctor was forced to admit that "enteric fever occurred in a considerable proportion of houses in which unwholesome conditions were not pronounced." So, although housing was bad it did not apparently itself give rise to fever.

Drainage pipes were next scrutinised and some especially bad ones in the Derby area were singled out for special comment. It appeared, however, that as soon as the fever began the worst pipes were rebuilt and, in any case, the pattern of cases bore little connection to the pattern of bad drainage pipes.

Dr Wheaton then looked at milk supplies noting that the 49 fever sufferers had obtained their milk from at least 14 different milk sellers. One retailer in particular aroused suspicion. This was because the man had suffered "some obscure illness" before the main fever outbreak, but after tests had been carried out the dairyman was declared innocent.

Attention then switched to ice cream, the report noting that "it appeared that ice cream was consumed to a very large extent by the working classes in Barnstaple throughout the hot summer of 1911." The ice cream was obtained from two itinerant vendors one of whom "is said not to be at all cleanly" though as he spent the entire Summer plying his trade in Ilfracombe he was ruled out as a cause of the fever.

The last possibility looked at was personal infection and the doctor thought that this was almost certainly an important part in the spreading of the disease He recognised that the working classes often visited each other's houses and that "when illness occurs there is a still greater tendency for visits to be made to the affected household." Several cases were traced directly to personal contact but this could not explain all cases.

In his conclusion Dr Wheaton could only say that "there were so many possible sources of enteric fever in operation in Barnstaple at the same time that it was impossible to fix upon any of them as the principal one concerned in the causation of the outbreak." His own belief was that the generally insanitary condition of certain parts of the town was the main cause along with the poor state of sewage disposal. Clearly if the doctor returned today he would be hugely gratified to see how the quality of housing had improved tremendously over the intervening years – though one wonders how he would view our still relatively primitive methods of sewage disposal?

North Devon Gazette 3.2.1984

135. WHEN THE FAIR BROUGHT FREAK SHOWS TO TOWN

Barnstaple Fair has been famous for hundreds of years. In the past it provided a welcome break from the monotony of small town life and restricted entertainments. Most of the fair, of course, consisted of confectionery stalls and catchpenny side-shows – and amongst the latter was the Freak Show.

To modern ways of thinking the exhibition of human freaks to morbid sensation seekers smacks of the worst kind of inhumanity and exploitation. From the point of those exhibited, however, being a fair side-show was probably a far better fate than being left to the taunts of unfeeling neighbours.

Recently I purchased a handbill entitled "Human Curiosities" which is dated "Barnstaple Fair 1935". Five exhibits are listed by their stage names – Colourado, Shadola, Lanky, Titania and Karo.

The most famous was Titania who was "admitted by all to be the most beautiful of all giant girls." She was nearly six feet tall, weighed 29 stone and had been born in Staffordshire of "humble parents". On a visit to the USA she "startled even the shock proof Americans." Her write-up ended with the bizarre phrase, "The Pick of the Freak Pit".

In contrast was Shadola "the thinnest boy in the world" or "the living skeleton." He was 18 years old, six-foot-three yet weighed "just under six stone, even though we are led to believe he has an excellent appetite" and enjoyed good health. Lanky was similar, being very tall though his height isn't given. Karo on the other hand was only 29 inches high. To add to his drawing power he claimed Eskimo ancestry, the handbill adding that he "is very good tempered, smokes a pipe, and generally smiles up at a world he can never understand." Completing the roster of exhibits was Colourado "the human fresco." His description was lengthy and obviously exaggerated, but basically he was a negro with albino patches.

Although this show was here some 60 years ago, can any readers remember "The Freak Pit", and do any of them still have a postcard memento of that visit to Barnstaple fair?

North Devon Journal 20.4.1989

136. POP MUSIC HITS TOWN

The Beatles scored their first British number one in 1963 thus giving birth to the whole pop industry as we now understand it. That North Devon was as affected by this as anyone else is shown by reference to the *Journal* of that year. Dances were advertised weekly for many towns in the area under the headings "Rock & Twist", "Big Beat", "Hully Gully Nite" and the catch-all "Rock-Twist-Teenbeat-Jive".

Young North Devonians had a huge choice of local groups to see. I have found mention of at least 20, including The Barracudas, Zodiacs, Heartbeats, Mustangs, Starfires, Tycoons and The Phantoms. The most popular group by far, however, were The Summits who played all over North Devon. Voted "Best Rock Group in the West Country" they had five members – Gil Jones, John Knill, Chris Verney, John Sweet and Robert Moore. Their popularity extended beyond Devon as in February 1963 they turned down an offer of a six month tour of France, in order to finish their apprenticeships to local firms.

These home-grown groups often provided support to nationally famous acts who played at the Queen's Hall in Barnstaple. Amongst the big names who came to this venue in 1963 were the Tornadoes, Mike Berry, Sounds Incorporated and Emile Ford and the Checkmates. At the latter's show 600 fans turned up and "on several occasion he appealed to the girls to stop screaming but it was of no use." Indeed, on four occasions he was nearly dragged from the stage! Perhaps the biggest name to play the Queen's Hall, however, was Gene Vincent along with his group the Blue Caps. The only comment on this legendary singer appeared in an irate letter to the *Journal* complaining that the "Wonder Boy from America" only came on stage at 10.45 p.m. and then performed for just 20 minutes.

Attendances at the Queen's Hall had shot up with the coming of pop music as a journalist noted in January when writing about more traditional dances. The reason was that "Teenagers, apparently are simply not interested in any other form of dancing than rock'n'roll, jiving and twist." This comment led to a reply from a pair of readers who signed themselves "Regular Dancers" and referred to "two chord twanging guitars and the hysterical knee knocking 'Yea, Yea' singers." They were "quite sure that this kind of music will soon pass."

This negative attitude to the birth of the pop industry resurfaced regularly in 1963. In July the *Journal* editor commented on the Bachelors' show being marked by "none of the deafening noise created by so many of the modern pop groups." In September "amplifiers transmitting pop music" at the Bideford Church Institute were denounced and in October stilettos were banned from the new wooden dance floor at South Molton's Assembly Rooms (even though one town councillor reckoned the floor to be "exceedingly smoochy!")

Perhaps the oddest comment on young people and their tastes came from local author R F Delderfield who, speaking at West Buckland School Open Day referred to a survey of North Devon teenagers he had carried out. He found them intelligent though he admitted, "I almost expected to be set on by young girls and boys in skin tight jeans and, when I went into parks, to find orgies going on."

Rather over-stated, one might think. In fact, the strongest condemnation of pop music came from local jazz fans. North Devon Jazz Club wrote to the *Journal* saying rather sniffily, "There is a difference between teenagers who scream at writhing pop, for want of a better word, singers and the serious minded young people who appreciate jazz as a recognised art form."

The clearest sign of whose view would prevail came from a report about two Barnstaple Grammar School girls, Diane Westmoreland and Anne Smeedle, who had written and published *The Beatle Maniac's Manual*. This included hints on "how to scream" and how Beatle fans should act. It included pen portraits of the "Fab Four" and some 250 copies were printed and sold in aid of the Freedom from Hunger Campaign. Do any survive? They will have become real collectors' items.

Today's record collectors love musical trivia and I will end with one fascinating titbit. In January 1963 Torrington's champion town crier Bert Waldron went to London to record his "cry" and bell on the latest record by the star Craig Douglas. Released soon after under the imaginative title 'Town Crier' it was played on television's Juke Box Jury and voted a hit but seems never to have entered the charts.

Happy days indeed – and perhaps far more innocent than our contemporary world?

North Devon Journal 29.11.1990

137. THE POP SCENE IN '64

Some months ago Peter Christie wrote about the history of pop music in North Devon in 1963. In this article he carries the story on a year to 1964, the year when the "beat boom" hit North Devon with a vengeance. The Beatles were the heroes of an entire generation and gave rise to huge number of local beat groups made up of young hopefuls. Some of these bands were very ephemeral – who for example, now remembers The Stringbeats, The Shandells, The Druids, The Cordettes or the String Beatles. Others won a degree of local fame such as the Pirates of Penzance advertised as "Cornwall's Top Recording Group". Another group B. Friendly and the Mates came to public notice when their manager was hit over the head with a microphone during a fight as they played at Bideford – so much for being friendly.

The leading local group of 1963 had been the Summits and they were still very popular. In May it was announced that they were booked to play a summer season at the Runnacleave Hotel in Ilfracombe and this left a gap in the local dance circuit. Two other groups quickly came forward to fill it – the Mysterymen from Bideford and the Chevrons from Ilfracombe. The former were famous for their gimmicks. They originally wore white masks when playing but graduated to performing under an ultra-violet lamp "to give them an aura of mystery" as the *Journal* reported in September. They also gained press coverage by being the first North Devon group to include a girl in their line-up – Sally Dibble, aged 19.

One other local group deserves mention – Graham and the Green Echoes who came from Shebbear. The year 1964 was a 'leap' one and in March lead singer Graham was complaining that he had to keep his phone off the hook as there had been so many offers of marriage – which sounds suspiciously like an early publicity stunt to me.

If these were the local groups what of the nationally known ones who came to North Devon to play? A 'beat' music fan in 1964 was spoilt for choice as during the year the following stars came to play – Brian Poole and the Tremeloes, The Swinging Blue Jeans, Wayne Fontana, Big Dee Irwin, Millie, The Four Pennies, Shane Fenton and the Fentones and Peter Jay and the Jaywalkers.

When Brian Poole played at the Queen's Hall in July 900 fans turned up and Barnstaple Town Council, who promoted the show, made a clear profit of £130 – a lot in those days. In April Johnny Kidd and the Pirates' visit to Ilfracombe gave rise to the *Journal* headline "Pop group brings teenage invasion" as 500 fans from all over Devon came to see their idol. Millie, a 16-year-old whose jolly hit song 'My Boy Lollipop' was on everyone's lips that summer, played Barnstaple in July and took time off to visit the Abbeyfield School in the town. Here she chatted to students and signed numerous autographs.

If she was young what is one to make of the lead singer of the rather obscure Vendettas? When they appeared at the Queen's Hall their lead singer who was just 14 had to bring a "nanny" with him in order to be allowed to perform under contemporary laws. In addition to the Vendettas other rather less famous national acts came to North Devon including the wonderfully named Rip Van Winkle and the Age Beaters.

All of these visits, whether by the famous or less-so were eclipsed in March, however, when half the entire front page of the *Journal* was filled with photos of the Beatles at South Molton railway station. They, along with Wilfred Brambell, arrived in a five coach train to shoot part of their first film. The visit was brief and only Ringo got off the train. Although the train was mobbed by fans only one was lucky enough to get any autographs – a Mrs Friend of Kingsnympton who said she got them for her son.

Interestingly it was the Beatles who gave rise to the longest running saga of readers' letters in the 1964 *Journal*. It began in January with a short news item that the headmaster of Bideford Grammar School had put a ban on Beatle-style haircuts and ordered two boys to visit the barbers to have their offending locks sheared. The mother of one of them said she would be taking the matter up with her MP, while one of the boys was reported as saying "I suppose the next target will be our waistcoats."

The following week a letter was printed supporting the headmaster, "Now that girls wear jeans it is difficult to differentiate the female sex from the male when they have full

Beatle haircuts." This inspired other writers and the correspondence continued over the next five weeks and included letters from a mother who liked her three sons' Beatle haircut. One of these sons is now a well-known teacher at Pilton School so I won't divulge his name!

Not only haircuts were attacked. In March there were complaints about "hooliganism" at Braunton Youth Club dances, while a dance at South Molton in April ended in fighting between "long haired louts from Bideford, Torrington and Barnstaple." In July J B Morris retired as headmaster of Shebbear College and was given a send-off by the school's own beat group. Afterwards he (rather ungraciously) deplored such music but was interrupted by pupils suggesting loudly that he should "get with it."

The church seemed to be divided on the issue of pop music. At Hartland, "a local electric guitar beat group" called The Lektrons played at a "beat service" but at Hatherleigh the vicar gave a public assurance that there would be no "Beatle Services" to try and attract young atheists. The parish council at nearby Shebbear had no qualms about pop music. They reported that by holding just two "beat dances" a year they could raise enough money to pay for 18 months worth of village lighting!

I will finish this survey of 1964 with just two other items. In July the "pirate radio ship" Radio Caroline sailed past North Devon, its broadcasts being picked up loud and clear. In the same month the first topless dress to be sold in North Devon was purchased in Bideford after being on display for a few days during which it had "attracted a lot of attention." The *Journal's* Bideford correspondent reported that two elderly women viewing it came out with the immortal phrase, "they did not know what the world was coming to."

North Devon Journal 30.4.1992 & 7.5.1992

GUIDE TO SOURCES

1. NDJ 11.10.1827 4c
2. NDJ 6.10.1836 4a
3. NDJ 16.8.1877 3c, 23.8.1877 2e & 3a, 18.10.1877 5d-e
4. NDJ 6.11.1851 8a, 13.11.1851 5c
5. 1851 Census held by the North Devon Record Office
6. NDJ 4.12.1879 8a
7. Sherborne Mercury 24.12.1821 4c
8. NDJ 24.12.1824 4b
9. NDJ 1.1.1829 4d
10. NDJ 13.11.1828 1c
11. NDJ 3.4.1834 4b-c
12. NDJ 27.3.1851 8a
13. NDJ 16.11.1854 3d, 5.4.1855 8b, 6.1.1859 5b
14. NDJ 21.4.1881 5c
15. NDJ 6.5.1886 8e
16. NDJ 15.6.1827 4b
17. NDJ 2.4.1896 3d, 16.4.1896 3b
18. NDJ 9.4.1840 3a, 18.2.1841 2e
19. St.Mary's, Bideford Parish Registers are held by the North Devon Record Office
20. NDJ 12.8.1875 6e
21. NDJ 11.8.1892 2b-c
22. *Jerome K.Jerome. A Critical Biography* by Joseph Connolly (1982), NDJ 25. 12.1851 8b, 7.9.1854 8b, 14.9.1854 3b, 25.10.1855 4c, 24.7.1856 1a
23. NDJ 24.5.1855 8a
24. NDJ 2.2.1865 5c
25. NDJ 25.11.1869 7a
26. NDJ 12.8.1875 5d
27. NDJ 9.4.1908 2c
28. *West Country Poets* by W.H.K.Wright pp.211-214 (London 1896)
29. NDJ 7.1.1909 2e,5e & 6c
30. NDJ 23.10.1913 6f
31. NDJ 14.6.1849 6b-d
32. Tape deposited with Bideford & District Community Archive
33.   "   "   "

34. Typescript held by North Devon Athenaeum
35. *Reprint of the Barnstaple Records* Vol.II p.193 by J.Chanter & T.Wainwright (Barnstaple 1900), NDJ 17.3.1887 3b & numerous references in NDJ for 1859 - see card index held by North Devon Athenaeum
36. *The Rural Economy of the West of England* by William Marshall in *Early Tours in Devon and Cornwall* edited by R.Chope (1918)
37. NDJ 27.3.1862 6b
38. *North Devon Miscellany* June 1824, *A short sketch of the interesting scenery and historical records of Bideford and its vicinity* by John Wilson (Bideford 1860-61)
39. NDJ 26.1.1827 4b, 18.7.1839 2d
40. NDJ 10.12.1835 4d
41. *BARUM; or North Devonshire: A Poem* by Henry Staveley (Bideford 1860)
42. *Braunton: A descriptive poem* by Thomas Mortimer (Barnstaple 1856)
43. NDJ 17.2.1870 5c, 5.10.1871 8c, 19.6.1873 8a, 5.2.1874 8b, 19.2.1880 6c, 20.5.1880 8a 18.11.1926 6c-d
44. NDJ 8.3.1877 6a, 12.4.1877 8b, 17.5.1877 8b, 9.5.1878 3b, 16.5.1878 1a, 31.8.1882 2e
45. NDJ 8.7.1880 2b
46. NDJ 24.5.1883 8a, 31.5.1883 8c, 14.6.1883 6b & 8b, 28.6.1883 8c, 19.7.1883 6b, 26.7.1883 8c
47. NDJ 28.4.1887 5a, 22.9.1887 4a, 12.4.1888 4a
48. NDJ 17.2.1887 5d, 24.2.1887 8a, 17.3.1887 8a, 12.5.1887 6b
49. *Original Poems and Prose* by George Whitaker p.90 (1895), Census & Land Tax records held by North Devon Record Office, various Directories & NDJ 6.11.1845
50. NDJ 10.5.1928 7d
51. *Survey of West Country Manors 1525* by T.Stoate (Bristol 1979)
52. NDJ 26.1.1827 4b, 6.7.1827 4d, 2.5.1833 4c, 13.6.1833 1a, 14.11.1833 4b, 3.7.1845 2e, 5.10.1848 2g, 12.10.1848 3b
53. NDJ 11.3.1830 1b-c, 8.4.1830 1b, 20.5.1830 1c-d
54. NDJ 30.5.1872 5e-f
55. NDJ 1.7.1841 1a
56. Devon Record Office 53/6 Box 73 Bankruptcy Papers

57. Microfilm held by North Devon Record Office
58. NDJ 12.9.1867 8e, 26.9.1867 1f & 8a, 16.1.1868 7c, 27.2.1868 1f
59. NDJ 8.2.1872 2b-c, 15.2.1872 4f & 5a-b, 22.2.1872 5c & 8a-b, 29.2.1872 6a
60. Personal communication from the late Dick Cleaver & NDJ 26.2.1874 1b
61. NDJ 22.8.1907 5d, 29.8.1907 5e
62. NDJ 27.6.1912 5e, 4.7.1912 5d-e, 11.7.1912 5e
63. Original copies of the Hartland Chronicle are held by North Devon Athenaeum. Also see *Cory's Chronicle* by Alan Vanstone (1981)
64. Devon Record Office Chanter 879
65. Devon Record Office 799A P1 367-369
66. NDJ 8.4.1886 2c
67. NDJ 6.3.1873 2b-d
68. NDJ 27.11.1828 4c, 19.2.1829 1d
69. NDJ 15.9.1836 1c, 6.10.1836 1c-d
70. NDJ 21.10.1841 3d, 6.1.1842 3b, 10.3.1842 3b, 31.3.1842 3b, 14.7.1842 3b
71. NDJ 15.8.1850 8d, 26.1.1854 8d, 3.8.1854 8a, 4.12.1856 5a, 28.5.1857 5b, 21.1.1858 4e
72. NDJ 11.1.1872 8d
73. NDJ 17.3.1887 3a
74. NDJ 15.8.1895 5c
75. NDJ 8.3.1928 7c-d
76. Devon Record Office Quarter Sessions Documents (9) Maimed Soldiers
77. *A Concise History of Bideford* by Inkerman Rogers (1938), *Western Antiquary* Vol.9 p.109, *The Plymouth Magazine* (1758), NDJ 2.5.1867 5d
78. Original documents held by North Devon Athenaeum
79. NDJ 21.3.1895 8d, 6.6.1895 8e, 13.6.1895 3b, 20.6.1895 8d, 8.8.1895 5f, 12.12.1895 8c
80. NDJ 2.4.1908 5f
81. Devon Record Office 1843 A/PM1-2
82. Tape deposited with Bideford & District Community Archive, NDJ 13.2.1919 2a
83. Booklet held by Bideford Library
84. NDJ 1.11.1838 3c

85. NDJ 2.3.1882 8c-d, 9.3.1882 7a, 16.3.1882 8c, 13.4.1882 8d, 27.4.1882 8a
86. NDJ 1.9.1887 2a & 8c-d, 8.9.1887 3b & 8d, 15.9.1887 3c & 8c,e-f, 22.9.1887 3b, 29.9.1887 5f
87. Original copy in my possession
88. NDJ 13.7.1911 8b-d
89. Typescript held by Devon Record Office
90. Devon Record Office QS 129/16
91. NDJ 23.2.1827 4b, 2.3.1827 1b
92. Exeter Flying Post 23.5.1816, Devon Record Office - Sidmouth Papers 152M Correspondence 1816
93. *Devon Extracts from the London Gazette* edited by M.Snetzler (Devon Family History Society 1987 & 1989)
94. Sherborne Mercury 25.3.1822 4b-c, 1.4.1822 4b
95. NDJ 2.4.1829 4a, 21.5.1829 4b, 9.7.1829 1c, 17.2.1831 3d
96. NDJ 16.12.1830 4b-c, 6.1.1831 4a, 13.1.1831 3b-c   97. North Devon Record Office - Barnstaple Borough Council Minutes BC p.128, NDJ 4.2.1836 4b-c, 18.2.1836 4c, 21.4.1836 4c, 26.5.1836 4b
98. NDJ 12.1.1837 4c
99. NDJ 18.7.1839 2d, 8.8.1839 2b
100. NDJ 4.1.1844 2e, 11.1.1844 3c, 18.1.1844 1e & 3d
101. NDJ 14.2.1850 5d, 15.8.1850 5d, 7.11.1850 5e, 22.5.1851 5a, 24.7.1851 4d, 4.5.1854 8a
102. Report held by North Devon Athenaeum
103. NDJ 29.5.1852 8b, 23.2.1854 8c, 1.6.1854 6e, 6.7.1854 8a, 13.7.1854 6a, 22.5.1856 5e
104. NDJ 18.5.1854 8c and weekly until 31.8.1854 4c & 8c
105. NDJ 20.9.1855 7a
106. NDJ 7.2.1850 5c, 14.2.1850 5d, 25.4.1850 4e, 29.8.1850 5c, 24.4.1851 5b-e, 1851 Census held by North Devon Record Office
107. NDJ 22.2.1872 5c
108. NDJ 19.6.1873 2a-b
109. NDJ 8.5.1866 3a
110. NDJ 13.6.1935 3c
111. St.Peter's, Barnstaple Parish Registers are held by the North Devon Record Office
112. North Devon Record Office B1/3044
113.   "   "   B1 p.298

114. Gentleman's Magazine 1745 p.582
115. For references see my introductory article in *An Essay towards a History of Bideford* by John Watkins (Bideford 1993)
116. NDJ 25.9.1828 1a, 30.10.1828 4e, 25.12.1828 4d
117. North Devon Record Office - Inland Revenue Wills 1812-56
118. NDJ 11.5.1827 4b, 27.7.1827 4b, 16.8.1923 2a-c
119. NDJ 16.7.1824 4b
120. NDJ 15.4.1825 4a, 22.4.1825 4b, 6.5.1825 4b, 13.5.1825 4a
121. Microfilms held by North Devon Record Office
122. NDJ 28.10.1830 1b
123. NDJ 2.2.1832 4a-b
124. NDJ 9.6.1842 1d, 22.12.1842 3e
125. NDJ 29.1.1852 5d
126. NDJ 24.1.1856 5a, 31.1.1856 6d, 7.2.1856 5b, 14.2.1856 5c, 26.6.1856 5d, 20.11.1856 5a, 5.2.1857 5b
127. NDJ 2.8.1866 5d, 9.8.1866 5e, 16.8.1866 5d, 23.8.1866 8a, 6.9.1866 8a, 13.9.1866 8b, 27.9.1866 5e
128. NDJ 11.4.1878 3a, 2.5.1878 2e
129. NDJ 24.3.1881 8a
130. Booklet held by North Devon Athenaeum
131. NDJ 15.4.1852 5b, 19.1.1865 5c, 14.11.1867 5c
132. NDJ 27.5.1909 8e, 5.8.1909 2c
133. NDJ 15.8.1889 6c
134. Booklet held by North Devon Athenaeum
135. Leaflet in my possession
136. & 137. References drawn from two years run of NDJ

Index

Readers Notes